D1553722

WITHDRAWN

Porfirio Díaz

PROFILES IN **POWER**

General Editor: Keith Robbins

. . . .
PORFIRIO DÍAZ

Paul Garner

An imprint of **Pearson Education**

Harlow, England · London · New York · Reading, Massachusetts · San Francisco
Toronto · Don Mills, Ontario · Sydney · Tokyo · Singapore · Hong Kong · Seoul
Taipei · Cape Town · Madrid · Mexico City · Amsterdam · Munich · Paris · Milan

Pearson Education Limited
Head Office:
Edinburgh Gate
Harlow CM20 2JE
Tel: +44(0)1279 623623
Fax: +44(0)1279 431059

London Office:
128 Long Acre
London WC2E 9AN
Tel: +44(0)20 7447 2000
Fax: +44(0)20 7240 5771
Website: www.history-minds.com

First published in Great Britain in 2001

The right of Paul Garner to be identified as Author of
this Work has been asserted by him in accordance with
the Copyright, Designs and Patents Act 1988.

ISBN 0 582 29267 0

British Library Cataloguing-in-Publication Data
A catalogue record for this book is available from the British Library

Library of Congress Cataloging in Publication Data
A CIP catalog record for this book can be obtained from the Library of Congress

10   9   8   7   6   5   4   3   2   1
05   04   03   02   01

Typeset by 35 in 10/12pt Jansen Text
Printed in Malaysia,LSP

The Publishers' policy is to use paper manufactured from sustainable forests.

CONTENTS

CONTENTS

PREFACE AND ACKNOWLEDGEMENTS

The informal and hierarchical systems of personal authority, and the complex networks of kinship and patronage which characterise political and social life in Latin America are apparent to any student or perceptive visitor to the region. What is less obvious to the visitor, and often perplexing to the student, is the clash of political cultures which has been the reality of political life in Latin America for nearly two centuries. The clash is manifest most clearly in the paradoxical relationship between Latin America's tradition of constitutional principle and liberal democratic ideals, and the parallel, but contradictory, traditions of authoritarianism and personal power. One recent analysis of Mexico's political culture has succinctly described this phenomenon as a clash between the 'culture of citizenship' and the 'culture of the pyramid'.[1] It is by appreciating the aspirations, disillusionments and inevitable tensions which this relationship has generated that the political history of Latin America can best be understood. The format offered by the series *Profiles in Power*, with its examination of the relationship between personal power and political structure, is therefore an entirely appropriate vehicle for an exploration of the political history of the region.

The difficulties encountered in the management of contrasting political cultures can be clearly identified in the long political career of Porfirio Díaz, President of Mexico from 1876 to 1880, and subsequently, without interruption, from 1884 until his forced resignation in 1911. Díaz succeeded in manipulating Mexican political life for the best part of three decades. He thus holds the record, and the dubious honour, of being the longest-serving constitutional leader during the often painful evolution of the Mexican state since 1821, the year in which 300 years of Spanish colonial rule formally came to an end (1521–1821).

The significance of Díaz's long tenure of office can only be properly understood in the context of Mexico's early experience as an independent state. In the 75 years between the consummation of independence in 1821, and the accession of Porfirio Díaz to the presidency for the first time in 1876, Mexico's political history was nothing if not turbulent. It would be no exaggeration to suggest that the new republic experienced almost permanent crisis throughout most of this period. Indeed, given the extent of domestic tensions and the external threat posed by the territorial and colonial ambitions of Mexico's European adversaries (Spain and France) and her immediate North American neighbour (the USA), it is remarkable that Mexico survived at all as an independent state.[2]

The transition from colonial status to independence and nationhood was inevitably protracted and painful. Ethnic, cultural and regional tensions, and the fragmentation of central political authority which accompanied the process of independence itself (1808–21), severely hampered the establishment of a strong central state. The struggle for power after 1821 between Mexico City and the provinces, and the conflicts which arose from the attempt to extirpate Mexico's colonial legacy (represented above all by the Catholic Church) dominated the politics of the first half-century after independence.

Mexico's early national history was pock-marked by bouts of constitutional proclamation and reform, military *pronunciamientos* and *coups d'état*, factionalism and civil war, and punctuated by wars of resistance against foreign invasion (from the USA in 1847–48, and from France between 1862 and 1867). Political stability, as measured by the frequent turnover of governments and occupants of the presidential chair, was the most obvious casualty of this degree of turbulence. The contrast represented by Porfirio Díaz's almost continuous occupation of the presidency for 31 years after 1876 is, therefore, remarkable in itself. The central purpose of the book is to explain why and how this was achieved.

But the Díaz era is significant not only for the longevity of presidential authority, but also for the fact that so many of the roots of Mexico's identity as a modern nation in the twentieth century – its political system, its economic structure, its cultural projection – are to be found during this period. This is still a somewhat controversial view outside the rather confined world of professional Mexican historiography, since it has long been argued, particularly in the official, popular and post-Revolutionary version of Mexican history, that Mexico's status as a modern nation-state was not defined in the

Díaz era, but during the Mexican Revolution (1910–20) which re-moved Díaz from power. Another of the aims of this book is, there-fore, to continue the process of re-evaluation of a regime which has been subjected to persistent historiographical and political distor-tion. It is for this reason that the book begins with an evaluation of the various ways in which the image of the Díaz regime has been manipulated over the past century, before examining in detail its origins, character and evolution.

I owe a considerable debt of gratitude to many friends and col-leagues both in Mexico and the UK who have assisted me in my pursuit of Don Porfirio in recent years. I would like to mention in particular my fellow *oaxacólogos* Brian Hamnett and Colin Clarke, who formed the nucleus of the now-dormant Oaxaca Seminar which was inaugurated at the Institute of Latin American Studies in Lon-don in 1989. During my years at the University of Wales, Swansea, my colleagues David George and Rhys Williams were always a source of encouragement and support. I must also thank the University of Wales, Swansea, and Goldsmiths College, University of London, for granting me a period of sabbatical leave to devote to the project. In Mexico, the assistance and friendship of the staff of the Porfirio Díaz archive at the Iberoamerican University have been invaluable. I would particularly like to thank Teresa Matabuena, María Eugenia Ponce and Georgette José for their many kindnesses. Without the generosity and hospitality over many years of my *compadres* in Coyoacán, Eduardo Antúnez and Amparo Maza, this book would never have been written. I must also express my gratitude for the support and patience of the editorial staff at Pearson Education, who have heard more excuses for the late submission of the manu-script than they would care to remember. The book is dedicated to my children, Daniel, Tessa and Dominic, who, while they have not exactly accelerated its completion, have always been its major source of inspiration.

· · ·

NOTES AND REFERENCES

1. W. Pansters (ed.), *Citizens of the Pyramid: Essays on Mexican Political Culture*, Amsterdam, 1997.
2. B. Hamnett's profile of President Benito Juárez, in this series, describes this process in detail; B. Hamnett, *Juárez*, Harlow, 1994.

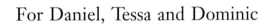

For Daniel, Tessa and Dominic

Chapter 1

PORFIRIO DÍAZ AND MEXICAN HISTORIOGRAPHY: PORFIRISMO, ANTI-PORFIRISMO AND NEO-PORFIRISMO

History is history. There can be no 'patriotic history', in the same way that there can be no patriotic chemistry, patriotic astronomy, nor anything scientific which is not governed by laws based upon the truth. (Francisco Bulnes, 'Rectificaciones y Aclaraciones a las *Memorias* del General Díaz', 1922)[1]

Few dictators in the history of Latin America are better known than Porfirio Díaz. It is one of the premises of this book that, until very recently, few have been more misunderstood or maligned. It is therefore crucial to any survey or analysis of the career of such an important but controversial figure to examine some of the ways in which the image of Díaz has been fashioned, denigrated and, above all, appropriated over the last century. This is a topic of intrinsic interest to any political biography, but it is of special interest in Mexico, where political mythology has been particularly powerful over the last three generations since the Mexican Revolution of 1910.

While this pervasive revolutionary mythology has made an important contribution to Mexican political stability in the twentieth century – for example, by promoting Mexico's identity as a *mestizo* nation and by linking post-Revolutionary nationalism to the nineteenth-century liberal state-building project – this has been achieved at the cost of distorting the analysis of Mexican history. This chapter argues that those distortions have been particularly acute in the case of the regime of Porfirio Díaz. At the same time, however, the contemporary (i.e. late nineteenth-century) interpretations of the Díaz regime before 1910 were no less distorted. In effect, the different representations of the Díaz era can be seen as a clear example of changes in both historiographical fashion and in national politics

over the course of the twentienth century.[2] These conflicting interpretations have made it very difficult to find a balanced interpretation of either the man or his regime.

Porfirian historiography falls into one of three broad categories,
each of which has a specific chronology and approach to its subject:
these are, in turn, *Porfirismo*, *anti-Porfirismo* and *neo-Porfirismo*. The
favourable portrayal of Díaz (*Porfirismo*) dominates the historiography
of the period before the Revolution of 1910, although some notable
contributions to *Porfirismo* were made during and after the Revolution. *Porfirismo* emphasises, above all, the longevity of the regime,
especially in contrast to its predecessors in nineteenth-century
Mexico, and its success in achieving political peace and stability for
a period of nearly 35 years. *Porfirismo* also stresses the personal
qualities which justified Díaz's monopolisation of political office for
over 30 years: *inter alia*, his patriotism, heroism, dedication, self-
sacrifice, tenacity and courage.

The typical frontispiece of the numerous biographies of Díaz which
were published during the latter years of the regime was chosen with
the specific purpose of portraying an image of the austere but benign
patriarch, the military hero, the nation-builder and the elder statesman
fully in control of the destiny of the nation: in short, a hero in the
classical republican mould. This deliberate cult of personality was
actively promoted throughout the lifetime of the regime, especially
after Díaz's third re-election in 1892, and saw its apotheosis in the lavish
celebrations in September 1910 which marked the centenary of
Mexican independence from Spain.[3] With supreme irony, the celebrations of 1910 also represented the regime's nemesis. Less than two
months later, in November 1910, the Revolution which would remove
Díaz from power was launched. Six months later, Díaz had resigned
and had been forced into exile, from which he would never return.

One of the many consequences of the Mexican Revolution was
the destruction of the cult of *Porfirismo* and its replacement by an
equally powerful *anti-Porfirismo*. *Anti-Porfirismo* was not, however,
exclusively a product of the Revolution, although it was most forcefully expressed after 1911 in what became the standard, orthodox,
pro-Revolutionary interpretation. According to *anti-Porfirismo*, the
Díaz regime was the supreme example of tyranny, dictatorship and
oppression, and Díaz himself was condemned for his corruption, his
authoritarianism and his betrayal of national interests.

Anti-Porfirismo dominated Mexican historiography for almost two
generations after the Revolution. However, over the course of the

1990s there have been strong indications that the image of Díaz and the interpretation of his regime have undergone a distinct transformation. The Díaz era has, as a result, been interpreted in a much more positive light. Indeed, it could be argued that *neo-Porfirismo* now constitutes the latest form of historiographical orthodoxy. An important stimulus to this profound re-evaluation has been the scope and sophistication of recent research carried out by the current generation of both Mexican and non-Mexican historians. As a consequence, new trends in social, regional and cultural history have profoundly altered the traditional depiction of Porfirian Mexico. Equally important has been the transformation of national politics since the 1980s.

In this wider political context, the change in public and official attitudes towards the Díaz regime in contemporary Mexico is clearly a reflection of the radical restructuring of Mexico's political economy which took place in the wake of the devastating impact of the debt crisis during the 1980s.[4] It is obviously no coincidence that the recent positive re-evaluation of Porfirian economic strategy, for example, coincides with the neo-liberal strategy of successive administrations after 1982. Neo-liberal economics in Mexico and Latin America have been characterised by a return to the positive endorsement of foreign investment, a renewed stimulus to export-oriented development and the drive towards de-regulation and privatisation – the hallmarks of Porfirian policy before 1910 – in stark contrast to the post-Revolutionary orthodoxy of state intervention, nationalisation and import-substitution.

There is abundant anecdotal evidence of the shift in perceptions within Mexico over the 1990s. In August 1992, for example, the influential Mexico City political journal *Proceso* published a benign, avuncular portrait of Díaz on its cover, accompanied by a feature article titled 'The Return of Porfirio Díaz'. Even more striking was the decision by President Salinas de Gortari in the same year to grant permission to the television company *Televisa* to film part of a new historical soap opera on the life of Díaz, in the National Palace. This constituted clear evidence of official endorsement of *neo-Porfirismo*. The series, which ran to over 100 episodes at an estimated cost of 30 million *pesos*, was finally shown in 1994 under the enigmatic title *El Vuelo del Aguila* (The Flight of the Eagle). While it received a mixed critical response, the extensive publicity which it received and generated, and the award of a prime daily broadcasting slot, were further indications of a profound revision of previous prejudice.[5]

Also in the summer of 1992, considerable public debate and controversy was stimulated by the proposed publication of new compulsory primary and secondary school history textbooks. The new texts substantially revised the 'official' view of the Díaz era and portrayed it not as a negative period of tyrannical and oppressive dictatorship, but as a positive and constructive period of modernisation and economic development. The controversial text was withdrawn by Minister of Education Ernesto Zedillo prior to his election as President in 1994. It must be emphasised, however, that this act of official censorship was not carried out primarily because of the *neoporfirista* interpretation of the Díaz era. Rather, it sought to suppress criticism in the new textbook of the ruling *Partido Revolucionario Institucional* (PRI, Institutional Revolutionary Party), which had won all presidential elections in Mexico since its creation in 1946, and of the army, especially for its role in the massacre of hundreds of student demonstrators in the Plaza de Tlatelolco in Mexico City in 1968.

Throughout the 1990s there has been a pervasive sense of imminent and profound transformation in Mexico, to which the events during the term of office of President Ernesto Zedillo (1994–2000) have clearly contributed. During that time, Mexico has seen the direct challenge posed by the EZLN (The Zapatista Army of National Liberation) to the PRI's rhetoric of social redistribution. In addition, the country has suffered the resurgence of economic crisis and a series of political assassinations and scandals. It has also been the period in which the remarkable electoral domination of the PRI has finally been broken, with the loss of the presidential elections in July 2000. These significant shifts have been identified for some time. In the prophetic words of two of Mexico's leading contemporary historians and political commentators, Lorenzo Meyer and Hector Aguilar Camín, in the preface to their survey of post-Revolutionary history, *In the Shadow of the Mexican Revolution*, published in 1993:

> we have – as many Mexicans do – the impression that Mexico is moving forward to a new historical period, which will dispel some of the most cherished traditions and the most intolerable vices of the historical legacy that we know as the Mexican Revolution.[6]

It is the contention of this profile that one of those most cherished traditions, and one of the most intolerable vices of the historical legacy of the Revolution, has undoubtedly been the vilification and satanisation of the figure who was removed from power in its wake. The portrayal of Porfirio Díaz as brutal dictator followed a very clear logic, a logic directly related to the process of mythification of the Revolution itself.[7] In the context of post-Revolutionary Mexico, the principal justification for Revolution became the overthrow of what became perceived as an oppressive, tyrannical dictatorship. Under these circumstances, a balanced evaluation of Díaz or of his regime was, at best, difficult and, at worst, impossible.

. . .

ANTI-PORFIRISMO

From the perspective of 'official' pro-Revolutionary and *anti-porfirista* history, Díaz became, in the famous phrase of journalist Filomeno Mata, 'the monster of evil, cruelty, and hypocrisy'.[8] For the outside world, Díaz was portrayed as a ruthless tyrant, 'the most colossal criminal of our times . . . the central prop of the system of slavery and autocracy', as defined by North American journalist John Kenneth Turner in his influential and widely-read *Barbarous Mexico*, first published in 1909.[9]

Turner's portrait epitomised *anti-Porfirismo*: he accused Díaz of conspiracy and treason, inhumanity, brutality and duplicity. According-ing to Turner, Díaz was 'the assassin of his people . . . [and] . . . a base and vile coward. . . . The President of Mexico is cruel and vindic-tive, and his country has suffered bitterly.' It was a grossly distorted picture, and Turner was quite prepared to use unsubstantiated and even ludicrous anecdote for sensational effect. Turner's distortions were little more than caricature. As evidence for his personal pen-chant for cruelty, Turner cited what he claimed was an 'incident' from Díaz's childhood: 'annoyed with his brother Félix over some trivial matter, he placed gunpowder in his nose and set fire to it'.[10]

The most virulent examples of *anti-Porfirismo* in Mexico are to be found in the 1920s. Typical of this period is Luis Lara Pardo's quasi-historical account, *De Porfirio Díaz a Madero*, published in 1921. According to Lara Pardo:

> Under the trappings of wealth and benevolence, cruelty, intran-sigence, unlimited ambition, and self-centred despotism began to appear . . . the true characteristics of the regime were then exposed: extermination and prostitution. . . . General Díaz believed firmly in

extermination as the principal tool of government ... [and] ... few leaders, even kings, emperors, pharaohs or sultans have done more to prostitute their peoples than General Díaz has done to degrade Mexicans. ...[11]

The pervasive influence of *anti-Porfirismo* is also to be found in other parts of the Hispanic world during this period. The Spanish essayist and dramatist Ramón del Valle Inclán's classic and widely-read novel of dictatorship, *Tirano Banderas*, first published in 1926, took Díaz as one of the models for an archetypal nineteenth-century Latin American dictator, a merciless and cynical tyrant character-ised above all by his cruelty and sadism.[12] Other Spanish writers of the period shared this view and were clearly more interested in demonisation than in historical accuracy. In an essay on Mexican militarism written in 1920, novelist and essayist Vicente Blasco Ibáñez described the *pax porfiriana* which Díaz had brought to Mexico as no more than 'a series of unwitnessed shootings and assaults on individual liberty ... more people were silently and clandestinely exterminated over a period of 30 years than in all the battles of the subsequent revolution'.[13]

Within Mexico, *anti-Porfirismo* continued to exercise a powerful influence over what became the 'orthodox' interpretation of the Díaz regime. The orthodox view emphasised the authoritarianism and tyranny of the regime and argued that it represented a distor-tion of Mexico's nineteenth-century liberal traditions. Traces of this orthodoxy continued to predominate even in the more scholarly and incisive analyses which appeared in Mexico after 1940, such as the influential studies of Mexican historians José Valadés, Jesús Reyes Heroles and Daniel Cosío Villegas, and the *Historia Moderna de México* project.[14]

José Valadés, whose three-volume study of the Díaz regime, *El Porfirismo: Historia de Un Régimen*, was published between 1941 and 1948, stated that he was seeking, with an 'open mind', to investigate the predominant perception of the Díaz regime as 'an almost text-book manifestation of tyranny'. His conclusion, nevertheless, was unequivocal:

It is true that the President [Díaz] had the qualities of a statesman: that his word was law; that he combined energy with perseverance; that he possessed undeniable personal qualities; and that he loved his country intensely. However, because his power was unconstitutional,

the Republic was plagued by sorrow and disaffection, and its foundations lacked solidity and balance . . . [his power] was, ultimately, sinister and bitter.[15]

Daniel Cosío Villegas, the co-ordinator of the *Historia Moderna de
México* project which published a ten-volume history of the Restored
Republic (1867–76) and the Díaz era (1876–1911) between 1955 and
1972, was more circumspect, and even expressed admiration, albeit
grudgingly, of Díaz's political skills. He recognised that Díaz 'was
neither an angel nor a demon, nor even a mixture of the two'. But
he nevertheless endorsed the broad thrust of post-Revolutionary
anti-porfirista historiography by explaining the Revolution of 1910
in terms of a reaction to the regime's accumulation 'of a degree of
power, which cannot be called absolute, but which, it can be safely
asserted, was incontrovertible'. In Cosío Villegas's view, the Díaz
era (or, as he called it, the Porfiriato) should be seen fundamentally
as an aberration in Mexico's slow evolution during the nineteenth
century towards political liberty. According to Cosío Villegas, 'Porfirio
Díaz raised the banner of material progress . . . [while] failing to
secure, and even sacrificing political freedom'.[16]

The Cosío Villegas project, the single most important contribution to our understanding of the Díaz era, thus qualified, but did
not fundamentally challenge, the prevailing historiographical orthodoxy. The orthodox view was more forcefully expressed by Jesús
Reyes Heroles, who, in his survey of Mexican liberalism, published
between 1957 and 1961, denied Díaz or his regime any place within
the nineteenth-century liberal tradition. Reyes Heroles's view was
that 'the Porfiriato did not represent the continuity of liberalism,
but was instead a substitution and a real discontinuity'.[17]

· · ·

PORFIRISMO

The work of Valadés, Reyes Heroles and, especially, Cosío Villegas
provided important insights and qualified some of the worst excesses
of *anti-Porfirismo*, but they did not challenge its basic approach, nor
its fundamental conclusions. An obvious parallel exists, therefore,
between the distortions of post-Revolutionary *anti-Porfirismo* and
the distortions of *Porfirismo* provided by the apologists of the regime
at the end of the nineteenth century.

Díaz emerges from the pages of contemporary accounts, written for both domestic and international consumption, as a wise patriarch, a republican patriot and positivist statesman, awarded such accolades as the 'Master of Mexico' (in the 1911 biography by US journalist James Creelman) or the 'Master Builder of a Great Commonwealth', as in the biography published by Mexican diplomat José Godoy in 1910.[18]

Contemporary reverence for Díaz as patriarch and national hero is most clearly to be found in a series of hagiographies which appeared with increasing frequency between 1900 and 1910. Perhaps not surprisingly, some of the most extreme manifestations of *Porfirismo* came from the pens of *oaxaqueños*, natives, like Díaz himself, of the state of Oaxaca in southern Mexico. In a commemorative volume to mark the centenary of Mexican independence (1810–1910) compiled by Andrés Portillo as a celebration of the material progress of Oaxaca, and the contribution made by *oaxaqueños* (most notably, Díaz and Benito Juárez) to national development, we find the following anonymous tribute to Díaz, as patriotic and romantic hero:

De las playas del Sur en las ignotas y vírgenes regiones,
Albergues de panteras y leones,
Una pleyade heróica de patriotas sola con su valor, sin experiencia,
Desnuda y desarmada
Pudo emprender la épica cruzada,
Que obtuvo la segunda independencia.
¿Quien en aquella lucha de gigantes,
Dio senales de arrojo y de talento,
Más dignas de la pluma de Cervantes y la lira dorada de Sorrento?
Himnos de gloria, cánticos fervientes,
Patrióticas y justas alegrías
Declararon espejo de valientes
Al noble General Porfirio Díaz.[19]

(From the unknown and virgin beaches of the South, the home of panthers and lions, an heroic constellation of patriots, naked, inexperienced, armed only with their courage, led the epic crusade for Mexico's second independence [the struggle against the French Intervention between 1862 and 1867]. Who, in that titanic struggle, showed more boldness and talent more worthy of the pen of Cervantes and the lyric poets of Sorrento? Celebratory hymns and passionate songs, patriotic and worthy celebrations declare the noble General Porfirio Díaz to be the very image of valour.).

Examples of adulation and deference to Díaz the patriarch were to be found across the social spectrum of Porfirian Mexico, from the inhabitants of remote rural *pueblos* to cabinet ministers and intimates of the President. In Díaz's private correspondence there are numerous examples of petitions for patriarchal favour, expressed in highly deferential and emotional language. These range from requests for Díaz to act as godfather (*padrino*) to numerous children to begging letters for pensions or employment from the President's numerous *compadres* and to petitions from *pueblos* and village authorities for the patriarch to intervene in search of a solution to a broad spectrum of local problems.

The language of deference also permeated the discourse of the Porfirian political elite. For example, Díaz's former Finance Minister, José Yves Limantour, one of the most influential figures during the last two decades the regime, was moved to respond to the unflattering obituary of Díaz published in the London *Times* in July 1915. The original text of the obituary had highlighted not only the mixture of ignorance and racial and cultural prejudice frequently demonstrated by British observers of Mexico, but also the fact that *anti-Porfirismo* had already become well established by 1915:

> Porfirio Díaz has shared the fate of numbers of South and Central American rulers. He has outlived his greatness and died in exile. He ruled Mexico with practically despotic power from 1876 until his downfall in 1911, and to that rule his country owed the first and only prolonged period of fairly settled government which she has enjoyed since she overthrew her allegiance to Spain. Under Republican hands, Díaz governed with an iron hand, but only an iron hand could have imposed respect for public order and fear of the constitutional authorities on a nation four-fifths of whom were of mixed or Indian blood, and who had been demoralised by over 60 years of anarchy, corruption and massacre.[20]

Limantour's indignant riposte was unapologetically *porfirista*, describing Díaz as the consummate patriot who single-handedly brought peace, order and material progress to his country:

> General Díaz was indeed the creator of modern Mexico. After the sixty years of turmoil which preceded his administration the country was brought by him to a state of progress unsurpassed by any of the Latin American countries. . . . Under his guidance order was brought

out of chaos, prosperity was consistently developed among all classes, and a new country was made. The greatness of General Díaz [was] as a statesman, a ruler of men, and a patriot.... General Díaz was a tireless worker, devoting the whole of his time, his remarkable ability, and his great strength of character to the welfare of his people, and the advancement of his country. No ascetic cared less for his own interests, pleasures, or comforts.[21]

Praise for Díaz from his contemporaries did not come exclusively from his political supporters. Perhaps the most unlikely source of praise for Díaz was Francisco Madero, the wealthy landowner (*hacendado*) from Coahuila who initiated the Revolution which toppled Díaz from power in 1910 and who became the first President of Revolutionary Mexico after Díaz's exile in 1911. In his influential and widely-read critique of the Díaz regime published in 1909 (*La Sucesión Presidencial de 1910*), which subsequently launched the Anti-Re-electionist Movement and his own candidacy for the presidency in 1910, Madero wrote:

I admire General Díaz, and can only reflect with respect on a man who has been one of the most staunch defenders of the nation's territory, and who, after wielding for more than 30 years the most absolute power, has exercised it with such moderation.[22]

Outside Mexico, contemporary praise for Díaz also came from some surprising sources. In 1894, José Martí, the radical Cuban intellectual and leader of the Cuban Revolutionary Party in its protracted struggle for independence from Spain, wrote to request an interview with Díaz during a fundraising visit to Mexico. While bearing in mind that Martí was seeking financial assistance and moral and political support for the Cuban cause, and therefore was hardly likely to insult a potential benefactor, Martí nevertheless openly revered Díaz as a wise patriot who had struggled consistently on behalf of the independence of the Americas:

A cautious Cuban has come to Mexico, trusting the profound and constructive wisdom, and absolute discretion of General Díaz, to explain in person to one of the foremost thinkers in the Americas . . . to the brave man who has made many sacrifices in the defence of the liberty of this continent and who today governs Mexico, the significance and scope of our sacred revolution for independence.[23]

Some of the most effusive and extravagant contemporary prose in praise of Díaz originated in the Anglo-Saxon world. As Robert

Skidelsky comments, 'the Victorian age was an age of hero-worship. In a period of religious doubt, morals increasingly needed the support of exemplary lives: lives, which, in particular, stressed the strong connection between private virtue and public achievement.'[24] Nevertheless, it is also clear that many of the accounts were based upon a combination of ignorance and an uncritical regurgitation of much of regime's own self-projection, self-promotion and propaganda in the international arena.[25]

Mrs Alex Tweedie, one of that indefatigable band of Victorian travellers from the British Isles, described Díaz in her 1906 biography simply as 'the greatest figure in modern history', and compared him to the Tsar of Russia and the Pope: 'yet', she affirmed on the same page, with a less than sure grasp of either political science or Mexican political realities, he was a 'democratic ruler'. Her description of Díaz as 'a fine, strong, handsome man . . . with deep, dark, penetrating eyes' also suggests that she may have been one of the many victims of what José Valadés later described as Don Porfirio's sexual magnetism.[26]

North American contemporaries were equally fulsome in their praise. José Godoy, the Mexican *chargé d'affaires* in Washington in 1909, solicited the opinions of prominent congressmen, senators, officers in the armed forces, civil servants and university presidents across the United States for his biography published in 1910. In the text which resulted, a remarkable mixture of purple prose, unadulterated fantasy and pure ignorance, Díaz emerges as a mythical figure of quasi-divine status, who had created the Mexican nation single-handedly. His US contemporaries compared him, variously and simultaneously, to Moses, Joshua, Alexander the Great, Julius Caesar, Cromwell, Napoleon, Bismark, Lincoln, Washington, Grant, Gladstone, Disraeli and, even, to the Mikado.

The descriptions and references most frequently used by Díaz's US admirers in Godoy's hagiography follow a predictable pattern. The most frequent reference was to Mexico's achievement of progress under the wise stewardship of Díaz. Other references emphasise the qualities of patriotism, personal morality, abnegation and humility, emphasising Porfirio's humble origins and citing his career as an example of rags to riches, the Mexican equivalent of the log-cabin to White House story. Congressman Charles Landis from California provided perhaps the most evocative expression of the apotheosis of late nineteenth-century *porfirista* mythology: 'we speak the name of Mexico, and think of Díaz . . . Díaz is Mexico, and Mexico is Díaz'.[27]

Ultimately, of course, the concerted and orchestrated efforts to promote both Díaz and the regime in a positive light both at home and abroad collapsed in the aftermath of the Revolution of 1910. Hagiography was rapidly replaced by the vilification and character assassination as *anti-Porfirismo* became the norm. Yet *anti-Porfirismo* itself was not an exclusive product of the post-Revolutionary period, and had clear pre-Revolutionary roots. The most striking example of the challenge to the cult of *Porfirismo* prior to the Revolution is the polemic which ensued from the decision to commemorate the centenary in 1906 of the birth of Benito Juárez, Mexico's mid-nineteenth-century liberal hero.

Given the heightened political tensions surrounding Díaz's sixth re-election in 1906, the attempt by the regime to exploit the myth of Juárez by casting him in the role of precursor to the Díaz era was bound to be controversial.[28] The historiographical outcome of the controversy was distinctly unfavourable to Díaz, and has been so ever since. While Juárez became firmly identified with nationalism and self-determination, political democracy and civil liberty, the rule of law and the secular state (and, subsequently, with indigenous rights and resistance to colonialism), Díaz became firmly associated with their antithesis: dictatorship and repression, the abuse of constitutional authority, pro-clericalism and the wilful violation of Mexican sovereignty, with Díaz in the role of arch xenophile and traitor.[29] The mud has subsequently stuck very firmly.

. . .

NEO-PORFIRISMO

The demonology of Díaz and the Porfiriato has proved stubborn and resistant throughout the twentieth century, despite some superficial indications of relaxation of official condemnation. President Avila Camacho (1940–46), for example, allowed Díaz's second wife, Carmelita, to return to Mexico. Despite the efforts of the family, however, Díaz's remains are still buried in Paris, in the cemetery at Montparnasse. This, above all, symbolises of the failure of the post-Revolutionary state to come to terms with the legacy of the Díaz regime.[30]

Nevertheless, the re-evaluation of the Porfiriato during the 1990s has finally begun to restore a degree of balance to both the *porfirista* and *anti-porfirista* interpretations. As indicated earlier, the roots of contemporary *neo-Porfirismo* are not only to be found in the official response to political and economic crisis, but also in the re-evaluation of the Díaz era by a new generation of Mexican historians. One of the central tenets of what is now classed as 'revisionist' history is the emphasis on the continuity (rather than the rupture) between the Porfiriato and the Revolution, and the consequent recognition of the debt which is owed by the post-Revolutionary political system to its Porfirian predecessor.

Neo-porfirista revisionism is not, however, a new phenomenon in Mexican historiography, and itself owes a good deal to the biographies of Díaz by Francisco Bulnes (1921), Angel Taracena (1960) and Jorge Fernando Iturribarría (1967). In recent years the case has been re-stated with renewed vigour, most recently in the revisionist biographies by Enrique Krauze (1987) and Fernando Orozco Linares (1991).

The maverick intellectual Francisco Bulnes, who managed to be both an active collaborator and a trenchant critic of the regime, provides the following assessment of the Díaz regime in 1921:

> Whatever the enemies of *Porfirismo* may say, the dictatorship was welcomed as a tremendous benefit by all social classes. Peace was a novel and attractive development for the country, and [the regime] inspired loyalty and gratitude amongst the people for the *caudillo* who had pacified his *patria*, in the belief that peace would be ever-lasting.[31]

Angel Taracena's biography of Díaz, published in 1960, could also be seen as a precursor of *neo-Porfirismo*:

> The Mexican people in general, and Mexican youth in particular . . . ought to be familiar with all of the details of the life of Porfirio Díaz, in order to be able to appreciate both his failures and successes, of which the latter were of significant benefit to the *patria*.[32]

Fernando Orozco Linares, in his 1991 biography, succinctly summed up revisionist *neo-Porfirismo*:

> Since 1930 the campaign to defame Porfirio Díaz has increased in intensity. There is no historical account or text book in which the author has failed to revile his memory. This is not only a travesty of the truth, it has also distorted the education of thousands of students, who are absolutely certain that Díaz was a tyrant, a murderer, a traitor, and a thief.[33]

Of the contemporary generation of historians, Enrique Krauze has been the most prominent and the most eloquent advocate of a balanced interpretation of the Díaz era. Krauze was one of the main promoters of the project for the television series on the life of Díaz, and in his 1987 biography he was highly critical of *anti-porfirista* interpretations. Krauze is not only interested in historical accuracy, however, since his revisionism also has overtly political overtones. He has been an influential member of the group associated with the cultural journal *Vuelta* (which included, before his death in 1997, Nobel laureate Octavio Paz) which has opposed the continued domination of the Institutional Revolutionary Party (PRI) in contemporary politics. Krauze sees significant parallels between the Díaz era and the PRI's stranglehold on Mexican politics since 1946. For Krauze, the continuities between *Porfirismo* and *Priismo* lie in the maintenance by both of a pernicious form of anti-liberal authoritarianism. He argues that Mexico has experienced since the Revolution only a superficial transition from a personal dictatorship to dictatorship of the party, or to what the Peruvian novelist Mario Vargas Llosa, on a visit to Mexico in 1990, controversially called 'a perfect dictatorship'.[34]

For Krauze, both the Porfirian regime and the PRI are analogous in terms of their 'political inertia' and of their 'stifling paternalism', both of which have long outlived their usefulness. As Krauze commented most perceptively and, perhaps, prophetically in 1992:

> the (post)-Revolutionary regimes cannot condemn Díaz without condemning themselves . . . there are two most appropriate courses of action; the return of [Díaz's] remains to Oaxaca, and the death of the PRI: a common epitaph should be inscribed on both graves: they served their *patria*, but they corrupted its civic life and denied its citizens their legal rights for a hundred years.[35]

The inherent danger of the new revisionism manifest in the recent outbreak of *neo-Porfirismo* is that, by transforming the image from diabolical dictator back to that of patriot and benign patriarch, Díaz will find his place once again in the pantheon of national heroes. This would represent a missed opportunity. As those who have grappled with the question of myth and history in Mexico and elsewhere have consistently identified, mythification tends to suffocate, if not entirely obliterate, the historical context. As Roland Barthes reminds us:

myth does not deny things, on the contrary, its function is to talk about them . . . purify them, make them innocent, give them a natural and external justification. . . . It abolishes the complexity of human acts . . . it does away with all dialectics . . . it establishes a blissful clarity . . . myth is constituted by the loss of the historical quality of things.[36]

In the case of Porfirio Díaz, the restoration of this elusive 'historical quality' to the myth has been long overdue. It is not without irony that, in 1911, the staunch *porfirista* Enrique Creel, Governor of Chihuahua and former Mexican Ambassador to the USA, wrote to Díaz in his Parisian exile and, in a vain attempt to console the exiled President, made the following prediction: 'you can be sure that history and the Mexican people will treat you with the utmost fairness'.[37] It has, however, taken a very long time for Creel's prediction to come true. One of the central purposes of this profile is to extend the process of historical re-evaluation.

. . .

NOTES AND REFERENCES

1. F. Bulnes, 'Rectificaciones y Aclaraciones a las *Memorias* del General Díaz', published in M. González Navarro (ed.), *Memorias de Porfirio Díaz*, 2 vols, Mexico City, 1994, Vol. II, p.298.
2. C. Hale, 'Los mitos políticos de la nación mexicana: el liberalismo y la revolución', *Historia Mexicana*, Vol. XLVI, 1997, pp.821–37.
3. M. Tenorio Trillo, '1910 Mexico City: Space and Nation in the City of the Centenario', *Journal of Latin American Studies*, 28(1), 1996, pp.75–104.
4. E. Williamson, *The Penguin History of Latin America*, London, 1994; P. Smith 'Mexico since 1946', in L. Bethell (ed.), *Mexico since Independence*, Cambridge, 1991, pp.321–96.
5. E. Krauze, 'Diez Mentiras sobre Porfirio Díaz', *Progreso*, Mexico City, Vol. 822, 3 August 1992, pp.45–9. Renewed interest in the life of Díaz is also exemplified in the publication of the new edition in 1994 of his memoirs, first published in 1892. This is the first major edition of the text since 1922.
6. H. Aguilar Camín and L. Meyer, *In the Shadow of the Mexican Revolution*, Austin, TX, 1993, p.viii.
7. I. O'Malley, *The Myth of the Revolution: Hero Cults and the Institutionalisation of the Mexican State 1920–40*, New York, 1996.
8. *Diario del Hogar*, Mexico City, July 1911.
9. J.K. Turner, *Barbarous Mexico*, London, 1911.

10. Ibid., pp.261, 269.
11. Luis Lara Pardo, *De Porfirio Díaz a Madero*, cited in José López-Portillo y Rojas, *Elevación y Caída de Porfirio Díaz*, Mexico City, 1921, pp.484–5.
12. The other models, as Valle-Inclán explained to Alfonso Reyes in 1923, were two other archetypes of nineteenth-century Latin American dictatorship: Doctor Francia in Paraguay and Juan Manuel de Rosas in Argentina: V. Smith *Tirano Banderas*, Critical Guides to Spanish Texts, London, 1971, pp.43–6.
13. V. Blasco Ibáñez, *El Militarismo Mexicano*, Valencia, 1920, p.149.
14. José Valadés, *El Porfirismo: Historia de un Régimen*, 3 vols, Mexico City, 1941; Daniel Cosío Villegas (ed.), *Historia Moderna de México*, 10 vols, Mexico City, 1955–72.
15. Valadés, *El Porfirismo*, Vol. I, p.xvi.
16. Cosío Villegas (ed.), *Historia Moderna de México*, Vol. X.
17. J. Reyes Heroles, *El Liberalismo Mexicano*, 3 vols, Mexico City, 1957–61, Vol. 3, p.xvii.
18. J. Creelman, *Díaz, Master of Mexico*, New York and London, 1912; José Godoy, *Porfirio Díaz, President of Mexico: Master Builder of a Great Commonwealth*, New York and London, 1910.
19. Andrés Portillo, *Oaxaca en el Centenario de la Independencia*, Mexico City, 1910, pp.501–4.
20. 'Death of Porfirio Díaz', *The Times*, London, 2 July 1915; R. Miller, *Britain and Latin America in the Nineteenth and Twentieth Centuries*, Harlow, 1993.
21. José Yves Limantour to the London *Times* 6 July 1915: a copy of the letter can be found in the private papers of Sir Weetman Pearson (later Lord Cowdray), held in the Science Museum Library at Imperial College, London: Box A4.
22. F.I. Madero, *La Sucesión Presidencial de 1910*, Mexico City, 1909, p.27.
23. José Martí to Porfirio Díaz, 23 July 1894: Porfirio Díaz Archive (*Colección Porfirio Díaz*), Iberoamerican University, Mexico City (hereafter CPD): File/*Legajo* (hereafter L) 19: Box/*Caja* (hereafter C) 21: Document/*folio* (hereafter f.) 10440; the importance of Cuba for the foreign policy of the Díaz regime is discussed in Chapter 6.
24. R. Skidelsky, 'Biography and Truth', in E. Homberger and J. Charmley (eds), *The Troubled Face of Biography*, Macmillan, 1988, p.5.
25. G. Yeager, 'Porfirian Commercial Propaganda: Mexico in the World Industrial Expositions', *The Americas* 34(2), pp.230–43.
26. A. Tweedie, *Porfirio Díaz. Master of Mexico*, London, 1906.
27. José Godoy, 'Opinions of Prominent Men Regarding President Díaz as Soldier and Statesman', published as an appendix to his *Porfirio Díaz, President of Mexico: The Master Builder of a Great Commonwealth*, New York, 1910, pp.124–93.
28. C. Weeks, *The Juárez Myth in Mexico*, Tuscaloosa, AL, 1987.

29. B. Hamnett, *Juárez*, Harlow, 1994, pp.244–51.
30. E. Krauze, *Porfirio Díaz: Místico de la Autoridad*, Mexico City, 1987, p.150.
31. F. Bulnes, *El Verdadero Díaz y la Revolución*, Mexico City, 1921.
32. A. Taracena, *Porfirio Díaz*, Mexico, 1960.
33. F. Orozco Linares, *Porfirio Díaz y Su Tiempo*, Mexico City, 1991, p.8.
34. 'La Dictadura y Mario Vargas Llosa', *ABC*, Madrid, 1990.
35. E. Krauze, 'Diez Mentiras', 1992.
36. R. Barthes, *Mythologies*, London, 1972, pp.142–3.
37. Creel to Díaz, CPD:L36:ff.9661–8.

Chapter 2

THE FOUNDATIONS OF PORFIRIAN MEXICO: LIBERALISM, AUTHORITARIANISM AND THE PATRIOTIC STRUGGLE, 1855–67

Never can I recomend to you too strongly that you should pay close attention to the consideration which the Indians deserve, for they have been the cannon fodder on which we have based our efforts to change the moral and political situation of the country. (Porfirio Díaz, 1894)

As Chapter 1 argued, one of the fundamental distortions of *anti-porfirista* historiography is the tendency to interpret the Díaz regime exclusively through the prism of the Revolution of 1910 which removed him from power. This has inevitably highlighted the regime's many shortcomings during its last years and, consequently, has tended to obscure the importance of its nineteenth-century origins. The aim of this chapter is, therefore, to explore the antecedents and foundations of the regime. Díaz's rise to power in 1876 cannot be understood without an appreciation of his participation in the political struggles of the 1850s and 1860s.

This chapter examines the evolution of Díaz's career before 1867. It will explore Díaz's early immersion into radical liberal politics in the provincial city of Oaxaca after 1849, and his highly successful military career which began during the Revolution of Ayutla in 1854 and blossomed during the Wars of the Reforma (1858–61) and French Intervention (1862–67). His parallel military and political careers witnessed his transformation from rebel *guerrilla* in 1854 to Divisional General in 1863, and from his appointment as sub-prefect of the district of Ixtlán in his native Oaxaca in 1855 to presidential candidate in 1867. Rather than attempt a detailed narrative, the emphasis here will be on the foundations of liberalism and *caudillismo* on which Díaz constructed his career.

One of the fundamental premises of this book is that the political success of Díaz and his regime lay in the construction of a *modus vivendi* between the most important components of nineteenth-century Mexican and Latin American politics: first, nineteenth-century Mexican liberalism, with all its contradictions and variations; and second, the traditions of patriarchal authority and the complex network of patronage represented by *caudillismo*. In other words, the exercise of personal, authoritarian and non-institutional power which is so common in the Hispanic world.

Liberalism constituted the ideological foundation of the Díaz regime. Inspired by US, French Revolutionary and Spanish precedents, nineteenth-century Mexican liberals sought to replace the *ancien régime* of absolutist monarchy, corporate privilege and colonial restriction with a federal republic based upon popularly-elected, representative institutions which would foster and protect citizenship, legal equality and the secularization of civil society. The essential dilemma was how to bring these aspirations to fruition within a political culture characterised by the maintenance of colonial institutions, and by distinctly authoritarian and anti-liberal practices, without resorting to the very evils liberalism was trying to destroy – namely, *caudillismo* and dictatorship.[1] The ability to maintain an equilibrium between these conflicting traditions would be the key to the success or failure of all nineteenth-century liberal administrations. Constantly subverted by the many personal, factional and ideological divisions within the liberal camp, and the persistent need to adapt liberal principle to political reality, it was to prove an immensely difficult balance to achieve.

The period 1855–67 is a crucial one in modern Mexican history and in the history of Mexican liberalism. It saw the promulgation of the sacred text of nineteenth-century liberalism, the Constitution of 1857, the authors of which identified the maintenance of colonial, corporate institutions and their legal privileges, and colonial restrictions on the free circulation of private property as the principal obstacles to Mexico's progress as a modern nation. Their principal target was the Catholic Church, the institution which represented the colonial, corporate legacy *par excellence*. The Constitution failed to recognise Catholicism as the religion of state, and the Church's legal immunity, control over education and its extensive properties came under concerted attack. The hostile response that the package of liberal measures provoked led directly to civil war after 1858.

Liberal victory in the civil war of 1858–61 came at a considerable cost. The election of Benito Juárez in March 1861 was followed by his declaration that Mexico's financial penury as a result of the cost of the war required the suspension of the interest payments on its accumulated debt to overseas bondholders (estimated at 82 million *pesos* in 1861). The governments of France, Britain and Spain then signed the Tripartite Convention which authorised a joint military expedition to occupy Mexico's customs houses until payments resumed. Britain and Spain withdrew once it became clear that Napoleon III was not just anxious to secure the repayment of interest, but aspired to bring Mexico into France's expanding empire. The invading French army, which entered Mexico City in June 1863, threatened the very existence of the Mexican Republic.

Mexican conservatives, monarchists and the ecclesiastical hierachy rallied to support the restoration of what they hoped would be a conservative Mexican empire under a European prince. The invitation was extended to Archduke Ferdinand Maximilian of the House of Habsburg, who arrived in Mexico with his wife Carlota in June 1864. However, Maximilian's flirtation with moderate liberalism soon alienated his conservative supporters, while failing to persuade his republican opponents in Mexico, under the tenacious leadership of Benito Juárez, to capitulate. Napoleon III, disillusioned with the failure of his Mexican experiment and fearful of potential hostilities with the USA following the end of the American Civil War in 1865, ordered a phased withdrawl of French troops after January 1866, but failed to persuade Maximilian to abandon Mexico. Following direct orders from Juárez, Maximilian was arrested and executed in June 1867.[2]

Maximilian's execution represented not only the end of his imperial dream, and of French colonial ambition, but the final defeat of Mexican conservativism, and the definitive triumph of Mexican liberal republicanism. In short, the defeat of the empire, in which Díaz played a prominent part, ensured that liberalism would remain the predominant ideology within Mexican political life. Nevertheless, during the subsequent period of the Restored Republic (1867–76), despite the absence of a conservative opposition, Presidents Benito Juárez and Sebastián Lerdo de Tejada were unable to turn liberal victory into a period of sustained political stability. In effect, the conservative, moderate and radical wings of the liberal movement proceeded to abandon their own rules of conduct and resorted to decidely illiberal and even anti-liberal practices – electoral manipulation, imposition of candidates and, in keeping with nineteenth-century tradition, resorting to the military coup or *pronunciamiento*.[3] It appeared that liberal principles could only be implemented through anti-liberal practices. These contradictions were far from being resolved when Díaz became President for the first time in 1876. Díaz himself would certainly be guilty of adopting anti-liberal practices in pursuit of liberal ends, but he was not the first (nor the last) President to govern Mexico in this way.

. . .

PROVINCIAL ORIGINS: DÍAZ AND OAXACA, 1830–55

Porfirio Díaz was baptised in the provincial city of Oaxaca in southern Mexico on 15 September 1830, as Mexico was entering its tenth year as an independent political entity. As many of his biographers have pointed out, the date itself was significant, since it coincided with what is today the most important of all of the civic rituals which mark the modern political calendar in Mexico: the celebration of Mexico's independence from Spain.[4] The fifteenth of September is the eve of the date in 1810 on which Miguel Hidalgo y Costilla launched the *grito* or call to arms which sparked off the popular insurgency against the continuation of colonial government.

This fortuitous umbilical link between Porfirio Díaz and the destiny of the Mexican nation would later be exploited by the regime in order to forge the link in public consciousness between Díaz and the consummation of national independence and sovereignty. To this end, the annual commemoration of independence was reorganised during the Díaz regime. This involved the relocation, during his third term of office in 1895, of the original bell, reputedly rung by Hidalgo himself, from Dolores to the National Palace in Mexico City. Henceforth, the hallowed bell was rung on 15 September, thus combining the celebration of Díaz's birthday with the birth of the Mexican nation. Not without irony, given Díaz's fall from grace after 1911, it continues to be rung on 15 September to this day.[5]

The link between Oaxaca and the evolution of the Mexican state in the nineteenth century was not an arbitrary one. Oaxaca was one of the 'cradles' of nineteeth-century Mexican liberalism, and produced the two most important political leaders of the second half of the century – Benito Juárez and Porfirio Díaz – who together dominated the political life of Mexico for half a century. Oaxaca's importance dated back to the late colonial period when the region had occupied a prominent position within the economic and political life of the Viceroyalty of New Spain. It had been the principal producer of cochineal and indigo dyes, which were in demand in the textile industry both in New Spain and, increasingly, in the international market. By the end of the colonial period, natural dyes had become, after silver, the second most important export of the viceregal economy.

Late colonial exports from Oaxaca had diversified into hides, wool, tallow, cotton and textiles. Mining also had showed a significant level of development in the late eighteenth century, as elsewhere in the Viceroyalty.[6] After 1800, however, and especially as a result of the economic dislocations of the independence period, the regional economy was plunged into a profound and prolonged recession. The recession was to last throughout most of the nineteenth century until the surge of domestic and international investment during the late 1880s and 1890s.[7]

The growing prosperity of late colonial Oaxaca had been reflected in the consolidation of a provincial elite which controlled the region's burgeoning commercial network from its provincial capital, Antequera (which became Oaxaca City after independence). It was also reflected in the growth in the influence and patrimony of the Church and the religious orders, not only through the ownership of rural and urban property and through the commercial activities which took place on those properties (agriculture, livestock farming, the processing of sugar, etc.), but also in the banking services it provided to merchants, miners and landowners (*hacendados*), in other words to the elite of colonial society.[8]

These patterns were repeated elsewhere in New Spain, but what was different about the colonial experience of Oaxaca was the cultural survival, political strength and economic independence of the indigenous *pueblo* or community. The direct economic and political control exercised by both the Church and the peninsular elite was largely limited to the city of Antequera and the surrounding Central Valleys. In 1832, a contemporary estimate calculated that the indigenous population of the state was 90 per cent of the total population (of some 484,000). Even at the end of the Díaz era in 1910 it still represented 77 per cent of the state's population.[9]

The indigenous communities of Oaxaca did not, however, conform to the characteristics attributed to them by many nineteenth-century liberals – as isolated, marginal communities, backward and resistant to change, tenacious in the defence of tradition. There can be no such simple categorisation, especially given the striking sub-regional diversity of Oaxaca's ethnic, economic and physical landscape, and the profound differences in material and non-material culture. Evidence from the colonial period indicates that the indigenous communities of Oaxaca had adapted over time, although to markedly different degrees, to the legal pressures and commercial opportunities offered by the colonial economy, and frequently engaged with the colonial legal system in the protection of their autonomy and territorial rights.[10]

In short, the distinctive features of late colonial and early nineteenth-century Oaxaca were, therefore, a provincial elite whose wealth was based upon trade and commerce (rather than the ownership of large rural estates); a Church whose influence was limited to the regional capital; and a diversity of indigenous communities which had retained a significant degree of cultural, economic and political autonomy throughout the colonial period.

The Church and the indigenous communities shared very different fates during the struggle for independence and its aftermath. Both were destined to come under sustained attack from liberal attempts to eradicate the colonial legacy. In practice, their experiences in Oaxaca were very different. The Church bore the brunt of the liberal assault. Already bruised economically as a result of the forced loans demanded by the Spanish crown in the late eighteenth century, it struggled in vain to retain its role as the principal source of credit and the control of its properties and estates in the face of the liberal onslaught on corporate property.[11]

By contrast, the political survival of the indigenous communities in Oaxaca after independence was ensured by the State Constitution of 1824, with almost every former Indian *pueblo* receiving the status of *ayuntamiento constitucional* (municipality), which was certainly not the case in other states within the new republic.[12] And not only did the Indian *pueblos* of Oaxaca obtain legal status, they also managed to retain their communal lands throughout most of the century, despite liberal advocacy of the privatisation of all corporate property in the hands of both the Church and of the indigenous communities. This was because liberal leaders in Oaxaca, including some of the most ardent advocates of anti-corporate reform, were conscious of the need to deal sensitively with the interests of the indigenous communities on whose support they depended.

The other significant political legacy of the independence struggle in Oaxaca was the broad appeal of federalism and regional autonomy among the provincial elite, encapsulated in provincial resistance to the imposition of central authority from Mexico City. The balance between the re-establishment of central authority (centralism), and the defence of state sovereignty and decentralisation (federalism) which had characterised the process of independence, would become one of the central issues in nineteenth-century Mexican politics. The struggle for power between the centre and the states within the federation would be repeated on many occasions in nineteenth-century Mexico, and Oaxaca would be always at the forefront of the debate.[13]

In short, the colonial legacy inherited by post-independence political leaders in Oaxaca, like that of many other parts of the new republic, was distinctly mixed. Subsistence and pre-capitalist production, Hispanic tradition and indigenous autonomy co-existed with liberal constitutionalism and capitalist enterprise. The consolidation of the liberal project in the aftermath of independence would require the skilful and sensitive dismantling of colonial structures and the creation of new economic and political models: first, the creation of an infrastructure to support trade and commerce in order to restore a fragmented and dislocated economy; second, the inculcation of citizenship, nationhood, popular participation and the rule of law in a caste society riddled with ethnic and class discrimination; third, the preservation of a precarious and highly sensitive balance, on the one hand, between local, community, state and central power and, on the other, between the extension of political representation and authoritarian practice.

Faced with these daunting tasks, it is hardly surprising that Oaxaca's post-independence liberal politicians demonstrated a strong streak of pragmatism. Oaxaca produced two generations of talented and capable politicians who were very conscious of the economic, social, political and cultural realities of their region (*patria chica*), and who were able to translate their experiences on to the national stage. It was from this provincial milieu that Porfirio Díaz emerged.

. . .

DÍAZ'S 'CONVERSION' TO LIBERALISM

The economic difficulties and political uncertainties of post-independence Oaxaca were reflected in the hardships suffered by the Díaz family. Díaz's father, José Faustino Díaz, reputedly of Spanish descent, had pursued a variety of careers, taking advantage of whatever economic opportunities came his way in what were clearly difficult economic circumstances. He had worked in a mining camp in the district of Ixtlán in the Sierra Norte of Oaxaca and had grown sugar cane (and established a small sugar-mill) on the Pacific coast (the district of Ometepec). He had taught himself the skills of a vet, a tanner and a blacksmith, which he put to good use when he moved the family to Oaxaca, which is where Porfirio was born (the sixth of his seven children, two of whom died in infancy). In addition to establishing a tannery and a smithy, Díaz's father also set up an inn (*posada*) called the Mesón de la Soledad (named after the patron saint of Oaxaca, La Virgen de la Soledad). From a position of relative security and prosperity, the family fortunes declined considerably with José's death from cholera in 1833, leaving his wife as the sole provider.

It is worth noting here that there is some confusion over the true identity of Díaz's father. In the notes of the 1922 edition of Díaz's memoirs there is a reference to the claim of Agustín Rivera in his *Anales Mexicanos* (1904) that Díaz's father was Rafael Díaz de León, an itinerant *mestizo* muleteer (*arriero*) from Jalisco who made frequent trips to Oaxaca, during which he fathered a number of children with an '*india mixteca*'. An additional confusion arises with the name of Díaz's father as recorded on the official Certificate of Baptism, which Díaz attached to the original draft of the text of his memoirs, composed in 1892. The Certificate of Baptism indicates that Díaz's father was not José Faustino, but José de la Cruz Díaz. The advantages of the official version for Díaz were, perhaps, twofold. Parental legitimacy, a greater percentage of European ancestry and a degree of 'whitening' which might have found more favour in the context of the contemporary influence of the positivist notion of scientific racism popularised throughout Latin America by Herbert Spencer's interpretation of social Darwinism. It was certainly widely believed in late Porfirian Mexico, although there is little evidence other than that of contemporary photographs, that Porfirio attempted in his later years not only to whiten his ancestry, but also the colour of his skin by using face powder. There can be no doubt, however, about his *mestizo* origins, which Díaz himself never tried to hide.[14]

Díaz's mother was Petrona Mory, a native of Yodocono in the Sierra Mixteca and daughter of a Spanish father (himself the son of a immigrant from Asturias) and of Tecla Cortés, a *mestiza* (i.e. of mixed Indian and Spanish blood). Despite the family's very difficult economic circumstances following her husband's death, Petrona Mory clearly had ambitions for her sons. Porfirio was sent to a rudimentary primary school from the age of six. The professional careers available in early Republican Oaxaca and throughout Mexico in the 1840s were the army, the priesthood and the law. New career prospects were beginning to open up as a result of the creation of the machinery of state government after independence, with the creation of national and provincial legislatures and a bureaucracy to service the institutions of the state. The most favoured pathway to a political or administrative career remained the study of law.

Perhaps surprisingly, given his talent for politics, the career initially favoured by the adolescent Porfirio Díaz was the priesthood. This was a result not only of his own religious convictions, but because of his family's connections in provincial society. Both of his parents were devout Catholics, to the extent that his father, according to Porfirio's own account, occasionally wore a monk's habit from the Order of St Francis during his daily prayers. Porfirio's cousin and godfather (*padrino*) at his baptism was the priest of the parish of Nochixtlán, José Agustín Domínguez, who would later become Bishop of Oaxaca.

The patronage provided by Domínguez enabled the young Porfirio to enter the seminary of Oaxaca (*Colegio Seminario Conciliar de Oaxaca*) in 1843 at the age of 13. While he was never an outstanding student and, to judge from his handwriting, he never learnt how to spell, Díaz successfully completed his studies in Latin, mathematics, ethics, philosophy and theology.[15] In 1846, on the death of a distant relative, he was offered a chaplaincy with a regular monthly income. He was destined, it seemed, for a career in the church.

In that same year, two events prompted Díaz to reconsider his career. The first was the final outbreak of hostilities between Mexico and the USA which had been brewing since the secession of Texas in 1836, and the crossing of the frontier by US troops in April. A number of students in the seminary offered their services to the governor of the Oaxaca, Joaquín Guergué. When the governor sub-sequently organised two battalions of the National Guard, the student volunteers from the seminary joined the Trujano battalion. The battalion did not see active service, however, and the young patriots, including the 16-year-old Díaz, had to be content with the occasional military exercises and routine guard duties. From then on, Díaz's enthusiasm for military service and military life turned gradually into a life-long passion.[16]

The other significant event in Díaz's life in 1846 was the invitation to give private lessons in Latin to Guadalupe Pérez, the son of Marcos Pérez, who was Professor of Public and Constitutional Law at the secular Institute of Arts and Sciences of the state of Oaxaca. Founded in 1828, the Institute became the training and recruitment centre of two generations of Oaxaca liberals. Pérez, like his contemporary Benito Juárez, was a Zapotec from the Sierra Norte who had been sent to the state capital to learn Castilian and to train for the priesthood, but who had been persuaded to study law rather than theology. Pérez rapidly took on the role of mentor to the young seminarist. In 1847 he introduced Díaz to Juárez, who had just been appointed as governor of the state. The governorship of Juárez (1847–53) provided a new stimulus to the group of Oaxacan liberals, with whom Díaz was anxious to associate himself.[17]

Díaz then made a decision that would have very significant impact on his future career. Very much against the wishes of his mother and godfather, he abandoned the chaplaincy and the priesthood and enrolled to study law at the Institute in 1849. Because of the loss of income which his decision represented (he also forfeited a grant by leaving the seminary), Díaz was forced to balance his studies with a number of part-time jobs, in addition to his private teaching, as shop-assistant, shoe-maker and carpenter. He also worked as a librarian, a substitute lecturer at the Institute and completed two years of practical legal training in the law offices of his mentor Marcos Pérez. Although he had passed his fourth-year law examinations, he was prevented by the events of 1853 from receiving the certificate which would allow him to practise law.

The *coup d'état* in 1853 which brough General Santa Anna to power for the eleventh (and final) time was followed swiftly by the suspension of the Constitution of 1824 and the arrest and exile of prominent liberals. In Oaxaca, the military commander Ignacio Martínez Pinillos seized power in conjunction with the the leaders of a rebellion for regional autonomy in Tehuantepec, and declared for Santa Anna. Marcos Pérez was arrested and imprisoned in the Convent of Santo Domingo and Benito Juárez was exiled to New Orleans. Because of his loyalty to Pérez, Díaz was now firmly associated with the radical (*rojo*) liberal faction in Oaxaca, which led him automatically into conflict with the *santanista* state authorities. The events of 1854 would further cast him in the role of radical liberal and rebel.

Díaz's portrayal of his conversion to liberalism must be regarded as an unreliable narrative, if not, as Francisco Bulnes caustically remarked later, as a work of historical fiction.[18] His memoirs certainly provide a dry account of his early career, with the emphasis very much on the preparation for a life of abnegation, self-sacrifice, patriotic duty and, above all, public service. Nevertheless, it is apparent from his own acount that a number of factors influenced his 'conversion' to liberalism. He was clearly frustrated by the rigidity of the education provided in the seminary. By contrast, he found the camaraderie of the liberals in Oaxaca very appealing. 'I was seduced', he wrote, 'by the openness and frankness of these individuals, which I had never seen in the seminary . . . [the Liberals] treated the younger generation as friends, and as men who had rights'.[19]

There is a notable reluctance in Díaz's own account to explain his ideological affinity with the principles of political liberalism. His avoidance of and distaste for public political debate would become a distinguishing feature of Porfirian politics.[20] There is also anecdotal evidence of a profound contempt for intellectual debate (or, as Díaz is memorably said to have defined it, '*profundismo*') and for intellectuals in general. When forced to listen to intellectual debate, he is reputed to have responded with the observation that '*Ese gallo quiere maís* [sic]' ('That rooster needs feeding'), implying that the best way to deal with intellectuals was to provide them with a sinecure and a steady income in order to keep them silent and under control.[21]

If he found the cut and thrust of political debate distasteful, he was clearly inspired, nonetheless, by the association of Pérez, Benito Juárez and the radical (*rojo*) liberal group in Oaxaca with freemasonry. In Mexico, as throughout the rest of Latin America and in Catholic Europe, freemasonry played a significant role in nineteenth-century political life. First established by *criollos* in colonial Spanish America in the 1790s, Masonic lodges were voluntary but clandestine organisations which championed the rational ideals of the Enlightenment, democratic ideals, public service and patriotism. Although in ideological terms Masonry was neutral, in practice it exerted a strong appeal to liberal republicans who sought to challenge the institutions and beliefs associated with colonialism, privilege and the *ancien régime*. As a result, Masonic lodges became centres of political conspiracy and debate, and their role in the independence struggle and its aftermath throughout Spanish America is well known. The most prominent 'liberators' of Spanish America – Francisco de Miranda, Simón Bolívar, Bernardo O'Higgins, José de San Martín and many others – were all Masons.[22]

In post-independence Mexico, freemasonry became associated with political factionalism and competition between the more conservative and europhile Scottish Rite Masons and the more liberal and radical Masons of the York Rite. Masonic lodges continued to serve as important centres for the dissemination of liberal ideas, and of specific resistance to the Santa Anna dictatorship and to the French intervention under Maximilian (although both Santa Anna and Maximilian were also Masons). Many of the most prominent mid-nineteenth-century liberals (Valentín Gómez Farías, Benito Juárez, Sebastián Lerdo de Tejada) were Masons.

Díaz's personal links to freemasonry were significant. He had been very active in lodge activity in Oaxaca, once presiding as lodge Master, and had assisted in organising a grand lodge there. Like Juárez, he attained the highest Masonic grade, the 33rd degree. As his private correspondence shows, once in power after 1876, Díaz received frequent requests from fellow Masons, especially from the USA, for contacts and introductions to further their business interests in Mexico, which he readily obliged.[23]

In nineteenth-century Mexican politics, freemasonry provided a crucial link between liberal politics and the construction of political networks or factions which revolved around the leadership of particular individuals. These informal, personalist networks or cliques, known as *camarillas*, have been clearly identified by political commentators as one of the fundamental features of twentieth-century Mexican political culture. Their importance for the nineteenth century has been less widely recognised, but it is no less crucial.

Roderic Ai Camp, in explaining the importance of the *camarilla* to twentieth-century, post-Revolutionary Mexican politics, defines it as a group of individuals 'who have political interests in common and rely on one another to improve their chances within the political leadership'. He further explains that the leader of the *camarilla* uses his own career as a means to further the career of other group members, and that as the leader rises to higher-level political office, 'he places members of his group . . . in other influential positions either within his agency or outside it. The higher he rises, the more positions he can fill.' Furthermore, Ai Camp makes the important point that membership of *camarillas* is fluid, with frequent shifts of loyalty which reflect the success of the leadership in obtaining political office. Mexican political leadership, he concludes, should be understood as an overlapping and hierarchical structure of inter-related *camarillas*.[24]

Camarillas were no less crucial to nineteenth-century political life in Mexico and to the the the evolution of Díaz's political career. The liberal group with which he became associated in Oaxaca in the early 1850s can be seen as a *camarilla* of radical liberals – also known as 'reds' (*rojos*) or 'Jacobins' (*jacobinos*) – under the leadership of Marcos Pérez. Another prominent member of this *rojo camarilla* in Oaxaca was the lawyer Justo Benítez. Benítez's career highlights the fundamental importance of *camarilla* organisation not only to the fate of individual careers, but also to the functioning of nineteenth-century Mexican politics. He was a contemporary of Díaz in the Institute of Sciences and Arts in Oaxaca and, subsequently, a very close associate throughout the Wars of the Reforma and French Intervention, and during the Restored Republic. Throughout these years, he acted as Díaz's confidant, secretary and agent. Benítez was Díaz's agent on a vital expedition to Washington in search of arms and campaign funds in 1865, entrusted with explaining to liberal supporters in the USA that Díaz had escaped from capture and that the liberal cause was still very much alive. According to Díaz's own account, the success of this mission was vital to the campaign to retake Oaxaca in 1866 and the eventual triumph of the patriotic forces in the following year.

The personal and political links between Díaz and Benítez remained strong throughout the critical years of the Restored Republic. Benítez remained a loyal supporter and advisor of Díaz in both the Rebellion of La Noria (1871) and Tuxtepec (1876), and was rewarded with the post of Minister of Finance in Díaz's first cabinet in 1876. Benítez's presidential aspirations, however, made him a potentially powerful rival, and Díaz subsequently sought to undermine Benítez's influence by supporting the candidature of Manuel González in the elections of 1880.[25]

The construction of *camarillas* required the manipulation of personal and political loyalties in loose, informal networks associated with the leadership of a particular individual. The major benefit received by the participant in the *camarilla* was the patronage received in return for loyalty and support, which, in practice, meant political office or a government post once the leader of the *camarilla* was successful in obtaining office. The importance of personal networks based upon hierarchy, deference and the distribution of patronage makes the links between *camarilla* politics and the practice of *caudillismo* very apparent. Both constitute aspects of Mexican political practice which are far removed from the principles of constitutional liberalism. They belong to the authoritarian and personalist traditions within Mexican political culture, which are equally vital for the analysis of the roots of political authority in nineteenth-century Mexico and the career of Porfirio Díaz.

. . .

THE AUTHORITARIAN TRADITION: *CAUDILLISMO* AND MILITARISM

The *caudillo* tradition has profound roots in Latin America. While its social, economic and cultural roots, and its essential characteristics (a combination of kinship, clientelism and personalism), are to be found in both pre-colonial and colonial society, the *caudillo*'s rise to political prominence and power during the first half-century after independence in Latin America was a direct consequence of the gradual fragmentation and collapse of Spanish colonial government after 1810, and the failure to find an alternative means of reconstructing the state.

John Lynch describes the *caudillo* as a combination of 'warrior, patriot, regional chief and *patrón*'– an individual imbued with strong and 'charismatic' personal authority, political and financial acumen and, in many cases, a commerical or landowning base in a particular region. *Caudillos* lacked a coherent political ideology, but Lynch sees them as a mostly conservative force intent on preserving the social fabric of pre-independence Spanish America.[26] *Caudillos* were products of a colonial and rural society whose institutions had been placed under great strain since the late colonial period. They therefore sought opportunities to protect their interests through every means at their disposal. This meant not only the manipulation of the Hispanic cultural traditions of patriarchy and patronage, but, in a period of acute instability and volatility, this most frequently meant coercion, violence or intimidation.

There were a number of indications of a profound absence of political legitimacy within the new states of independent Spanish America, most clearly exemplified by recurrent constitutional crisis. Throughout the Hispanic world in the wake of the precedent set by the Constitution of Cádiz in 1812, there was a recognition that the form of the state, and the political structures which governed the state, should be determined by a written constitution. The central problem was finding a consensus on ideology and content. Should the new states be monarchist or republican, centralist or federalist? Should they seek to imitate European or North American models, or should they conform, as the liberator Simón Bolívar suggested, to Spanish-American experience and reality, and therefore afford due consideration to Hispanic political traditions of centralism, authoritarianism and hereditary power?

The constitutional debate could clearly not be divorced from the political realities of post-independence Spanish America: these were, in essence, the absence of central authority, the fragmentation and decentralisation of power and widespread militarisation. The achievement of political consensus, stability and legitimacy proved to be extremely elusive under these circumstances. The inherent weakness of the post-imperial state left a profound and disruptive legacy of factional conflict, civil war and military coups (*pronunciamientos*). As a result, in the early post-independence period, the *caudillo* stepped into the political vacuum, and *caudillismo* emerged as the predominant form of political authority across the continent.

One of the particular features of the Mexican case was that the maintenance of political authority relied not only on the mastery of informal, personalist or clientalist networks of power, but also on the ability to mobilise the support of the army. The army was to be of central importance in nineteenth-century Mexican politics because of the prominent role played by the former colonial militias in the consummation of independence in 1821, and in the subsequent defence of the fragile sovereignty of the new state. The new republic, formally constituted in 1824, faced innumerable threats, both internal and external. The threat of Spanish intervention (following the failure of Spain to recognise Mexico's independence until 1836) and the strength of regional and federal resistance to the centre highlighted the overwhelming political need for the early imperial (1822–23) and subsequent republican governments to sustain a regular army.

At the same time, domestic political realities strengthened the degree of political power enjoyed by local military commanders. As a result of the fragmentation of political authority within the new republic, regional military chiefs frequently combined civil and military functions and created personal fiefdoms beyond the reach or influence of central goverment. Under these circumstances it was no surprise that creole officers from the regular army were transformed into military *caudillos* and saviours of national sovereignty. Creole military officers (not only the notorious Antonio López de Santa Anna, but Mariano Paredes, José Joaquín Hererra, Nicolás

Bravo and Mariano Arista) thus controlled Mexico's political destiny and dominated the presidency for more than a generation until the ascendancy of Benito Juárez and the Liberal Party after 1855.[27]

Although it is undoubtedly correct to signal the predominance of authoritarian practices in early post-independence Mexico, the importance and vibrancy of civilian political debate should not be underestimated. Although the early Republican period is always referred to in general histories as the 'Age of Santa Anna', and was therefore by implication an era in which autocracy, *caudillismo* and dictatorship predominated, it is important to remember that Mexico had adopted the republican form of government in 1824, based upon a recognition of popular sovereignty and the need for representative institutions. No military president, not even Santa Anna himself (until his last period of office between 1853 and 1855), attempted to govern without some form of elected or representative assembly.[28]

As a consequence, from the early post-independence period, and throughtout the years of so-called political instability, regular elections were held at local, state and national levels, supported (at state and national levels) by the emergence of political clubs and newspapers supporting the candidacy of prominent or aspiring members of the political elite. This is not to say that electoral practices were always conducted in an open or democratic fashion. This is clearly not the case. Nevertheless, despite the extent of carpetbagging, gerrymandering, the imposition of candidiates and the bribery of voters, the traditions of electoral and representative politics (including those of electoral manipulation) were a well-established feature of Mexican political culture before Díaz came to power.

To what extent were the roots of Díaz's political career to be found in *caudillismo* and militarism? Was he an advocate of a 'praetorian state'? He clearly had neither the social background nor the economic resources of property or landownership which could qualify him for 'classic' *caudillo* status. In other respects, however, the connections are obvious – Díaz rose to national fame and notoriety as a result of his military exploits as a patriotic hero, and his image as providential saviour of Mexican sovereignty in the struggle against the French Intervention in the 1860s was a fundamental aspect of his appeal in 1867 when he first made his bid for presidential election. He also adopted the traditions of *caudillismo* in his manipulation of patriarchy and patronage in the creation of *camarillas* and broad networks of personal loyalty and deference which were vital to his eventual accession to the presidency in 1876.[29]

During the military campaigns of the period 1858–67, Díaz was able to build an important political base within the National Guard and the regular army. As a result, he was able to draw on an ever-wider circle of fellow officers, subordinates and admirers who would support his political campaigns between 1867 and 1876. It is also self-evident that in 1871 and 1876 he attempted to achieve and finally achieved power by means of a military *pronunciamiento*, which involved the collusion and support of key regional army commanders. The Plan of La Noria of November 1871 was supported by a series of regional rebellions by Generals Treviño (Nuevo León), Trinidad de la Cadena (Zacatecas), Manuel González (Tamaulipas), Luís Mier y Terán (Veracruz), Juan Crisóstomo Bonilla and Juan Nepomuceno Méndez (Puebla), as well as that of his brother Félix, the governor of Oaxaca since 1867. In 1876, the support of regional army commanders would also be vital to the success of the Plan of Tuxtepec.

But Díaz's early political career cannot and should not be interpreted as simply another chapter in the history of nineteenth-century Spanish-American militarism or *caudillismo*. His base of support before 1876 extended well beyond the boundaries of the regular army. After 1867 Díaz became the figurehead of radical (*rojo*) and popular liberalism in opposition to the abuses of the Constitution of 1857 committed by presidents Benito Juárez and Sebastián Lerdo. Díaz's liberal convictions therefore distinguish him from the archetypal *caudillo*, whose ideological neutrality or promiscuity concealed the fact that they were most frequently the allies, agents or subordinates of predominantly conservative interests.

. . .

THE ENTRY INTO POLITICS: THE REVOLUTION OF AYUTLA, 1854

Díaz's commitment to liberal politics was demonstrated during his first foray into the regional politics of Oaxaca in 1854. The national context was the challenge from a multifaceted opposition throughout Mexico under the banner of the Revolution of Ayutla to the dictatorial aspirations of Santa Anna who had been restored to power in 1853. These disparate forces, ranging from former republican insurgents such as Juan Álvarez (the nominal head of the Ayutla movement) in Guerrero, autonomous regional *caudillos* such as

Santiago Vidaurri in Nuevo León and Coahuila, moderate liberals such as Ignacio Comonfort, radical liberal intellectuals (Melchor Ocampo and Guillermo Prieto), disaffected military officers and dissident conservatives (such as Antonio de Haro y Tamariz) called for constitutional reforms, the end of autocratic government and the return to the rule of law.

After the initial persecution and the circulation of warrants for the arrest of its most prominent enemies (which in Oaxaca included former Governor Benito Juárez and Díaz's political mentor, Marcos Pérez), the Santa Anna regime called for a national plebiscite in December 1854. In Oaxaca, despite the official claim that the vote was to be a free expression of the popular will, voting took place in public in the central square of the city under the watchful gaze of the governor and the military commander of the state, General Ignacio Martínez y Pinillos. Díaz, following the completion of his studies at the liberal Institute of Arts and Sciences, had been appointed as a temporary instructor of Natural Law in that same institution. According the Díaz's own account, when it was publicly announced that the staff of the Institute unanimously supported the continuation of Santa Anna in office, Díaz requested an abstention, but, following a public accusation that he had failed to register his vote out of fear, he responded by openly declaring his support for the leader of the Ayutla rebellion in Guerrero, General Juan Álvarez. An order was issued for his arrest and Díaz was obliged to flee the city and to find refuge in the Sierra Norte of Oaxaca, to begin the life of a rebel *guerrillero*.[30]

. . .

NATIONAL GUARD COMMANDER AND POPULAR LIBERAL, 1855-67

The triumph of the Revolution of Ayutla and the overthrow of the Santa Anna government in 1855 gave a definitive boost to Díaz's career. Both the political and military aspects of his career developed in tandem. As he readily acknowledged himself, a significant part of his early military duties and responsibilities required him to exercise political skills:

> while I was in charge of companies of soldiers in my youth, there were times when I received absolutely no orders or assistance from

the government for long periods, which obliged me to think for myself and become the sole instrument of government.[31]

His career, and his responsibilities, evolved at a rapid pace. In 1855, at the age of 24, he was appointed sub-prefect for the district of Ixtlán in the Sierra Norte of Oaxaca by Governor Ignacio Martínez. The following year he was awarded his first formal military rank as captain of infantry in the Oaxaca National Guard by Governor Benito Juárez. After the promulgation of the Liberal Constitution of 1857 by President Ignacio Comonfort, and the hostile conservative reaction manifest in the Plan of Tacubaya in 1857, Díaz participated in the defeat of the conservative forces under José María Salado at the battle of Ixtapa (August), where he suffered wounds and, subsequently, acute peritonitis. Following the outbreak of the Wars of the Reforma in 1858, Díaz participated in the siege and capture of the City of Oaxaca, held by conservative General José María Cobos. In April 1859 he accepted the appointment as military commander and governor of the Department of Tehuantepec, after two other candidates had declined to accept on the grounds that the meagre resources given to the new commander in a notoriously hostile and conflictive region amounted to only 160 men and barely 100 rifles.

His appointment to Tehuantepec in 1858, where he stayed for two years, taught Díaz important lessons in the arts of political administration and *realpolitik*. This was a particularly tough assignment, given the ethnic and political divisions between the local Zapotec, Chontal, Zoque and Mixe communities, and the fierce commercial rivalries which existed between the two major urban centres in the region, Juchitán and Tehuantepec. In addition, in the Isthmus of Tehuantepec there was a strong tradition of the resolute defence of regional autonomy and fiscal independence from state and national government, and from outsiders (both Mexicans and foreigners) who had attempted since the late colonial period to exploit the region's natural resources of salt and livestock. Díaz's central task – to establish and represent the interests of a fragile central state in a region profoundly hostile to outside interference – was therefore a very difficult one.[32]

The complex local situation in the Isthmus of Tehuantepec was further complicated by geography and the geo-politics of the region. The topographical advantages of the Isthmus for canal or railway construction (it is a mostly flat, tropical zone), and the increasing importance to the growth of domestic commerce in the USA for a viable crossing which would link the Atlantic to the Pacific, inevitably focused both national and international attention on the region.[33]

As Benito Juárez had discovered as governor of Oaxaca in 1847, the Isthmus had proved consistently resistant to subtle political manipulation from the state capital, or to direct military intervention to suppress local demands for the separation of the Isthmus from the state of Oaxaca. The conflict had escalated to a full rebellion in 1847, and had necessitated the despatch of the Oaxaca National Guard in 1850 and the personal intervention of Governor Juárez in 1851. None of these measures had resolved the conflict. With the restoration of Santa Anna at national level in 1853, the Tehuantepec rebels were rewarded by the *santanista* governor of Oaxaca, General Martínez Pinillos, with the creation of a federal territory of the Isthmus of Tehuantepec. But this was far from the end of the constitutional or political conflict in the region. With the triumph of the Ayutla Revolution, the Isthmus formally rejoined Oaxaca in 1857.[34] In April 1858, Díaz thus inherited a particularly volatile and difficult political situation.

Díaz's memoirs admit to an initial ignorance of the political context of his appointment. He recalled that the task 'proved extraordinarily difficult . . . much more difficult than I imagined, since I was out of touch with the [state] government, and in a region which was entirely hostile'.[35] But his solution to the maintenance of peace in the region foreshadowed his talent for pragmatism. By his own account, he sought first to establish a reputation for toughness and ruthlessness, by threatening to execute all prisoners. Second, he applied the technique of divide and rule. The major threat to peace in the region was the possible alliance of Juchitán and Tehuantepec against the anti-clericalism of the Reform Laws, particularly those relating to obligatory civil marriage and civil registry promulgated by Juárez in Veracruz in July 1859. Díaz sought to drive a wedge between the two communities, and to revive their long-term hostilities by allowing the rumour to spread among the *tehuanos* that he had supplied the *juchitecos* with arms. When the inevitable hostilities broke out at the local *fiesta* to celebrate the New Year in Tehuantepec, Díaz took the opportunity to attack the *tehuanos*, enabling him to attract, he claimed, over 2,000 new *juchiteco* recruits to his depleted forces.

He also sought to accommodate, rather than to antagonise, what he later referred to as the religious 'fanaticism' of the local residents, for example by permitting the body of a local *juchiteco* dignitary to be embalmed, according to local religious practice. He also took great pains to reassure the *juchitecos*, ironically through the good offices of the local Zapotec-speaking Dominican priest, Mauricio López, that the Reform Laws did not constitute an attack on the church.

A visit to Tehuantepec in 1859 to assess the commercial viability of a trans-Isthmus railway by the French engineer Charles Etienne Brasseur offers an intriguing contemporary portrait of Díaz as local *Comandante Militar*:

> a pure-blooded Zapotec, the most handsome of all indigenous types I had encountered on my travels. . . . Tall, with a distinguished appearance and a noble and lightly-bronzed face, he seemed to me to present the most perfect traces of ancient Mexican aristocracy . . . it would be desirable if all of the Mexican provinces were governed by men of his mettle.[36]

Despite the fact that Díaz was a *mestizo*, Brasseur described him as a direct descendant of Cosijópi, the indigenous ruler of Tehuantepec at the time of the Spanish conquest, and the nephew of Moctezuma. Its factual inaccuracies aside, Brasseur's description raises two important aspects of Díaz's political authority. First, his 'natural' leadership qualities and, secondly, the extent of his personal identification with his indigenous ancestry and his empathy for the concerns and aspirations of Mexico's indigenous communities.

During the course of his military career, Díaz frequently demonstrated his natural affinity with the role of *caudillo*, patriarch and *patrón*, carving out for himself a reputation for generosity, bravery (and also cruelty), and developing a close personal relationship with the officers and men under his command. He took pains, for example, in true *caudillo* fashion, to ensure the physical and material welfare of his men. He ensured that salaries of the troops were paid before those of his officers, and that essential provisions were secured as a matter of priority – especially, for example, the distribution of *pulque*, a drink made from fermented cactus sap which was a staple of the indigenous diet.[37] He also claims that during his campaign in the Sierra Mixteca in Oaxaca in 1865 and early 1866, despite the fact that resources were so scarce that none of his officers could be paid, he nevertheless continued to pay the wages of his soldiers.

Often his ministrations to his men went well beyond the normal call of duty for an officer. On one occasion, Díaz was required to adapt his skill with a carpenter's saw to amputating the leg of one of his soldiers after the local doctor had fainted when faced with this disagreeable task.[38] The cultivation of trust, loyalty and deference among the troops in his charge was assisted by his prodigious memory for names, personal details and family connections, a skill which would later be put to good political use.

Díaz also showed a preference for *guerrilla* warfare, allowing him to exploit his talent for improvisation, cunning and deception, talents which would also prove to be of political use in his future career.[39] He was, nevertheless, an ardent believer in the need for military discipline, stating in 1866: 'my opinion on military orders is well-known: I always apply them with the utmost rigour'.[40] He also deliberately cultivated a reputation for ruthlessness, both among his own troops, as well as those of the enemy. He was harsh with deserters, but particularly so with prisoners who had been captured. He appeared to follow with some relish the directive of 1862 that all Mexicans in the service of Maximilian were to be summarily executed.

His was not a policy which responded to any personal blood-lust, but rather reflected a cool, even cold, calculation of the psychological effects that terror and fear held over both his enemies and his supporters. Díaz commented in 1866, during the campaign to recapture the City of Oaxaca, that he was encouraged 'to adopt a more threatening and implacable tone towards the traitors [the word he consistently used to describe the Mexican supporters of Maximilian] in my correspondence and in my actions, which had very favourable results for me'.[41] He further justified this course of action with the following analysis of human nature, which provides an insight into his views on the conduct of not only military, but also political life:

> unfortunately the human heart is guided more by fear than by any other emotion . . . and so in order to demoralise the enemy, exemplary actions, carried out with energy and rigour were indispensable, even if they might be subsequently regretted.[42]

Díaz's own account also hints at the popular support which he was able to generate from the indigenous inhabitants of central and southern Mexico for the liberal and patriotic cause. He claims to have respected local, indigenous traditions and customs, refusing to force local communities to provide funds and provisions for the campaign and, on occasion, even reducing taxes.[43] When resources were scarce, as they frequently were, he claims that he even refused to extract forced loans for the local *pueblos*. 'I did not want to extort', he wrote, 'since this would have gone against my character and education.'[44]

While *jefe político* of Ixtlán in 1855, faced with the reluctance and suspicion on the part of the local Zapotec inhabitants of the Sierra Norte of Oaxaca to enlist in the National Guard units he was organising, Díaz was obliged to negotiate with the local communities the terms and conditions of service. To those who agreed to enlist, he offered immunity from imprisonment for minor offences and, as an additional inducement, he granted them exclusive access to a gymnastic club which he, as a life-long fitness fanatic, had organised.[45]

In retrospect, Díaz's experience as a National Guard commander during the late 1850s and 1860s was not only a crucial part of his own political education, but also helps to explain the basis of his popular political support after 1867. As recent research has indicated, the National Guard became the crucial agency through which the ideology and values of liberalism were filtered to the rural communities of central and southern Mexico from the Revolution of Ayutla to the Wars of the Reforma and French Intervention. Some of the central tenets of liberalism – local representative government and municipal autonomy, the defence of village lands, the abolition of compulsory ecclesiastical tithes and labour services, and civic defence based upon a locally-recruited and locally-accountable National Guard – found an enthusiastic response in central and southern Mexico.[46]

According to Marcelo Carmagnani, the formation of National Guard units in the 1850s and 1860s aimed to create local militia which would not only 'keep the peace' in areas of rural unrest (of which there were many), but also ensure the dominance of '*hispano-mestizo*' power: in other words, to control the insurrectionary tendencies of the Indians. As a result, the organisation of the National Guard served only to confirm, rather than to undermine, the ideological and social gulf which separated the liberal creole bourgeoisie and the traditional Indian *pueblos*.[47] By contrast, Guy Thomson argues that, in the context of a weak central state, local National Guard units were able to act as the guarantor and protector of village autonomy. Furthermore, the emphasis upon soldiers' rights and the popular election of local commanders extended the scope of popular sovereignty.[48]

Díaz's own experience as the commander of National Guard units in Oaxaca in the 1850s suggests that both types of National Guard unit could, and did, exist in this period. The type of military organisation and its impact on local society clearly depended upon the regional and sub-regional context and local circumstance. The unit which he organised as *jefe político* of Ixtlán in the Sierra Norte in 1855, a region with a strong tradition of communal ownership of land, election of municipal officers and reciprocal labour systems, seems to correspond more closely to Thomson's model. But the military organisation of the *juchitecos* undertaken by Díaz as military commander of Tehuantepec in 1858–59 appears to have been more in keeping with Carmagnani's model, since in the Isthmus the authority of the state was fundamentally weak and the need to control insurrectionary tendencies correspondingly greater.

Recent investigations into the nature of popular mobilisations during the military campaigns between 1855 and 1867 have, therefore, raised crucial questions as to the constituency of support for the liberal cause in rural Mexico. The emerging evidence suggests strongly that mid-nineteenth-century liberalism should no longer be understood, as more traditional historiography has suggested, either as a 'top-down' process of modernisation supported only by a liberal elite or as a project which had fundamentally failed to remove the vestiges of the colonial past prior to the Revolution of 1910. Instead, we now have a far more subtle picture of an interactive process in which rural communities were able to identify distinct advantages in some of the reforms advocated by liberalism, while rejecting others, and thereby to evolve what Florencia Mallon calls a 'counter-hegemonic discourse' through which to negotiate with regional elites and local political authorities in return for mobilisation and support for the liberal cause.[49]

This helps to explain the crucial support which Díaz received throughout central and southern Mexico for his political campaigns after 1867. There can certainly be no doubt that Díaz was acutely aware of the fundamental contribution made by the indigenous inhabitants of rural Mexico to the victory of the liberal cause. Without not simply their mobilisation, but their active participation, Díaz knew that the liberal triumphs between 1855 and 1867, and indeed his own accession to the presidency in 1876, would not have been possible. At the same time, he was also aware of the contradictions which state-building, political centralisation and economic modernisation posed to the interests of the indigenous communities. He wrote to the governor of Puebla, Mucio Martínez, in 1894, looking back to the years of the Reforma, clearly sympathetic to indigenous suffering at the hands of the agents of modernisation:

> Never can I recommend to you too strongly that you should pay close attention to the consideration which the Indians deserve, for they have been the cannon fodder on which we have based our efforts to change the moral and political situation of the country. . . . With that we have arrived at a plausible victory which is peacefully being converted into a defeat by the ambitions of speculators to whom the nation owes not so much as a breath.[50]

Nevertheless, at the same time, Díaz shared the view of the majority of nineteenth-century Mexican liberals that the traditional belief-systems and practices of indigenous Mexicans were examples of 'fanaticism' and that the most pressing need for indigenous communities was 'scientific education'.[51] His experience in the Isthmus, as Enrique Krauze contends, may well have put him in touch with his ethnic roots, but he came away with the conclusion that his allies the *juchitecos* were fanatical and fundamentally unreliable. If they were ever forced to leave Juchitán for a military campaign, then not only were they highly likely to desert, but 'they get so riotously drunk that they create all manner of disturbances, wounding and killing each other in large numbers'.[52]

As a result of both experience and conviction, Díaz certainly shared the view of urban and educated 'elite' liberals that the economic, social, political and cultural practices and structures of rural Mexico constituted an obstacle to material and social progress, to economic development and citizenship, and that the central mission was to deliver them from ignorance.[53] In this way, Díaz's affiliations were clearly on the side of 'progress', which he was convinced would be for the long-term benefit for the *pueblos*. He nevertheless understood the causes of community resistance and was always prepared to negotiate and convince rather than to cooerce.

Díaz's low-key and very dry account of his military career in his memoirs is clearly intended to impress the reader with his qualities of leadership, wisdom, discipline, self-sacrifice and heroism. It should be read with extreme caution. The context of its composition nearly 30 years later (in 1892) as part of the strategy to create a cult of personality should also be taken into account. In the highly critical view of Francisco Bulnes, Díaz's memoirs should be read alongside the classics of nineteenth-century romantic fiction, and he compares them to Alexandre Dumas' *The Three Musketeers* and *The Count of Monte Cristo*. For Bulnes, Díaz was guilty of indulging in the 'gluttony of glory, in pursuit of his ambition . . . certain that it was possible to deceive the world, and especially Mexico, with the most barefaced lies'. Other evidence would suggest that the memoirs present, at best, an incomplete picture.[54]

Díaz's own account is even less forthcoming on the details of his early political career. After the restoration of Juárez to the presidency in June 1861, and following orders for the demobilisation of all National Guard units in every state, Díaz 'discovered' on his return to Oaxaca in June 1861 that he had been 'elected' as representative in the second National Congress for the district of Ocotlán. The implication is that he had neither requested nor campaigned for this post and that, in accordance with the familiar electoral practices of the Restored Republic, he had been nominated rather than elected.

His participation in the Congress was short-lived, however, since with the news of a conservative attack on Mexico City in the same month, Díaz made his inaugural and only speech in the Congress, seeking permission, as a soldier, not to waste his skills on political debate, but to use them for combatting the enemy. A number of biographers have suggested, according to their *porfirista* or *anti-porfirista* stance, that this was an early indication of either his distaste for, or his ineptitude in, political debate.[55] For the next six years his career was necessarily focused on military affairs, culminating in his most resounding military successes in the recapture of Oaxaca, Puebla and Mexico City in 1866 and 1867.

The memoirs end abruptly in 1867, with the defeat and execution of Maximilian and the restoration of the Republic under the presidency of Benito Juárez. Díaz claims that, having done his patriotic duty in freeing Mexico from the yoke of foreign domination, he was content to retire to his private life, and to his *hacienda* in his native Oaxaca to exploit the fruits of his honest labour. Accordingly, when the State Congress of Oaxaca awarded him the title of *Benemérito* of Oaxaca and granted him the *hacienda* of La Noria close to the state capital, he declares that he happily embarked upon a new career as businessman and family man. It is here, however, that the memoirs are at their most deliberately disingenuous. Díaz's involvement in radical liberal politics, the success of his military career, his status as national patriotic hero, his political experience in the areas under his military jurisdiction and, last but by no means least, his personal ambition, meant that it was inevitable that he would become more deeply involved in national politics.

. . .

NOTES AND REFERENCES

1. L.B. Perry, *Juárez and Díaz: Machine Politics in Mexico*, DeKalb, IL, 1978, p.5.
2. B. Hamnett, *Juárez*, Harlow, 1994, p.184.
3. B. Hamnett, 'Liberalism Divided: Regional Politics and the National Project during the Mexican Restored Republic 1867–76', *Hispanic American Historical Review*, 76(4), November 1996, pp.659–89.
4. It was for this reason, undoubtedly, that the date of baptism, rather than the date of birth, was always celebrated. The actual date of birth is unknown. One of Díaz's biographers has suggested it may have been as early as 1828; see José López Portillo y Rojas, *Elevación y Caída de Porfirio Díaz*, Mexico City, 1921, p.22.
5. A. Lempériere, 'Los dos centenarios de la independencia mexicana (1910–21): de la historia patria a la antropología cultural', *Historia Mexicana*, Vol. XLIV, 1995, pp.317–52; for the growth of patriotic ritual in mid-nineteenth century Mexico, see G.P.C. Thomson, 'Bulwarks of Patriotic Liberalism: The National Guard, Philharmonic Corps, and Patriotic Juntas in Mexico 1847–88', *Journal of Latin American Studies*, 22(1), 1990, pp.31–68.
6. B. Hamnett, *Politics and Trade in Southern Mexico 1750–1821*, Cambridge, 1971, p.119.
7. P. Garner, *Regional Development in Oaxaca during the Porfiriato (1876–1911)*, Liverpool, 1995.
8. W. Taylor, *Landlord and Peasant in Colonial Oaxaca*, Stanford, CA, 1972, pp.173–6.
9. *Estadísticas Sociales del Porfiriato, 1877–1910*, Mexico City, 1956.
10. Ma. de los Angeles Romero Frizzi (ed.), *Lecturas Históricas del Estado de Oaxaca*, Instituto Nacional de Antropología e Historia, 4 vols, 1990, Vol. III, pp.20–3.
11. C. Berry, *The Reform in Oaxaca, 1856–76. A Microhistory of the Liberal Revolution*, Lincoln, NB, 1981.
12. P. Gerhard, 'La evolución del pueblo rural mexicano', *Historia Mexicana*, 24, 1975, pp.566–78.
13. W. Pansters and A. Ouweneel (eds), *Region, State and Capitalism in Nineteenth- and Twentieth-Century Mexico*, Amsterdam, 1989.
14. Gonzálex Navarro (ed.), *Memorias de Porfirio Díaz*, 2 vols, Mexico City, 1994, Vol. II, pp.150–1; on the influnece of social Darwinism in Latin

America, see R. Graham (ed.), *The Idea of Race in Latin America*, Austin, TX, 1990, pp.1–5. For the multiple inaccuracies and inventions (and therefore general unreliability) of Díaz's memoirs, see F. Bulnes, 'Rectificaciones y Aclaraciones a las *Memorias* del General Díaz', in Gonzálex Navarro, *Memorias,*, Vol. I, pp.247–325.

15. C. Beals, *Porfirio Díaz: Dictator of Mexico*, Philadelphia, PA, 1932, p.241 provides examples of Díaz's appalling handwriting and spelling.
16. Díaz, *Memorias*, Vol. I, p.36.
17. Ibid., p.38.
18. Bulnes, 'Rectificaciones', in *Memorias*, Vol. II, p.325.
19. Díaz, *Memorias*, Vol. I, p.38.
20. Díaz, *Memorias*, Vol. II, p.40.
21. E. Krauze, *Porfirio Díaz: Místico de la Autoridad*, Mexico City, 1987, p.84. Krauze is implying that Díaz favoured the tradition of the co-option of intellectuals by the state through their appointment to govenment or diplomatic posts, which became standard practice in post-Revolutionary Mexico.
22. A. Carnicelli, *La masonería en la independencia de América (1810–1830)*, 2 vols, Bogotá, 1970.
23. T. Davis, *Aspects of Freemasonry in Modern Mexico*, New York, 1967, pp.278–9.
24. R.A. Camp, *Politics in Mexico*, Oxford, 1993, pp.103–7.
25. Díaz, *Memorias*, Vol. II, pp.37–41. See below, Chapter 4, for details of the presidential elections of 1880.
26. J. Lynch, *Caudillos in Spanish America 1800–1850*, Oxford, 1991, p.407.
27. J. Bazant, 'From Independence to the Liberal Republic 1821–1867', in L. Bethell (ed.), *Mexico since Independence*, Cambridge, 1991, pp.1–48.
28. M. Costeloe, *The Central Republic in Mexico 1835–46*, Cambridge, 1993.
29. R. Buve, 'Transformación y patronazgo político en el México rural: continuidad y cambio entre 1876 y 1920', in A. Annino and R. Buve (eds), *El Liberalismo en México*, Hamburg, 1993, pp.143–76.
30. Díaz, *Memorias*, Vol. I, pp.49–50.
31. E. Krauze, *Porfirio Díaz*, p.15.
32. L. Reina (ed.), *Historia de la cuestion agraria mexicana: Estado de Oaxaca*, 2 vols, Mexico, 1988, Vol. I, pp.181–267.
33. P. Garner, 'The Politics of National Development in Late Porfirian Mexico: The Reconstruction of the Tehuantepec National Railway 1896–1907', *Bulletin of Latin American Research*, 14(3), 1995, pp.339–56; see Chapter 6.
34. B. Hamnett, *Juárez*, Harlow, 1994, pp.40–5, 78–9.
35. Díaz, *Memorias*, Vol. I, p.83.
36. Charles Etienne Brasseur, *Voyage sur l'Isthme de Tehuantepec, dans l'Etat de Chiapas et de la République de Guatemala, executé dans les années 1859 et 1860*, Paris, 1861, pp.150–7.

37. The memoirs indicate also a profound interest in prudent and frugal financial management of scarce funds during long campaigns. This was so successful that Díaz claims to have been able to susbsidise, from the surpluses generated from his campaign funds, the salaries of President Juárez's entire cabinet as well as those of his military escort, following the fall of Mexico City in 1867. *Memorias*, Vol. II, p.124.

38. Alberto María Carreño, *Archivo del General Porfirio Díaz*, 30 vols, Mexico City, 1947–51, Vol. I, pp.172–3.

39. Díaz, *Memorias*, Vol. I, pp.103, 241–65.

40. Ibid., p.265. Díaz to Matias Romero, 28 June 1866.

41. Ibid., p.272. Following the encounter at Miahuatlán in October 1866, 22 officers were summarily shot on Díaz's orders. Díaz also recounts that, in fit of anger, he personally executed with his sword one of the captured officers who had previously fought alongside Díaz (Captain Manuel Álvarez). Although he claims (writing 26 years later in 1892) that he considered this action to be 'deplorable' and a source of continuing anguish (*me ha apenado profundamente*), the incident clearly also served to enhance his reputation for ruthlessness. Díaz, *Memorias*, Vol. II, p.21.

42. Díaz, *Memorias*, Vol. II, p.20.

43. He wrote to Matías Romero, the Minister in Washington, requesting that campaign funds be raised outside Mexico, and also explaining that 'I have reduced the capitation tax to one *real*' in the Sierra Mixteca. Díaz to Romero, January 1866, *Memorias*, Vol. I, p.244.

44. Díaz, *Memorias*, Vol. I, p.264.

45. Ibid., p.56.

46. G.P.C. Thomson, 'Popular Aspects of Liberalism in Mexico 1848–88', *Bulletin of Latin American Research*, 10(3), 1991, pp.265–92.

47. M. Carmagnani, *El regreso de los dioses. El proceso de reconstitución de la identidad étnica en Oaxaca Siglos XVII y XVIII*, Mexico City, 1988, p.234.

48. Thomson 'Popular Aspects of Liberalism', p.280.

49. F. Mallon, *Peasant and Nation: The Making of Postcolonial Mexico and Peru*, Berkeley, CA, 1995. What recent research shows, above all, is that the response to liberalism varied tremendously from region to region and from municipality to municipality, even within the same region. The local context (geographic location, the dynamics of particular economic and social structures and historical precedent) was crucial to the reception or rejection of liberal aspirations, which makes generalisations very difficult to sustain.

50. Díaz to Mucío Martínez, quoted in D. Stephens, 'Agrarian Policy and Instability in Porfirian Mexico', *The Americas*, 39(2), 1982, pp.153–66.

51. See, for example, the disparaging remarks in Díaz's account of the medical treatment he received for a bullet wound from an '*indio*' (from Cacahuatepec) who thought he had some scientific knowledge of

medicine because he had spent some time as an inmate of the San Cosme hospital in the city of Oaxaca, and who succeeded only in infecting the wound. *Memorias*, Vol. I, p.63.

52. Díaz, *Memorias*, Vol. I, p.93.
53. Díaz, *Memorias*, Vol. I, pp.85–9.
54. Bulnes, 'Rectificaciones', in *Memorias*, Vol. II, pp.258, 273. For very different account of one of Díaz's military 'victories', see A. Valadés, 'La marcha de Díaz a Oaxaca durante la Intervención', *Historia Mexicana*, Vol. VII, 1957, pp.92–115; Valadés suggests that Díaz, despite his claim that he always maintained rigorous discipline among his troops, did little to prevent looting, theft and attacks on the lives and property of the enemies of the patriotic cause.
55. Díaz, *Memorias*, Vol. I, p.116.

Chapter 3

THE LONG ROAD TO THE PRESIDENCY, 1867–76

No honourable or patriotic soldier ought to support a government which has broken the pact with the people which the Constitution represents. (Porfirio Díaz, 1876)

It is apparent from Díaz's career since 1854 that he was, at heart, an intensely political animal, and a highly ambitious one. His immersion in radical (*rojo* or *jacobino*) liberal politics in Oaxaca, his tenure as military commander of Tehuantepec and, above all, his period as Commander of the Army of the East between 1863 and 1867 provided him with vital political experience and real political power, given that he was obliged to fulfil not just military, but administrative, judicial and legislative functions in the area under his command.

Díaz had also established himself as a figurehead of the radical wing of the Liberal Party (referred to as *puros* or *jacobinos*), as a defender of the 1857 Constitution and a champion of local and municipal rights. During his long campaigns he had made alliances across a broad spectrum of Mexican society, in the long-standing *caudillista* traditions of Mexican political culture. He had developed an extensive network of contacts within National Guard units and the patriotic army, and he had made a number of military and political appointments in his area of jurisdiction (military commanders and *jefes políticos*), many of whom would remain loyal to him throughout the turbulent years of the Restored Republic. He was, therefore, also clearly identified with the defence of the interests of the army, profoundly disturbed after the end of the war by the imminent demobilisation and the reduction in active units from 60,000 to 20,000.

Of equal, if not greater significance was the fact that he had acquired the status of a popular and respected national hero, praised in the national press as the most outstanding and successful defender of the nation's integrity and sovereignty in the face of foreign aggression. He enjoyed very favourable press coverage in 1867, a factor which is often overlooked.[1] Not only was he praised for being the only Mexican commander who had successfully routed the French army (at Miahuatlán, La Carbonera and Oaxaca in 1866), but he was also praised for his administrative and personal qualities – financial probity, military discipline, moral rectitude and the absence of either public or private scandal. He was widely lauded in the national press for evidence of the lack of personal ambition manifest in his decision 'to retire from public life' in order to devote himself to business and family on his *hacienda* of La Noria in Oaxaca, and to resign his commission in 1867 (although it was highly likely that had he not done so President Juárez would have removed him). He was, in short, dubbed as the Mexican incarnation of one of the classical heroes of the Roman Republic, Cincinnatus, the peaceful tiller of the soil, 'called from the plough to assume the dictatorship and to defeat the enemies of the Republic, and then to return to his farming'.[2]

If 1867 represented a new phase in Díaz's political career, it also represented a new phase in his personal life. In March 1867 he had married his 20-year-old niece, Delfina Ortega, the daughter of his sister Manuela.[3] Their first son was born in 1868, although he died two years later. Tragedy continued to plague to Díaz-Ortega family, with their first three children dying in infancy. Díaz's first son, Porfirio Germán, and his second, Camilo, born in 1869, died in 1870. Their third child, Luz, was born in 1871 but died in 1872. Only their fourth and fifth children, Deodato Lucas Porfirio (known as Porfirito) (b. 1873), and Luz Aurora Victoria (b. 1875) survived their infancy. The seventh child, Victoria Francisca, was stillborn and Delfina died soon afterwards in April 1880 as a result of complications arising from the birth. There can be little doubt that this tragic family history derived from consanguinity. Díaz demonstrated his trademark stoicism in the face of these tragedies, although he betrayed his true feelings in a letter to his 'dear *compadre* and friend' and future President Manuel González, following the death of his first two children in 1870: 'You know', he wrote, 'what it is like to lose a child; but you have no idea what it is like to lose two at the same time, or, more properly speaking, to lose all of your children; it is the same as losing one's love of life or work . . . which now seem meaningless.'[4]

Despite the tragedies of his personal life, in the prevailing political circumstances it was almost inevitable that Díaz would become a future candidate for the presidency. This became even more likely once profound divisions within the triumphant Liberal Party had developed following the successful conclusion of the military campaign against Maximilian in 1867. These bitter political conflicts characterised the entire period of the Restored Republic (1867–76), as the different factions within the Liberal Party – the supporters of Benito Juárez (*juaristas*), Sebastián Lerdo de Tejada (*lerdistas*), Porfirio Díaz (*porfiristas*) and José María Iglesias (*iglesistas*) – struggled to enjoy the spoils of political office. The intense factional conflict has often been interpreted on the basis of differences in personality or personal ambition, and partly on the basis of ideology ('pure' (*puro*) versus 'moderate' or conservative-liberal). However, it was widely perceived in contemporary political and journalistic circles that the candidates spoke for very different constituencies. As Ignacio Ramírez, one of the leading radical liberal intellectuals of the period (and a self-confessed *porfirista*) explained at the time, *juaristas* were the office-holders and bureaucrats of the Restored Republic, keen to hold on to power; *lerdistas* were men of wealth and intelligence (the economic and political elite), keen to preserve order and the *status quo*, while *porfiristas* were radicals and progressives and spoke as the party of 'the people'.[5]

The first serious schism to develop within the ranks of the Liberal Party had occurred in 1865 as a result of internal opposition to President Juárez's decree of November 1865 extending his term of office until such time as elections could be held. The challenge to this 'unconstitutional act' came from the President of the Supreme Court, held since 1863 by General Jesús González Ortega. Because the presidency of the Supreme Court was next in line to the office of President itself, the office became a source of significant political activity during the Restored Republic. Not only González Ortega but also both Lerdo and Iglesias would challenge for the presidency from their tenure of the office in 1872 and 1876, as Juárez himself had done in 1858. In the event, González Ortega was easily outmanoeuvred by Juárez, since he was arrested on his return from self-exile in December 1866, following a decree which called for the arrest of military or government personnel who had left Mexico during the Intervention. He was released on condition that he retired from political activity.[6]

The challenge from González Ortega was swiftly and effectively neutralised. Díaz, with characteristic caution and clearly not wishing to commit himself, refused to comment directly on Juárez's extension of his term of office, indicating only that he had complied with the government's instructions to publish the controversial decree in the area under his jurisdiction. His opposition was, however, only barely concealed. He wrote to Matías Romero:

> I have published the latest government decrees, which have been well-received. I have made no comment, because my behaviour has consistently been to obey or to resign whenever political developments have not been to my liking.[7]

The controversy highlighted what would become the principal *porfirista* challenge to both the Juárez and Lerdo administrations between 1867 and 1876: that the incumbent regimes were guilty of abusing the Constitution of 1857 by attempting, first, to create a self-perpetuating dictatorship through the manipulation of the electoral process and, second, the attempt to centralise political power and thereby undermine the political sovereignty of the states within the federal republic. In short, Juárez and Lerdo were guilty of 'executive centralism' and personalist despotism.

A second and more profound internecine conflict within the liberal camp resulted from the *Convocatoria* for popular elections of August 1867. In the *Convocatoria*, Juárez attempted not only to introduce constitutional reform (including the creation of a second chamber, or Senate, within Congress and the introduction of a presidential veto over legislation), but also to circumvent the constitutional procedure by which such amendments could be made. Electors were asked, by means of a plebiscite, to endorse the principle that Congress would be empowered to ratify the amendments without the prior approval of the majority of state legislatures.[8]

Juárez's backing for constitutional reform thus prompted accusations, primarily from the radical (*rojo*) wing of the Party, of his 'presidentialist' or dictatorial aspirations, and served to extend the divisions that had long been brewing within the Liberal Party. The extent of radical opposition to the *Convocatoria* added extra spice and momentum to the presidential elections of October 1867, since the radical liberal wing of the Party now actively campaigned for the candidacy of Porfirio Díaz and against Juárez. In fact, without the growth of opposition to Juárez in the summer of 1867, it is doubtful whether Díaz would have stood at all.

. . .

THE PRESIDENTIAL CAMPAIGN OF 1867

Díaz's presidential candidacy of 1867 sought to make political capital out his military record, his defence of Mexican sovereignty and of the Constitution of 1857, and his implacable opposition to the conservatives, whom he referred to as the 'traitors' who had sided with Maximilian. In his reply in 1864 to his former comrade-in-arms, the conservative General José Uraga, who had invited Díaz to join the imperial cause in 1864, Díaz adopted the discourse of patriotic struggle and argued that to side with Maximilian constituted 'the destruction of the national flag, the symbol of the freedom and the independence of Mexico . . . [and] of the free and sovereign Republic'.[9]

What prompted Díaz's candidacy in 1867 was less a reflection of personal differences with Juárez, or even of a clash between the advocates of civilian rule (*civilismo*) and military rule (*militarismo*), than the articulation of the serious disquiet within the radical (*puro* or *rojo*) wing of the Liberal Party which had been voiced over the *Convocatoria*.[10] That concern was expressed most clearly in the vocal protest of a majority of the liberal newspapers published in Mexico City after August 1867, most of which had been, until then, unequivocal supporters of Juárez. So vociferous was the protest that Juárez was forced to capitulate on the proposed reforms, particularly on the procedure for ratification of constitutional amendments.[11]

It is significant that a number of Mexico City newspapers not only expressed their opposition to the *Convocatoria*, but began simultaneously to advocate the candidacy of Díaz following its publication. Favourable editorials in Manuel María de Zamacona's *El Globo*, Ignacio Altamirano's *Correo de México* and Ireneo Paz's *El Padre Lobos* indicated that Díaz now enjoyed the support of some of Mexico's leading liberal intellectuals. The groundwork was therefore laid for an anti-Juárez faction, and even a party, calling itself the Constitutionalist or the Progressivist Party, to emerge with a coherent platform, choosing Díaz as their candidate.

Díaz's own reaction to growing public declarations of support was typically reserved and cautious. As was the convention of electoral campaigns in nineteenth-century Mexico, he did not make campaign or political speeches (and neither did his opponents) and refused to commit himself. He appears to have closely followed the advice of his closest political associate, Justo Benítez, as he had done since their early association in the radical liberal *camarilla* in Oaxaca in the 1850s. Benítez 'implored' Díaz

> to assume systematically a character of reserve, complete reserve, and to everyone who speaks to you . . . remember to answer that the nation has the right to entrust its destiny to whomsoever it wishes. Moreover, it is better to keep silent than to enter discussion . . . .[12]

Nevertheless, the growing momentum of the electoral campaign towards the end of 1867 was insufficient to ensure victory for Díaz. Juárez's prestige, if not his popularity, in combination with some adroit electoral manipulation, won the election for the incumbent President. According to Ballard Perry, Juárez had, for example, re-placed political opponents in the governorship of key states (especially Guanajuato and Puebla), and these appointees had, in turn, replaced district *jefes políticos* in order to ensure that electors from the district electoral colleges would return a favourable vote. Juárez obtained 7,422 votes, Díaz 2,709. And in the simultaneous election for the important position of the President of the Supreme Court, Sebastián Lerdo had obtained 3,874 votes, and Díaz 2,841.[13]

Díaz's reaction to the failure of his first attempt to conquer the presidency was, understandably, one of disappointment and frustration. He wrote to Miguel Castro, provisional governor of Oaxaca, who was an intimate associate and close friend of Juárez:

> although you declare that the victory of Juárez was the will of the state, we already know that the will of the people is more powerful than that of the governing authorities, and that it has elected the man who, before August 14, was our flag, our pride, and the basis of our hopes; but that with his actions of that date [a reference to the *Convocatoria*], he demonstrated that he is not a man in whose hands we ought to place the future of the nation; I know the opinion of the whole Republic well, and I do not believe he has been elected.[14]

Díaz's claim to speak for the 'opinion of the whole Republic' demonstrates not only his popular liberal constituency and his patriotic rhetoric, but also his determination to return to politics when the opportunity presented itself. In the short term, he returned to Oaxaca, and to his *hacienda* at La Noria, granted to him by the state legislature in reward for his services to the state and to the nation. He became a farmer and a businessman, growing sugar cane and demonstrating his commitment to material and economic progress by helping to establish the first telegraph link between Oaxaca and Mexico City. At the same time, he established a munitions and weapons factory at La Noria, indulging in what was not only a life-long passion, but also, in preparation for possible eventualities. As Francisco Bulnes later commented, with characteristic irony, the machinery installed in the factory was 'obviously designed to extract more juice from the *hacienda*'s sugar cane'.[15]

It would certainly be wrong, therefore, to assume that his political ambitions had diminished, since in Oaxaca he had the ideal political base from which to make his subsequent bid for the presidency in 1871. In the reconstruction of his political alliance he had a valuable, if sometimes inconsistent and headstrong, ally – his brother Félix (known by his nickname *El Chato*) who had won the Oaxaca governorship elections of November 1867.

. . .

THE DÍAZ BROTHERS IN OAXACA, 1867–71

Porfirio Díaz had made an important contribution to his brother's political career by appointing him military commander of Oaxaca in the spring of 1867 while Porfirio was still commander of the Army of the East. Nevertheless, political victory in Oaxaca for the Díaz brothers in 1867 required the effective neutralisation of the strong support for Juárez among more moderate liberals (known as *borlados*) in the state capital, and especially in the mining stronghold of the Sierra Norte, Juárez's birthplace. Here, Juárez's lieutenants Miguel Castro, Fidencio Hernández and Francisco Meixueiro maintained a powerful influence, backed up by local units of the National Guard. It was also necessary to heal the rift which developed between Porfirio and *El Chato* over the latter's rejection of his older brother's advice that any *rapprochement* with *juaristas* would compromise his freedom of action.

Relations between the two brothers improved during 1868, and their control over state politics was extended through political appointments (in particular, of *jefes políticos*) and the reconstruction of the National Guard units within the state.[16] The success of this strategy was confirmed by the state congressional elections of November 1869, which increased the number of Díaz supporters.

As a result, they were able to challenge the attempt by Juárez and his agents in Oaxaca to influence the subsequent governorship elections of June 1871, when *El Chato* was re-elected unopposed. The simultaneous results from the electoral districts of Oaxaca for presidential candidates confirmed the hegemony of the Díaz bothers within the state – not one single vote was registered for either Juárez or Lerdo.[17]

Despite these voting figures, it was clear, however, that key areas of Oaxaca, particularly the Sierra Norte and the Isthmus of Tehuantepec, were still beyond the control of the Díaz brothers. According to Porfirio's memoirs, Fidencio Hernández had initially supported their cause but had then defected, subsequently being rewarded by Juárez with promotion to Brigadier General. The lack of support from the Sierra Norte would have important repercussions for the success of the rebellion against Juárez which the brothers were now plotting. The support of the Sierra Norte of Oaxaca would once again be crucial to Porfirio's ultimate accession to power in 1876.[18]

The political machinations in Oaxaca between 1867 and 1871 demonstrate that Porfirio Díaz had certainly not retired from political activity. In fact, as the Juárez regime became increasingly plagued by regional political rebellions, and by peasant and agrarian rebellions across central and western Mexico during 1868 and 1869, Díaz's political activity increased. Although he had publicly refused, despite frequent invitations, to endorse any of these anti-Juárez revolts, it is clear that he had decided, long before the presidential elections of July 1871, that an armed uprising against the Juárez government was not only justified, but a manifestation of his political destiny.

· · ·

THE REBELLION OF LA NORIA, 1871–72

The abortive Rebellion of La Noria has often been interpreted as either a manifestation of Díaz's overwhelming personal ambition, or as a resounding triumph for Juárez and the rule of law. It is best understood, however, in the context of the overall failure of the liberal project of the Restored Republic, the deepening of factional schism within the Liberal Party, and the increasing recourse by all of the major political contenders (Juárez, Lerdo and Díaz himself) to unconstitutional practices in the achievement of political power.[19]

The profound schism within liberal ranks and growing dissatisfaction with the Juárez government became increasingly obvious during the course of 1869 and 1870. Sebastián Lerdo de Tejada, President of the Supreme Court and a loyal *juarista* since the early 1860s, had progressively cultivated, through the traditional modes of political patronage, a significant following within the National Congress and in key state governorships (particularly those of Puebla, Guanajuato, San Luís Potosí, Hidalgo, Morelos and Jalisco). Once it became clear that Juárez would be seeking re-election in 1871, Lerdo resigned from the cabinet in January 1871 to prepare his campaign. At the same time, the supporters of Díaz in the Congress, led by the tenacious Justo Benítez, continued to promote the General's political fortunes (and the cause of insurrection) through manipulation and intense negotiation.[20]

Díaz only formally accepted that his name should be put forward as a candidate in January 1871. His manifesto, published in the newspaper *El Mensajero* in the same month, outlined his political programme, and the basis of his challenge to Juárez and of the political stance he had adopted since 1867. It promised to respect the Constitution, ensuring free elections and the sovereignty of the states within the federation, and to fight corruption and bureaucratic waste and, ironically, military intervention in politics. Once again, according to the traditional practice of nineteenth-century politics, the candidate took no further role in the campaign, which was carried out through the press.[21]

The election result showed that none of the candidates had won an overall majority – the votes cast from the electoral colleges were as follows: Juárez 5,837; Díaz 3,555; Lerdo 2,874. As a consequence, the result would have to be decided after the inauguration of the National Congress in October. The political manoeuvring which took place over the summer of 1871, however, failed to cement the loose alliance between *lerdistas* and *porfiristas* which had functioned sporadically during the previous Congress, and Juárez was officially declared re-elected in October.

On 8 November 1871, Porfirio Díaz formally launched the Plan of La Noria, published by the state government of Oaxaca which was now under the control of his brother, Félix. Governor Díaz declared himself to be in rebellion against the Juárez government, under the banner of 'the Constitution of 57 and Electoral Freedom' and a slogan of 'less government and more freedom'.[22]

Despite the appeals to constitutional legalism and the claim to be upholding the cause of legitimate electoral practices, there is clear evidence that Díaz had been planning an armed insurrection months in advance of the elections of July 1871. In his correspondence with his closest military and political allies, there were scarcely veiled references to the need for an armed uprising from November 1870 onwards, and frequent references to the rumours in the press during the summer of 1871. The launch of the Plan itself in November had been preceded by a series of regional anti-Juárez rebellions by Generals Treviño (Nuevo León), Trinidad de la Cadena (Zacatecas), Manuel González (Tamaulipas), Luís Mier y Terán (Veracruz) and Donato Guerra (Durango), which had occupied the attention of the federal forces in the north, thus permitting Díaz to combine the forces from Oaxaca and Puebla in an assault on the capital.[23]

Díaz's military campaign was singularly unsuccessful, despite his appeal for support from what he described in the Plan of La Noria as a 'vilified and downtrodden' regular army, abused and neglected by the government. The Minister of War, the loyal *juarista* Ignacio Mejía, who was fully aware of the nature and extent of the *porfirista* plot, and the limited resources at their disposal, orchestrated a very successful military strategy to defeat the rebels. In the decisive military encounters, Generals Ignacio Alatorre and Sóstenes Rocha defeated rebel forces in Puebla (at San Mateo Xindihui in December 1871) and in Zacatecas (at La Bufa in March 1872). Significantly, the Díaz rebellion was unable to attract adequate support, even in Oaxaca, especially in the crucial region of the Sierra Norte, where the local *caciques* Fidencio Hernández and Francisco Meixueiro stayed loyal to Juárez.

There is a curious aspect of the rebellion which has never been fully explained. Díaz himself was not present at any of the military encounters, and there is little evidence that he provided either military or political leadership during the rebellion. He was largely out of touch with his allies after January 1872, seeking refuge in Chihuahua, across the border in Texas and California and subsequently in north-western Mexico (Tepic), in a vain attempt to elicit the support of one of nineteenth-century Mexico's most intransigent regional *caudillos*, Manuel Lozada. The most obvious explanation for his absence would appear to the combined desire to generate further support for the campaign and to avoid capture. It also underlines the point that Díaz's primary role in the rebellion was as the figurehead of a loose, heterogeneous and ultimately unco-ordinated coalition.

The definitive end to the Rebellion of La Noria did not come as a consequence of military defeat or inadequate leadership, but rather as a consequence of the sudden death of Benito Juárez in July 1872, thus removing the principal *raison d'être* of the rebellion. The next day (19 July), Lerdo de Tejada, President of the Supreme Court, was nominated as interim President, and a week later he called simultaneously for presidential elections in October and offered an amnesty to the *porfirista* rebels. Lacking in co-ordination and morale, and in any political justification for continuing the rebellion, the majority of Díaz commanders accepted the terms of the amnesty. Díaz remained elusive until his final acceptance of defeat in October 1872. The extent of the decline in his political fortunes was under-lined that same month by the virtually unanimous election of Lerdo as constitutional President.[24]

. . .

THE CAMPAIGN AGAINST LERDO, 1872–76

It was apparent from the outset that the presidency of Lerdo de Tejada would retain the same policies and general political strategy pursued by Juárez since 1867 – to uphold the supremacy of the civil power, to maintain the rule of law but, at the same time, to introduce constitutional reform which would enhance the role of the execu-tive by increasing the authority of central government *vis-à-vis* the authority of the states, and that of the office of President in relation to Congress. This moderate, legalistic strategy was bound to clash, as had Juárez after 1867, with the radical liberal (*puro*) tradition which supported the 'purity' of the 1857 Constitution, the preservation of popular sovereignty, the supremacy of a unicameral Congress, and local and municipal autonomy. Since Díaz had acted as the figurehead of the radical liberal cause since 1867, and still commanded wide-spread popular and loyal support outside the confines of formal politics, he remained Lerdo's principal political adversary.

Following the disaster of La Noria, however, Díaz had lost vital political support both within Congress and among the state gov-ernors, most of whom were the appointees or associates of either Juárez or Lerdo. The task of the subsequent four years would be to reconstruct the opposition coalition but, in contrast to the failed strategy 1867 or 1871 through which Díaz had initially sought power through the electoral process, his preferred tactic after 1872 became military rebellion. That he chose to uphold the sanctity of the Con-stitution by means of a military coup highlights one of the central paradoxes of nineteenth-century liberal politics in Mexico – the pursuit of representative institutions by authoritarian means. In the abuse of constitutional practice, however, especially in the manipulation of electoral advantage, it would be difficult to argue that, prior to 1888, Díaz was any more guilty than either Juárez or Lerdo.[25]

Lerdo's government between 1872 and 1876 courted controversy and political opposition in a number of areas – the creation of a second chamber or Senate (one of Juárez's proposals in the *Convocatoria* of 1876) met opposition within Congress and the enforced implementation of the Reform Laws (The Law of Regulation) brought accusations of anti-clericalism and stimulated popular pro-Catholic (*cristero*) rebellions in north-western Mexico in 1874 and 1875. The Lerdo government was also faced with a series of regional rebellions (such as, for example, from the *caudillo* Manuel Lozada in Tepic and the Yaqui rebellion under José María Leyva Cajeme in Sonora). Lerdo also clashed with the *Gran Círculo de Obreros de México* in a series of textile and mining strikes, and with business interests over the refusal to approve a railway concession which, for the first time, would link Mexico directly with the USA. Lerdo preferred to maintain the territorial separation of Mexico and the USA because of the threat to Mexican political sovereignty. He is frequently quoted to have insisted on maintaining 'between strength and weakness, the desert'.

Above all, it was Lerdo's overt intervention into the conduct of politics at the state level which gave a legitimate focus to the opposition's accusations of corrupt, authoritarian and unconstitutional practice. One of the *causes célèbres* which antagonised the *porfirista* opposition was the conduct of the Lerdo administration in the state of Nuevo León, where federal troops stationed in Monterrey (under the command of General Carlos Fuero) enforced a 'state of siege' and prevented the election of *porfirista* sympathiser Francisco González Doria. Lerdo was also accused, with some justification, of interference in the internal politics of Jalisco, where *lerdistas* clashed with former *juaristas* Ignacio Luís Vallarta and Jesús Camarena, and federal troops under the command of *lerdista* General José Ceballos were sent in to supervise the contested elections of 1875. The political situation remained unresolved on the outbreak of the Tuxtepec Rebellion in 1876 and it was noticeable that support for *porfirismo* was strong in both states.[26]

One of the most significant executive interventions and abuses of state sovereignty made by Lerdo during his term of office, which would have a significant impact on the outcome of the Tuxtepec Rebellion in 1876, was in Díaz's home state of Oaxaca. Here, the internal political conflicts centred upon the clash between the supporters of *juarista* Miguel Castro, who had been appointed by Juárez as interim governor since the failure of the La Noria Rebellion in December 1871, and *lerdista* José Esperón. The governorship elections of 1874 had produced a split local legislature and accusations of the usurpation of legislative powers by Castro. The case was heard eventually in the National Congress, which found in favour of Esperón, and federal troops were despatched, under the command of *lerdista* General Ignacio Alatorre, with orders to depose Castro and install Esperón. Far from bringing political peace to the state, the events in Oaxaca served to alienate the supporters of Castro, especially the *juarista caciques* of the Sierra Norte, who subsequently entered into an anti-Lerdo alliance with Díaz, who had previously been their sworn enemy during the La Noria Rebellion in 1871. As a result, the local events in Oaxaca ensured that Díaz had a solid base in his native state from which to build the Tuxtepec campaign from the south.[27]

Francisco Bulnes, a supporter of Lerdo between 1872 and 1876, proposes the interesting hypothesis that events in Oaxaca were precipitated by a series of manipulations by Minister of War General Ignacio Mejía. Mejía, a *oaxaqueño* and loyal *juarista*, had become the widely-acknowledged leader of the *juarista* faction following the death of Don Benito in 1872. Apparently piqued at the efforts of *lerdistas* in Congress to promote the candidacy of Manuel Romero Rubio (rather than his own) as the successor to Lerdo in the forthcoming elections of 1876, Mejía took revenge on the *lerdistas* by giving overt military advantage to his supporters in Oaxaca (Castro, Meixueiro and Hernández) in opposition to *lerdista* governor Esperón. Bulnes argues that Mejía's deliberately inadequate support for the federal garrison in Oaxaca, and for the subsequent campaign to restore Esperón, thus guaranteed not only the success of the anti-Esperón rebellion of January 1876, but its survival as a bastion of *anti-lerdismo*. According to Bulnes, Mejía's betrayal of Lerdo, and the indirect support this provided for the Díaz campaign, was the principal reason for the victory of the Tuxtepec Rebellion.[28]

Lerdo's most controversial political manoeuvre, and one which played directly into the hands of the *porfirista* opposition, was his decision to seek re-election in 1876. Although the justification for the decision was the maintenance of political stability, in fact it produced the reverse. As demonstrated on many occasions during the Restored Republic, anti-re-electionism had become one of the central and most controversial questions of late nineteenth-century Mexican politics. It had formed a vital plank in the opposition to Juárez in 1865, 1867 and 1871, and would remain one of the major rallying points for the opposition to Díaz throughout the Porfiriato.[29] In 1876, not without considerable irony in the context of Díaz's own subsequent re-elections, it became the principal *raison d'être* of the Tuxtepec Rebellion.

. . .

THE TUXTEPEC CAMPAIGN, 1876

There has been a good deal of speculation over Díaz's motives in leading a second military rebellion against an incumbent government, especially after the first had been such an abject disaster. It is generally assumed that personal ambition was the principal motivation. Díaz's critics frequently point out that the Tuxtepec Rebellion, unlike that of La Noria, could not be justified as a response to a fraudulent election, since the original Plan was launched in January 1876, six months before the presidential elections scheduled for July. While personal ambition is undeniable, it is important not to underestimate the extent of political and popular opposition to Lerdo upon which Díaz was able to capitalise in 1876. It is also important to emphasise the fact that the *porfirista* cause had been associated with anti-re-electionism since before the Rebellion of La Noria.[30]

It is clear that in 1876 Díaz had prepared his campaign far more thoroughly than in 1871. Precisely because of the débâcle of La Noria, Díaz and his associates throughout the Republic devoted considerable attention to the evolution of a military and political strategy. Even before the launch of the Plan of Tuxtepec, Díaz had left his home in the *Hacienda La Candelaria* in Tlacotalpan, Veracruz, for the USA, establishing a base of operations in Brownsville, Texas, in December 1875.[31]

Political preparations were as important as the military strategy. Invitations to join the rebellion were extended to all state governors and regional military commanders. The political message in these invitations was explicit: Lerdo had violated one of the most cherished notions of late nineteenth-century liberalism – the sanctity of the 1857 Constitution – and therefore deserved to be deposed. Díaz's invitation to General José Guillermo Carbó, a former companion-in-arms in both the Wars of the Reforma and French Intervention, in an attempt to persuade him to endorse the Tuxtepec cause, is representative. It exonerates Díaz from the accusation that he was only marginally committed to the cause of radical liberalism.

> As a gentleman and a man of patriotism, a brother and colleague of the second war of Independence [i.e. the struggle against the French Intervention], in your hands lies the rapid and permanent organisation of the next government. . . . I am incapable of recommending any course of action to you which is not noble or dignified . . . remember that I was forced to turn against Juárez politically, in spite of the close personal bonds of friendship which united us, only because I judged that the Constitution had been damaged . . . and Juárez's actions were nothing by comparison to the political crimes committed against the Constitution by [President] Lerdo. The government has lost its legitimacy. A country can never call itself truly constituted unless its citizens, including those who command its troops, are resolved only to follow the government if it abides by the rule of law, the standard bearer of its liberties. No honourable or patriotic soldier ought to support a government which has broken the pact with the people which the constitution represents.[32]

The political strategy, however, had only limited success among incumbent military commanders and state governors, since most of these were *lerdista* appointees. As might be expected, the response was far greater among those who were political opponents of the Lerdo administration. As a further inducement to rebel, those who endorsed the Plan of Tuxtepec (subsequently 'reformed' in Palo Blanco, Tamaulipas, in March 1876) were to have their posts, their titles and their military honours recognised, with the further promise of political office to follow.[33]

From the outset, the military campaign had one major objective – the creation of multiple centres of rebellion through *guerrilla* activity, which would not only give the impression of widespread national and popular support, but also occupy the attention of the government and thus prevent a concerted campaign to destroy rebel forces.[34] After the first few months of the campaign, the strategy was adapted towards the establishment of two principal concentrations of rebel forces, the first in the north-east and the second in the south-east (based in Oaxaca and Puebla), under the general command of one of the most powerful *caciques* of the Puebla Sierra,

Juan N. Méndez. Díaz himself led the campaign in the north-east until the 'defeat' at Icamole (Nuevo León) in May, after which Díaz took command of the south-eastern campaign and Manuel González that of the north-east.[35]

The military campaign did not always run smoothly or to plan, and suffered from a lack of resources, especially of funds to pay for arms and equipment. The northern campaign was largely unsuccessful in generating widespread support. Here, the largest contingent of government troops, under the command of General Mariano Escobedo, kept rebel activities in check. In that sense, it has often been portrayed as a failure, although Ballard Perry suggests that, by drawing the attention of the Lerdo government to the northern campaign, this allowed the campaign in the south-east to flourish by default. It was the convergence of the rebel forces of the south-east and those of the north-east which achieved the decisive military victory at Tecoac, Puebla, in November 1876.

There is one further element which was crucial to the victory of the Tuxtepec Rebellion – the fact that, following Lerdo's re-election in July 1876, he was faced with not simply an escalating *porfirista* insurrection, but a second 'legalistic' revolt led by José María Iglesias, who challenged the legitimacy of the elections. As President of the Supreme Court since 1873, Iglesias had become embroiled in constitutional conflicts with the Lerdo government long before 1876 over the right of the Supreme Court to overturn the decisions of the electoral colleges in the individual states.

In 1876 the confrontation between Lerdo and Iglesias came to a head over the presidential elections. Iglesias claimed that Lerdo's re-election was fraudulent and illegal because in some cases the elections had been manipulated and in others they had been cancelled. Claiming, not for the first time in nineteenth-century Mexican history, that his constitutional position as President of the Supreme Court justified his accession to the presidency, Iglesias launched his revolt from Salamanca, Guanajuato, in October 1876. However, he was able to achieve only a limited level of political support, despite professions of loyalty from leading officers of the federal army, for example from Generals Felipe Berriozábal, Sóstenes Rocha and Ignacio Alatorre.[36]

Ultimately, however, the Iglesias challenge was profoundly and decisively upstaged by the military victory for the *tuxtepecano* rebellion at Tecoac, Puebla, on 16 November 1876, where Díaz himself presided over the defeat of federal troops under the command of

Alatorre. In the subsequent confusion throughout the Republic over the locus and tenure of central political authority, exacerbated by Lerdo's flight from Mexico City, a number of governors and regional military commanders (in Michoacán, Coahuila, Durango, Sonora, Colima and Morelos) officially 'recognised' Iglesias and his 'Government of Legality'. Others were clearly confused and proceeded to recognise Iglesias as interim President and Porfirio Díaz as General in Chief of the Army.[37] In reality, the relative strength of *iglesismo* meant that negotiations between the two rebel camps would be necessary in order to settle the final outcome.[38]

In those negotiations, which became known as the Convention of Acatlán, Díaz offered Iglesias the role of 'provisional president' provided that future cabinet posts be divided equally between *porfiristas* and *iglesistas*, and that Díaz should occupy the Ministry of War. Iglesias refused to accept these terms. He argued that his challenge to Lerdo had been based upon the fact that no member of the interim government would become an official candidate, and therefore, because Díaz would undoubtedly be a candidate in any subsequent elections, he should not form part of the interim cabinet. The real reason for Iglesias's refusal was, it seems, the fact that power would rest with whoever controlled the army following Lerdo's overthrow.[39]

After the failure of these negotiations, Díaz took the decisive step to occupy Mexico City on 23 November, at the head of the self-styled 'Constitutionalist' army. He assumed executive power by decree one week later, nominating his close ally from the Puebla Sierra, General Juan N. Méndez, as provisional President so that he could lead the military campaign against the remaining pockets of *iglesista* resistance. A final meeting between Iglesias and Díaz took place at the *Hacienda de La Capilla* near the city of Querétaro in December, but the scope of the *porfirista* victory made any concessions to *iglesismo* largely unnecessary. As Díaz's troops subsequently marched triumphantly into Querétaro, and then to Celaya and Guadalajara, the number of *lerdista* defections grew. Eventually, like Lerdo, who had sought exile in the USA (New York), Iglesias sought refuge in San Francisco.

The triumph of the Tuxtepec Rebellion brought Porfirio Díaz the presidential office he had coveted since 1867. It had been achieved not simply as a reflection of the ruthless pursuit of personal ambition, but as a result of a combination of significant popular support in central and southern Mexico and careful military and political preparation. Those who had supported the Plan of Tuxtepec represented an eclectic coalition, including former conservatives and former supporters of Maximilian who opposed Lerdo. Nevertheless, the triumph of the Tuxtepec campaign should principally be seen as the culmination of the radical (and popular) liberal (*rojo/jacobino*) challenge to the constitutional abuses committed by Juárez and Lerdo since 1867, supported by National Guard units from Puebla, Oaxaca and Veracruz which sought redress for Lerdo's failure to implement the constitutional guarantees of effective suffrage and municipal autonomy. The Tuxtepec rebellion, in other words, had a genuinely popular base. The opportunity provided by the parallel rebellion of José María Iglesias in October was crucial to the eventual success, but in his negotiations with Iglesias and the eventual neutralisation of the threat which *iglesismo* posed to his authority, Díaz demonstrated considerable political skill. Those same skills would be needed over subsequent years in order further to consolidate his national political authority, which was still extremely precarious in 1876.

. . .

NOTES AND REFERENCES

1. I. Paz, *Algunas Campañas*, 2 vols, Mexico City, 1997, Vol. 1, pp.11–19.
2. H. Scullard, *A History of the Roman World from 753 to 146BC*, London, 1935, p.74; for references to Díaz as Cincinnatus, see *inter alia* F. Bulnes, 'Rectificaciones y Aclaraciones a las *Memorias* del General Díaz', in Gonzálex Navarro (ed.), *Memorias de Porfirio Díaz*, 2 vols, Mexico City, 1994, Vol. II, p.304.
3. According to Díaz's great-great-grandson, Carlos Tello Díaz, although Delfina's birth certificate claimed that she was the daughter of 'unknown parents', it was common knowledge that she was the daughter of Porfirio's sister, Manuela. C. Tello Díaz, *El Exilio: Un Relato de Familia*, Mexico City, 1993, p.188.
4. Díaz to González, Oaxaca, 7 May 1870, *Archivo Manuel González*, Iberoamerican University, Mexico City, Box 3, ff.1–37.
5. Ramírez, quoted in D. Brading, *The First America*, Cambridge, 1991, p.664.
6. L.B. Perry, *Juárez and Díaz: Machine Politics in Mexico*, DeKalb, IL, 1978, pp.36–8.
7. Díaz, *Memorias*, Vol. I, p.265. He was also clearly a believer in censorship. When Francisco Bulnes asked Minister of the Interior Manuel González Cosío why his study of the Díaz regime had not been accepted, he was told by González Cosío that 'General Díaz believes

that there are some things that the people should be told, and others that should be hidden'. Bulnes, 'Rectificaciones', in *Memorias*, Vol. II, p.248.

8. B. Hamnett, *Juárez*, Harlow, 1994, p.202.
9. Díaz, *Memorias*, Vol. I, pp.203–5.
10. C. Beals, *Porfirio Díaz: Dictator of Mexico*, Philadelphia, PA, 1932, p.158.
11. Perry, *Juárez and Díaz*, pp.42–3.
12. Letter from Benítez to Díaz, quoted in Perry, *Juárez and Díaz*, p.52.
13. D. Cosío Villegas, *Historia Moderna de México*, 10 vols, Mexico City, 1955–72 (hereafter *IIMM* followed by volume number), Vol. I, p.187.
14. Díaz to Castro, quoted in F. Falcone, 'Benito Juárez versus the Díaz Brothers: Politics in Oaxaca 1867–71', *The Americas*, 33(4), 1977, pp.640–1.
15. E. Krauze, *Porfirio Díaz: Místico de la Autoridad*, Mexico City, 1987, p.22; Bulnes, 'Rectificaciones', in *Memorias*, Vol. II, p.305.
16. B. Hamnett, *Juárez*, p.223.
17. Falcone, 'Benito Juárez', p.648.
18. Díaz, *Memorias*, Vol. I, p.59.
19. B. Hamnett, 'Liberalism Divided: Regional Politics and the National Project during the Mexican Restored Republic', *Hispanic American Historical Review*, 76(4), November 1996, pp.659–90. As Francisco Bulnes later pointed out, at the same time as the Díaz brothers were criticising the Juárez government for 'imposing' candidates against the will of the people, in the elections in Oaxaca for federal deputies to the National Congress in 1871, four of the candidates were either not from Oaxaca or had never visited the state: the candidates were Manuel María de Zamacona (from Puebla), Felipe Buenrostro (Zacatecas), Roberto Esteva (Veracruz) and Jesús Alfaro (Mexico City); Bulnes, 'Rectificaciones', in *Memorias*, Vol. II, pp.305–6.
20. F.A. Knapp, *The Life of Sebastián Lerdo de Tejada: A Study of Influence and Obscurity*, Austin, TX, 1951, p.150; for details of the labyrinthine negotiations between *juaristas*, *lerdistas* and *porfiristas*, see Perry, *Juárez and Díaz*, pp.153–200.
21. W. Scholes, '*El Mensajero* and the Election of 1871 in Mexico', *The Americas*, 5, 1948, pp.61–7; details of the campaign are in I. Paz, *Algunas Campañas*, Vol. 2.
22. The text of the Plan can be found in J.F. Iturribarría, *Historia de Oaxaca: Vol. IV 1867–76*, Oaxaca City, 1956, pp.96–100. There is general agreement that the authors of the Plan were Díaz's closest political allies, Justo Benítez, Manuel María de Zamacona and the *mestizo* intellectual Ignacio Ramírez; see, for example, José López-Portillo y Rojas, *Elevación y Caída de Porfirio Díaz*, Mexico City, 1921, p.83.
23. Perry, *Juárez and Díaz*, p.168.
24. Although Lerdo was, in fact, the only candidate; Knapp, *Lerdo*, p.164.

25. Hamnett, 'Liberalism Divided', p.688, and Perry, *Juárez and Díaz*, *passim*.

26. Perry, *Juárez and Díaz*, pp.192–6.

27. Iturribarría, *Historia de Oaxaca: Vol. IV*, pp.132–7.

28. Bulnes, 'Rectificaciones', in *Memorias*, Vol. II, pp.315–20.

29. Díaz, for this very reason, assiduously avoided the question of consecutive re-election until 1888; see Chapter 5.

30. Perry, *Juárez and Díaz*, p.188; for a critical view, see Bulnes, 'Rectificaciones', in Díaz, *Memorias*, Vol. II, p.312; J. López-Portillo, *Elevación y Caída de Porfirio Díaz*, p.102; this is the view sustained by Cosío Villegas, *HMM*, Vol. I, p.805.

31. While Díaz received no formal assistance from the US State Department, it appears that US military intelligence turned a blind eye to his recruitment activities in Brownsville; R. McCormack, 'Porfiro Díaz en la Frontera Tejana', *Historia Mexicana*, Vol. V, 1956, pp.373–410. See Chapter 6 for Mexico's relations with the USA in this period.

32. Díaz to Carbó, 8 November 1876, CPD:C1:f.047.

33. The text of the original and 'reformed' Plans, modified to include an extensive preamble listing the political crimes of the Lerdo government, can be found in López-Portillo, *Elevación y Caída de Porfirio Díaz*, pp.105–8.

34. Perry, *Juárez and Díaz*, Chapter 8, includes considerable detail on the military and recruitment strategies within the Tuxtepec campaign.

35. Díaz to Méndez, 8 July 1876, *Archivo Manuel González*, Box 3, doc. 1–00278. Ballard Perry is convinced that the battle of Icamole was very far from a defeat for Díaz, who was not present; Perry, *Juárez and Díaz*, Chapter 9.

36. Alatorre was reluctant to join the *iglesista* cause until the official end of Lerdo's term of office on 1 December: those military officers who subscribed to this view became known as 'Decemberists' (*decembristas*); Perry, *Juárez and Díaz*, pp.296–8.

37. Domingo Nava in Tepic to Díaz, quoted in Perry, *Juárez and Díaz*, p.318.

38. D. Cosío Villegas, *HMM*, Vol. IX, p.57; it is also important to note that Article 6 of the reformed Plan of Tuxtepec in March 1876 had already offered the provisional presidency to Iglesias, provided that he accepted the provisions of the Plan within one month. Iglesias had declined the offer.

39. Perry, *Juárez and Díaz*, pp.437–40.

Chapter 4

PRAGMATIC LIBERALISM,
1876–84

In the United States, democracy works because once a President is elected, everybody supports him. In Mexico, everybody immediately works to get him out of office. (Porfirio Díaz)[1]

The political survival of the Díaz regime following the Revolution of Tuxtepec in 1876 was far from inevitable or straightforward. The first Díaz administration seemed destined to share the experience, and even the fate, of all previous nineteenth-century governments, plagued by the continuation of the domestic political conflicts and international hostilities which had characterised most of Mexico's independent history. After nearly a decade of liberal government during the Restored Republic since 1867, Mexico in 1876 still lacked the basic requirements of political stability: clearly-defined or secure frontiers, or stable relationships with its hemispheric neighbours (both the USA and Guatemala) or with Europe. Financial and fiscal instability, exacerbated by the persistent problem of external indebtedness, remained an important obstacle to economic development. National and nationalist consciousness had undoubtedly been raised during the struggle against the French Intervention, and the impact of the Laws of the Reforma had had a decisive, albeit patchy impact on the restructuring of rural society and the extension of a republican political consciousness.

But there was little evidence of a coherent sense of national identity, of social or economic integration, or of profound social, material or political development. Above all, despite – or, as some contemporary observers saw it, because of – the adoption of the Constitution of 1857, the country lacked legitimate government or stable institutions, and the construction of both the state and the nation had yet to be consolidated. In short, while the liberal state can be said to have embarked on its precarious existence, there was precious little evidence of nation and even less of a solid basis for political stability by 1876. Despite the triumph of liberalism in 1867, the liberal project in Mexico – the establishment of representative institutions, the secularisation of civil society and the 'free-market' invigoration of a post-colonial economy – still stood on very unstable foundations. It is against this background that the nature of the Díaz regime must be understood, and its achievements assessed.

Before any of these political or developmental goals could be achieved, it was vital to establish, first and foremost, a period of internal political peace. This was the principal and central task of the first Díaz administration, and it remained a consistent priority throughout the history of the entire regime. Its contemporary apologists (and subsequent *porfirista* historiography) considered the establishment of the *pax porfiriana* as one of its principal achievements, and it became the main justification for successive re-elections after 1884. Despite these confident assertions of the definitive establishment of peace, it is nevertheless clear that, throughout the lifetime of the regime, political peace was far from complete. The regime was consistently buffeted by political turbulence, ranging from indigenous and agrarian rebellion to anti-re-electionist political agitation.

In addition, the supreme authority which Díaz claimed, and which his enemies accused him of abusing, was, in reality, much less supreme than it appeared. In the mosaic of Mexican politics at both the national and regional levels, the achievement and maintenance of power was a process of constant negotiation and renegotiation. Consequently, neither *porfirista* historiography, which praises Díaz as a supernatural man of destiny, nor its *anti-porfirista* counterpart, which caricatures him as a brutal tyrant, captures the essence of Porfirian politics.

There was certainly very little evidence of political peace before Díaz' second re-election in 1888. Nonetheless, the strategies for its ultimate achievement were adopted from an early stage after 1876. They included repression, coercion, intimidation and, in at least one celebrated case, in Veracruz in 1879, the assassination of political opponents. But, at the same time, such authoritarian practices co-existed with, and ultimately were less important than, mediation, manipulation and conciliation – in other words, the politics of pragmatism and *realpolitik*. For more than a decade, the implementation of multiple strategies proved to be a tentative and difficult process, given the political inexperience of Díaz and the majority of his *tuxtepecano* followers, and the scarce resources available to the central state in 1876.

. . .

THE PRINCIPLES OF PORFIRIAN POLITICS

It is appropriate to outline some key themes, preoccupations and strategies of Porfirian political practice which were crucial in the survival and the consolidation of the regime after 1876. First, the distinction between ideology and practice, and, in its wake, the strong advocacy of pragmatism as one of the hallmarks of the regime. Second, the importance of patronage in the construction of ties of personal loyalty and deference to the supreme authority of the President, which fuelled the entire Porfirian system. Third, the strict formal observance of constitutional practice, especially in the conduct of elections at state and national levels. Fourth, the maintenance of a delicate balance between central and state (federal) authority, perhaps the most intractable political problem in nineteenth-century Mexico, which was seen most clearly in Díaz's relationship with state governors. Finally, the adoption of force, intimidation and other authoritarian practices as necessary tools for the maintenance of political peace.

Ideology and practice

From the earliest days of the regime, despite the advocacy of *puro* liberalism in Díaz's political campaigns since 1867, the Porfirian political system would be based upon pragmatic political management, rather than constitutional principle. Nevertheless, during his first administration, Díaz showed a clear commitment to *puro* liberal principles, as enshrined in the Plan of Tuxtepec: first, the prohibition of consecutive re-election to political office; second, a commitment to electoral reform which would guarantee broader political representation and participation in the electoral process; and, third, a commitment to the *tuxtepecano* principle of the protection of local sovereignty and autonomy through the conduct of direct elections at municipal and district level (and direct elections for regional *jefes políticos*). In honouring these commitments, Díaz clearly reflected his own political affiliations and antecedents as the standard-bearer of radical or popular liberalism.

Díaz came to power in Mexico at a time of heightened ideological debate. Following the defeat of Mexican conservativism in 1867, the hegemony of mid-nineteenth-century radical liberalism was increasingly challenged and ultimately transformed by the development of conservative or 'developmentalist' liberalism, which itself demonstrated the growing influence of the doctrine of positivism. Mexican positivism drew on the theories of Henri de Saint-Simon and Auguste Comte, which had enjoyed considerable political currency in Europe after the 1820s, especially in France and Spain. Positivist or 'scientific' politics (whose adherents in Mexico therefore became known as *científicos* after 1893) advocated the application of scientific method, not only to the analysis of social, economic and political conditions, but also to the formulation of policies which would remedy their deficiencies and thus ensure material and scientific progress. In political terms, positivism challenged the excessive idealism or 'metaphysics' of doctrinaire liberalism and its emphasis on popular sovereignty, and advocated instead constitutional reform and strong central government which would avoid the descent into anarchy and revolution.[2]

During the course of the Porfiriato, positivism would exert a strong influence over the 'high politics' of the Díaz regime, particularly within the *camarilla* of the *científicos* led by José Yves Limantour after his appointment to the key post Minister of Finance in 1893. The influence of positivism outside the cabinet, or outside Mexico City, is open to question, and highlights one of the central problems in understanding the dynamics of national and local politics during the Porfiriato, about which relatively little is currently known. Nevertheless, the influence of the *científicos* over Díaz, and in the elaboration of patriarchal or elite liberalism was significant.[3]

Díaz's personal stance in the ideological debate between doctrinaire (*puro*) and conservative or 'developmentalist' liberalism is difficult to pinpoint with any degree of confidence and, in a sense, it is a futile quest. His political style emphasised reticence and caution, and his preference was always for political action rather than ideological debate. In addition, his contempt for what he referred to as *profundismo* or intellectual analysis has already been noted. He had an acute political brain and highly-sensitive political antenna, but he was no ideologue, much less an intellectual. Nevertheless, he personally approved the government subsidy to *La Libertad*, published as a daily newspaper between 1878 and 1884, which was the principal vehicle for the expression and exploration of positivist ideas during the early years of the regime.

Díaz's endorsement of conservative liberalism, like his earlier adherence to *puro* liberalism in the 1850s was based fundamentally on pragmatism. He thus always adapted and subordinated ideological principle to the needs of political management. Díaz never questioned the validity of the fundamental goals of Mexican constitutional liberalism – the creation of a sovereign, secular and federal state, with representative political institutions where citizenship and legal equality were protected by the rule of law – but the regime's priority was always the maintenance of political peace. This meant that the outcome of elections was too important to leave to chance. In Porfirian political practice, therefore, there was widespread electoral manipulation.

Positivism was similarly adapted to pragmatic ends. The positivist antipathy to the 'metaphysical' politics of doctrinaire liberalism and popular sovereignty and, by contrast, the endorsement of strong central government, mirrored perfectly Díaz's preference for authority and order. The positivist argument that the methods of scientific enquiry should be applied to the practical ends of economic development, social regeneration and political unity were perfectly in keeping with his belief in material and social progress. The emphasis placed by the advocates of scientific politics on 'Order and Progress' therefore became an entirely appropriate description of the central preoccupations of the Díaz regime.

Porfirian pragmatism was a product of its age and its dual liberal and anti-liberal antecedents. It was based on a highly personalist system which sought to preserve and extend ties of personal loyalty and collective deference to the supreme authority of the President. It was fuelled by patronage and maintained by a broad spectrum of strategies, ranging from flattery, duplicity, appeals to loyalty, patriotism and personal advancement to the overt use of threats and intimidation. At all levels Porfirian practice emphasised negotiation, conciliation and compromise rather than confrontation, much less the repressive tactics traditionally associated with authoritarian dictatorship. The guiding principle was the avoidance of conflict – many of Díaz's handwritten notes in the private correspondence indicate the need for caution and the recommendation that 'conflicts which might prejudice an eventual solution should be avoided'.[4]

This strategy necessarily required a regular flow of information from the wide network of correspondents from both military and civilian sources. This enabled Díaz not only to be fully aware of events, but also to be aware of the conflicting interests and viewpoints of the parties in any particular dispute, which allowed him the role of mediator, negotiator or arbiter. This knowledge was far more useful in preventing potential dissent or rebellion than the deployment of force. With detailed information at his disposal, Díaz was able to monitor the unpopularity of opponents and potential rebels, and to offer his services as mediator. He was able to calm the fears of his more anxious correspondents with a phrase that could well serve as a succinct motto for the Díaz style of government: 'We are on the alert, and in this way we shall avoid the only difficulty we could possibly fear: surprise.'[5]

Personalism and patronage

Porfirian politics was intensely personalist. Personal contact, whether by correspondence or private audience, was the principal means of communication between Díaz, his acolytes and *camarillas*, his subordinates, as well as his rivals and enemies.[6] Ably assisted by his private secretaries, Díaz was a prolific, always circumspect correspondent, with a prodigious ability to remember names and personal details, and family connections. One biographer claims that he was able to name from memory the entire officer corps of the Army of the East, and of all members of the Congress and Senate.[7] This enabled him to end his correspondence with a combination of patriotic exhortation and fraternal or paternal greetings for family and friends, which not only reflected social convention but was crucial to the maintenance of a personalist style of politics.

As the ample evidence of his private correspondence attests, he was a passive rather than an active correspondent, always careful to reply to the vast majority of his correspondents with tact and courtesy, displaying the interpersonal skills at which he was so adept. Even requests which were refused – which was frequently the case – were done so in a manner which attempted to seduce the correspondent with the possibility of future satisfaction. A typical response was: 'I shall do what I can, but if I am unable to do what you request, it is because there are so many pressing obligations and demands that it will be impossible to reconcile or satisfy all interests.'[8]

The apparent personal intimacy with a broad range of correspondents across a wide spectrum of social classes is also deceptive because the exercise of personal skills was aimed principally at the cultivation of deference. Automatic or unquestioning deference to higher and supreme authority, whether to the monarch or, in the nineteenth-century republican tradition, the president or chief executive, has long been a part of Mexican (and Hispanic) political culture. As suggested in Chapter 2, deference was one of the distinguishing features of Latin American *caudillismo*. As Díaz knew very well, the successful cultivation of deference facilitated the exercise of political authority, since the word of the *caudillo*/president/monarch was law. As his most loyal of supporters were accustomed to confirming: 'You know, sir, that the smallest word from you is an order for me.'[9]

The most extreme personal expressions of deference, which frequently bordered on adulation, came from his former comrades in arms, usually on the anniversary of his most renowned military exploits (5 May 1862, the defeat of French troops in the battle of Puebla; 18 October 1866, the victory over French troops at La Carbonera in Oaxaca; and 2 April 1867, the liberation of Puebla). In the copious correspondence from those who had served under Díaz in the National Guard or the patriotic army, Díaz is frequently referred to as 'my *compadre*' or 'our *caudillo*', 'the standard-bearer of peace' and the personification of 'the glory of Mexico'.[10]

The language of deference and adulation used to commemorate Díaz's military exploits was not restricted to his subordinates. One of the most illustrative examples is the case of General Manuel González, who had fought initially against Díaz and against the liberal cause during the War of the Reforma (1858–61) but who subsequently became an intimate ally and *compadre* of Díaz during the campaigns against the French Intervention (1862–67). The personal and political alliance between Díaz and González had been notably extended during the Tuxtepec campaign of 1875 and 1876, when González had accompanied Díaz during his preparations in Brownsville, Texas, and, subsequently, as a result of González's decisive intervention in the battle of Tecoac which secured a vital victory for the Tuxtepec campaign. The strength of the personal alliance would be fully demonstrated in 1880 when González was chosen by Díaz to succeed him as President after his first term of office.

González wrote regularly to his *compadre* Díaz on the anniversary of his major exploits. The correspondence began on the first anniversary of the battle of La Carbonera (31 October 1866) and continued even after the end of González's term as President in 1884. In the first letter in 1867, addressed to 'the Illustrious *Caudillo* of [the Army of] the East', González wrote:

> Today, after twelve months, as I recall this never-to-be-forgotten date, the most humble of the soldiers of [the Army of] the East seeks

out his General in Chief and congratulates him on his personal glories, which are the most cherished glories of the *patria*.[11]

Díaz's response to a very similar letter from González nearly 20 years later, in 1885, this time commemorating the battle of Puebla (2 April 1867), showed that he was still the target of adulation and deference from his former companion in arms, who was now himself a former President of Mexico. The reply also shows Díaz as a master of both patriotic discourse and the art of flattery:

> the benevolence of a friend always flatters; but the respect of a patriot swells me with pride. In your greeting, everything is there to behold: the memory of a friend, the appreciation of a valiant soldier of the Republic, who, wounded but disdaining death and mocking danger, entered the streets of Puebla amidst the stirring enthusiasm of our troops, who in those moments bestowed glory to the *patria*, and a *patria* to our children.[12]

Flattery was an important weapon in Díaz's personalist armoury, but it was exercised always with discretion. An early indication of his belief in the need for both discretion and flattery as essential tools in the successful stewardship of political office is illustrated by the advice given to his brother Félix following the latter's election as governor of Oaxaca in 1867. He emphasised, above all, the need to win over opponents by not drawing attention to their shortcomings. He criticised his brother's open and often intemperate complaints about his political opponents:

> I don't like it when you openly express your opinion of certain individuals: a man in your position ought to be a friend to all, and an enemy of no-one, however insignificant they may be. I don't mean that you should call a fool wise, or someone who has an overblown opinion of themselves dignified, but you should never explain their defects to them . . . silence compromises no-one and upsets nobody; listen to me and you will reap the rewards.[13]

The primacy of personal networks in the conduct of politics was emphasised in a letter to Díaz's former companion in arms and close ally in Oaxaca, Francisco Uriarte, in 1881:

> even if an individual may appear to be useless [literally a corpse or *cadáver*], that should not be a reason for us to be indifferent to the

potential help he might give us: . . . when it is a question of attempting to extend the influence of a party or campaign, every offer of help
should be welcomed.[14]

In the longer term, especially when political difficulties arose, the
cultivation of personal loyalties, although they required considerable
energy to sustain, would prove to be most useful in the exercise of
authority and the achievement of the principal long-term political
objective – peace, or, in other words, the absence of conflict. He advised his close ally and *tuxtepecano* Carlos Pacheco, who had just taken
up the governorship of Chihuahua (in 1884), to follow his example:

> I have taken upon myself the onerous obligation . . . of speaking to
> friends every day in order to recommend good judgement, prudence
> and calm, appealing to their professions of loyalty to me and their
> patriotism so that they cease all hostility and, instead, seek reconcili-
> ation, the only path along which the country can make positive,
> straightforward and unimpeded progress.[15]

The Díaz style of politics therefore contained a subtle combination of, on the one hand, compromise, negotiation and flattery,
and, on the other, the cultivation of loyalty and deference. The
maintenance and extension of a loyal network of personal contacts
required prodigious energy to sustain. At the same time, Díaz assiduously cultivated the image of a supremely and deliberately enigmatic
persona, unmoved by personal favouritism and aloof from political
factionalism. The writer and novelist Federico Gamboa provides an
intriguing portrait of the *caudillo*'s enigmatic qualities. Díaz was,
according to Gamboa, 'always serious, always in control, unsmiling,
his bearing and physique strong and upright: his features, which
never reveal whether he is pleased or displeased, are perfectly enigmatic, and never betray him'.[16]

Only on very few occasions did Díaz allow his enigmatic mask to
slip, revealing a sceptical, even cynical, view of his fellow Mexicans.
Francisco Bulnes claimed that he once overheard Díaz discussing
the true characteristics and motivations of his compatriots in 1884,
prior to taking up his second term of office as President. The anecdote is significant because it highlights the basis on which Díaz
sought to manipulate individuals and their careers:

> Mexicans are content to eat tasty snacks [*antojitos*] without self-
> control, to get up late, to be public employees with influential personal

contacts, arrive late at work, frequently take sick leave, seek paid absences, never miss the bull-fight, look for permanent entertainment, marry young and have unlimited children, spend more than they earn and get mixed up with money-lenders in order to throw children's and birthday parties. Fathers who have a large number of children make the best government employees, because of their fear of poverty – poverty is what Mexicans of the governing classes fear most, not oppression, servility, nor tyranny; [they fear] the lack of bread, a home, clothing, the harsh reality of having nothing to eat or of sacrificing their laziness.[17]

Bulnes argued that Díaz, having studied his country 'microscopically' during his extensive military campaigns, understood that the solution to Mexico's political problems was to be found in satisfying the individual's craving for security and economic satisfaction, and satisfying a collective and innate desire for patriarchal authority rather than the fulfilment of abstract ideals or ideology. Díaz understood, according to Bulnes, that in Mexico 'the problem of peace was the problem of hunger; the problem of justice a question of an iron hand; the problem of freedom, a bird-cage with birdseed'.[18] In other words, Díaz understood, according to Bulnes, that for the majority of his fellow Mexicans peace and security were always more important than liberty or democracy.

There is evidence of Díaz's deliberate manipulation of individuals, friends and enemies alike. The strategy was justified by the necessities of statecraft and *realpolitik*. As he explained in Machiavellian mode to Governor Martín González of Oaxaca, in order to preserve political order, it was necessary to abandon

even those friends with whom one has solemn and direct obligations . . . those of us who manage public affairs must be tough, and avoid letting personal considerations intrude, because the leader who does not know how to stand on his own will not be remembered by the people.[19]

The maintenance of a personalist network required not simply insight into the Mexican psyche and its conscious manipulation for political ends, but also the distribution of tangible and reciprocal rewards. The principal lubricant of the personalist system was the patronage at the *caudillo*'s disposal. Díaz's powers of patronage increased considerably after his accession to the presidency in 1876, and increased still further with the expansion of the state bureaucracy and, above all, with the rapid influx of foreign capital and the consequent benefits to be gained by acting as intermediaries for overseas business interests, as will be shown in Chapter 6.

In the distribution of patronage, Díaz was careful to reward the loyalty of numerous individuals who had fought with or supported him during his many military campaigns between the 1850s and the 1870s. He showed himself always responsive to requests from veterans of those campaigns for military pensions, for positions in the expanding government bureaucracy, either for themselves or for their offspring. He used his influence, for example, to obtain entry into the Colegio Militar, or in the provision of grants to study in the Escuela Nacional de Agricultura.[20] In 1881 he provided a sinecure for the son of one of his former teachers at the Instituto Libre de Enseñanza in Oaxaca.[21]

The same use of patronage was applied to the families of his long-term political allies and supporters. It is notable that this network was maintained by Díaz up until the very end of the regime, and that these contacts were maintained not just over one, but over two or sometimes three generations. For example, in February 1911, only three months before his forced resignation, he found a minor bureaucratic position for the great-grandson of his original political mentor, the lawyer Marcos Pérez, who had given Díaz his first political appointment as sub-prefect in the district of Ixtlán in Oaxaca in 1855.[22]

Personal networks also required new recruits. An example of how this broad network of personal loyalty was extended during the regime is Díaz's response to a request from a young telegraph operator from Oaxaca to send him a manual on 'Telegrafía' in order for him to be able to study for his professional examination. Díaz replied that he was sending the book via the governor, with an exhortation that the young man should make full use of the opportunity he had been given to study. The reply which Díaz received indicated that this small gesture would guarantee a lifetime of personal loyalty to the *caudillo*:

> I shall always treasure this undeserved favour. I have asked you, as I would a father, knowing that you would oblige, because I recall the affection you showed my own father, who always told me that you were a man of honour. I shall find an opportunity to express my gratitude.[23]

The network of personal loyalties was, therefore, well established before 1876, and became vastly extended during the lifetime of the regime. As the last example shows, patronage was not solely distributed to powerful or potentially dangerous individuals drawn from a narrow social elite, but across the social spectrum. It extended to entire communities, especially in the case of a number of *pueblos* in Díaz's native Oaxaca, where the *caudillo* frequently intervened in a personal capacity to ensure the provision of village schools and teachers, or for musical instruments for the local municipal band.[24]

Electoral practices

Personalism and patronage were the essential lubricants of Porfirian politics. They were employed openly, and paradoxically, to bolster an element central to the politics of the Díaz regime – the strict adherence to constitutional practice and, specifically, to the careful maintenance of the cornerstone of the liberal political system, that is the conduct of regular elections for political office-holders.

Patronage was widely used in the selection of non-elected office-holders within the Porfirian system. This applied, at one end of the spectrum, to the selection of cabinet ministers and, at the other end, to appointments within the burgeoning bureaucracy at state and national level; ministerial secretaries, governors' secretaries and *jefes políticos*, the regional representatives of executive authority throughout the republic who were nominated in most cases by the state governors in consultation with Díaz.[25] For example, the appointment of ministers to Díaz's first cabinet in 1876 clearly demonstrates the importance of patronage in rewarding the political loyalty of those who had supported the Tuxtepec campaign in 1876, in response to the code of conduct of *camarilla* politics.[26]

Patronage was equally ubiquitous in the selection of candidates for elected posts. It is worth noting here that the turbulent history of electoral participation and 'modern' forms of political representation in nineteenth-century Mexico dates back to model provided by the Constitution of Cádiz in 1812. Despite the obvious and regular abuses and imperfections of the electoral process during the nineteenth century, they should not divert our attention from their fundamental importance to the liberal project.[27] It is, in fact, in the arena of electoral practice that the contradictions between the personalist political culture of *caudillismo* and dictatorship and the legal and democratic culture of liberalism and citizenship, are most clearly highlighted. An understanding of these contradictions is indispensable to an understanding of the way in which Porfirian politics functioned.[28]

The Díaz regime was always fully committed to the holding of regular elections, in formal accordance with the practices laid out in the Constitution of 1857. At the same time, as already indicated, because of their significance, the outcome of elections was too important to be left to chance. As a consequence, throughout the Porfiriato, the supervision and selection of candidates was closely monitored. This applied not only to the elections of state governors, of congressmen (*diputados*) and senators (*senadores*) in the National Congress, but also to *diputados* in the state legislatures, as well as to members of the judiciary (*magistrados*) at both national and state level.

The nomination of candidates required either the direct or indirect *imprimatur* of the executive, and functioned as both a means of either creating, consolidating, or renewing a clientalist network. It was, however, far from being either a rigid or inflexible system, since the limitations of presidential authority, especially during the *tuxtepecano* era before 1884, were all too apparent, and especially apparent to Díaz himself. This inevitably meant that the exercise of presidential authority with regard to the nomination of candidates was always subject to negotiation with the state governors, and depended upon the particular set of circumstances which prevailed in each state.

In the management of elections Díaz, like his liberal predecessors Juárez and Lerdo, was primarily concerned with control, and here he demonstrated a pragmatic combination of tactics and strategies in the pursuit of his political objectives. While there were certainly occasions when direct intervention, or the threat of direct intervention, was deployed, the overriding preference was always for negotiation and compromise.

There had been early indications that the *tuxtepecano* regime might represent a new era of open political competition and free elections, in keeping with the commitments made in the Plan of Tuxtepec. Interim President Juan Méndez issued the *Convocatoria* for presidential elections in December 1876 and announced that 'the free vote, which has been one of the goals of the revolution [of Tuxtepec], will be henceforth a reality . . . the government is determined to avoid pressure on the public vote'.[29]

In practice, these pious commitments remained at the level of rhetoric only. The available evidence certainly indicates that, as his predecessors Juárez and Lerdo had done, Díaz and his close *tuxtepecano camarilla* used their influence unconstitutionally in the selection and appointment of both electors and candidates after 1876.

As a result, Treasury Minister Justo Benítez, the most powerful and influential figure in Díaz's first cabinet, at precisely the same time as Méndez was issuing his *Convocatoria* for open elections, made direct and blatant recommendations to *porfirista* sympathisers as to the suitability of certain candidates, such as in the case of the nomination of Ignacio Vallarta as President of the Supreme Court. Díaz himself, despite the highly-disciplined discretion of his later years, was far more open during his first administration about making direct recommendations for political office. In February 1877, for example, he openly suggested to Manuel González that 'José María Martínez Negrete would be an ideal candidate for the governorship of Michoacán, and I urge you to support and protect his candidature'.[30]

Also in the early years of the regime, Díaz was equally forthcoming with his advice on the criteria for the selection of suitable candidates for political office. Significantly, Díaz did not insist that absolute or slavish personal loyalty should be the only criterion for selection. 'Candidates should be', he wrote, without a hint of irony, in 1881, 'more or less friends of mine'. He went on to emphasise, however, that this did not mean that they should be dependent on any one faction, but that they should be independent, backed by 'independent support' (*elementos propios*), and they should, above all, not be subject to 'outside influences' (*influencias extrañas*) and thus open to manipulation by political enemies.[31]

There is still very little research into the detail of electoral practices during the early years of the regime, but it appears, on the basis of rather anecdotal evidence, that, once nominated, the electoral process itself was largely a formality. It is clearly the case, however, that practices varied considerably from state to state and from region to region. In some cases, Díaz's personal nomination of a candidate was clearly enough in itself to secure the result. In a blatant example of *caudillismo* in action, the *jefe político* of Tlaxiaco in the Sierra Mixteca of Oaxaca wrote to Díaz in 1877 to thank him for 'restoring, via the political creed of Tuxtepec, the sovereignty of the people, abused for so long', but, in the same breath, and without any apparent sense of irony, he announced that Díaz's choice of candidate for the governorship had been unanimously elected in his electoral district, solely because 'you have chosen him, and since your only aim is to look after the interests of the *pueblos*, then we elected him without delay'. The fact that the candidate concerned was not from the Mixteca himself but was a *zapoteco* from the rival Sierra Norte, and therefore not only lacked a local political base in the Mixteca but was viewed locally with universal suspicion, only serves to emphasise the extent of Díaz's *caudillista* authority.[32]

The tradition of the interference of central government in the selection and nomination of candidates, which had also been a feature of the liberal administrations of Juárez and Lerdo, was therefore fully embraced by the early Díaz regime. There is also evidence, however, that during the early years of the regime Díaz was also conscious of his role as the standard-bearer of the restoration of political representation to the municipalities and the states under the banner of the Plan of Tuxtepec. The *tuxtepecano* commitment to municipal autonomy led to the establishment of a Special Commission on the Independence of the Municipality, which recommended in 1878 that 'all local employees in the municipalities should be popularly elected'.[33] The recommendation was complemented by the parallel restoration of direct elections for *jefes políticos* in 1876, which had been introduced in 1861 but subsequently abandoned. It is clear, however, that different methods of selection of *jefes políticos* had always existed since their first introduction in the aftermath of independence. The Díaz era was certainly no different, and, as Romana Falcón concludes, throughout most of the Porfiriato *jefes políticos* continued to be appointed and removed from office by the state governors, to whom they were directly answerable. In other words, it appears that the early commitment by the Díaz regime to holding direct elections at municipal level in 1878 was more honoured in the breach than in the observance.[34]

Certainly during the first years of his administration, there were clear discrepancies and inconsistencies between policy and practice. Díaz's much-repeated official reply to those who suggested the nomination of particular candidates for elected posts was that: 'the government of which I am in charge is convinced of the need to abstain from interference in the affairs of the states, concentrating solely on the guaranteeing the expression of the popular opinion'.[35] Given the clear evidence of direct intervention in elections during the *tuxtepecano* years, such a reply was both duplicitous and disingenuous, and failed to describe the true dynamics of electoral practice.

The struggle between central and state authority

The balance of power between central government and the individual states within the federation was, as indicated in Chapter 2, one of the fundamental sources of political conflict in nineteenth-century Mexico. It is difficult to generalise about the process in Porfirian Mexico, since the differences in the circumstances which prevailed in each state were matched by the different personal and political relationships Díaz sustained with each of the state governors. Nevertheless, the shifts in the relationship between centre and state are crucial to the understanding of Porfirian political practice.

To a large extent, these shifts reflect the changing nature of the regime itself. The relative weakness of the Díaz administration during the *tuxtepecano* period, its wavering advocacy of *puro* liberal political decentralisation and the consequent autonomy enjoyed by the state governors meant that the process of asserting its precarious authority in the regions would involve a high degree of tact and negotiation. However, following Díaz's first re-election in 1884, described in Chapter 5, the autonomy of the state governors was gradually but progressively curtailed.

Two points need to the emphasised. First, that the autonomy of the state governors, even during the apogee of the regime's authority after 1884, was very far from being completely subordinated. And, second, that there were frequent tensions between the preservation of state and local autonomy and the constantly-expanding tentacles of the central state. These tensions became particularly acute after 1884. The protracted and delicate process of securing the constitutional amendments which resulted in the indefinite re-election of both the President, the state governors and the representatives in the national and state legislatures provoked a wave of anti-re-electionist protests in a number of states in 1891 and 1892.

During the early years, in keeping with the regime's *puro* liberal antecedents, Díaz was concerned to avoid accusations of interference in, or abuse of, state sovereignty. He was particularly circumspect, therefore, when it came to his dealings with state governors, since he was obliged to provide them with a good deal of discretion and power over the management of state politics. He felt free to dispense both criticism and advice but, as he explained to Governor Rosendo Márquez of Puebla in 1885:

> In the end, you are responsible for the situation, and you will have your own reasons for proceeding in the manner in which you have done. You should, therefore, accept my comments as no more than conversation or confidences which are entirely amicable in character.[36]

If conflicts arose over governorship elections, Díaz's instinct, as he outlined to one of his closest political allies, General Bernardo Reyes, in the context of the 1885 elections in Coahuila, was to find a third, compromise candidate acceptable to both factions, 'in order to preserve the peace and the welfare of the state, whose tranquillity must be maintained at all costs'. This was not only pragmatic, he explained, but a question of principle: 'the freedom of citizens to exercise their constitutional and legal rights must not be restricted in any way . . . above all, the will of the state must be respected'.[37]

It is evident that different regional socio-economic conditions and the complexities and idiosyncrasies of local politics inevitably necessitated the adoption of different strategies in the implementation of central authority. It is undoubtedly true that the underlying tendency in federal–state relations during the course of the Díaz era should be interpreted as a creeping process of political centralisation.[38] Nevertheless, the complete picture will only emerge following detailed investigation of political practice at municipal and regional level, and it is highly likely that the image of a ruthless and inexorable process of centralisation will have to be qualified. One recent study has even suggested that, in the nomination and selection of state representatives to the Congress and Senate, the authority of the state governors was not only maintained, but was even enhanced during the 1890s.[39]

Nevertheless, the process of centralisation was undeniable. An early example was the systematic and progressive erosion of the regional power base of *caciques* from the Sierra de Puebla (Juan Francisco Lucas, Juan C. Bonilla and Juan N. Méndez) during the late 1870s and early 1880s. The evidence from Puebla demonstrates Díaz's capacity for ruthlessness and manipulation in pursuit of his objectives, and the total absence of sentimentality towards former *tuxtepecano* allies. The Puebla *caciques* had each served the liberal cause on numerous occasions during the military campaigns during the Reforma and French Intervention and, most notably, as a bastion of political and military support for Díaz's political aspirations during the rebellions of La Noria and Tuxtepec. Their loyalty had been rewarded with the successive governorships of Puebla – in 1876 (in the case of Bonilla) and in 1880 (in the case of Méndez). As an indication of a close personal and political relationship with Díaz, Méndez had even served briefly as provisional President following the victory of the Tuxtepec campaign in 1876, while Díaz was engaged in the military campaign to suppress the challenge of José María Iglesias to the Tuxtepec campaign.

However, after 1876 Díaz was progressively reluctant to tolerate the political independence of the Sierra de Puebla, and even less inclined to tolerate the existence of an independent National Guard which was the basis of the authority of the Sierra *caciques*. Through a classic Porfirian combination of conciliation, negotiation and the strategic deployment of troops, their domination of the politics of Puebla was profoundly undermined by the election of General Rosendo Márquez in 1884, and effectively terminated with the re-election of Márquez in 1888.[40]

Authoritarian practices

As the fate of the *caciques* from the Sierra de Puebla shows, despite the emphasis that has been placed up to now on Díaz's instinctive preference for conciliation and negotiation, authoritarian tactics were certainly key components within the political armoury of the regime. These were strategies which had been employed consistently during Díaz's military campaigns between 1855 and 1867.[41] Once in power, and especially during the early years of the regime, Díaz frequently resorted to the tactical deployment of direct military intervention to suppress any armed challenge to state or national authority. Moreover, Díaz was fully prepared to sanction the use of arbitrary and summary execution. Whenever a rebellion occurred, whatever the justice of the complaints, however small the rebel band might be, the rebels must be punished 'severely' (a euphemism for execution) in order to set an example. The fundamental duty of the authorities, he explained in 1880, was to 'apprehend those who have rebelled, however much their Plan may be justified . . . and they must be punished with the utmost severity . . . because any leniency shown to them will later have fatal consequences, and will only encourage them to renewed and constant uprisings'.[42]

The uncertain political context following Díaz's accession to power in 1876, especially in the light of persistent rumblings of regional rebellion, meant that force would be used more frequently in the achievement of political peace during his first term of office, and that the resources allocated to the maintenance of order would continue to represent a high proportion of government expenditure.

The first serious threat to the survival of the new regime was the series of armed challenges from General Mariano Escobedo and the activities of the nucleus of pro-Lerdo conspirators in exile in New York during 1877 and 1878. Although the military threat had been effectively eliminated by March 1878 with the defeat of Escobedo at Matamoros, the climate of uncertainty which military rebellion induced, and the progressive abandonment of the political programme of the Plan of Tuxtepec, was fertile ground for a resurgence of regional political protest. The general climate of political instability was also reflected in a spate of banditry which drew extensive press comment and prompted a petition to Congress in 1879 from the Ministry of the Interior for the suspension of individual guarantees under the Constitution. Congress rejected the petition but, as the *Monitor Republicano*, which was always highly critical of the first Díaz administration, commented in February 1880: 'The outbreak of banditry has reached monstrous proportions; panic has spread throughout the whole society, and scarcely a day goes by without reports of new attacks on lives and property.'[43]

The regime's response was heavy-handed but conducted with the dual purpose not only of eradicating the problem, but also of instilling a reputation for ruthlessness which Díaz had found so effective during his military campaigns in the 1850s and 1860s. As a consequence, in 1878 and 1879 newspapers were full of reports of the application of the *ley fuga*, where prisoners were 'shot while trying to escape'. The policy had the desired effect, but the strategy would eventually return to haunt the regime and would become a weapon with which to attack its reputation during its last years in power.

The most notorious incident of repression during the first Díaz administration was what became known as the 'Veracruz Massacre' of June 1879. It is important to reiterate the context of uncertainty and instability in which the incident took place. Not only had the regime been unsettled by the persistence of political opposition, but the combination of falling customs receipts, banditry and smuggling threatened serious financial penury and the non-payment of public salaries, including those of the army, and, therefore, endangered the regime's survival.

The immediate response had been to increase the penalties on smuggling and to intensify the vigilance of opposition activity.[44] The agent entrusted with the implementation of this new tough policy in the strategically significant port of Veracruz was Governor Luis Mier y Terán, a fellow *oaxaqueño* and a close and long-time associate of Díaz.[45] Tension within the city increased significantly in June 1879, when smugglers from the port of Alvarado commandeered the government gunboat *Libertad*, with the help of some of the members of the crew, and escaped into the Gulf of Mexico. Mier y Terán's immediate and ill-considered response was to round up *lerdista* sympathisers and to carry out the summary execution of nine prisoners in the harbour fort of San Juan de Ulúa.[46]

Most accounts suggest that Díaz, on hearing the news of the capture and mutiny of the *Libertad*, sent a telegram which instructed Mier y Terán to 'Kill them in the act' (*'Mátalos en caliente'*). However, the telegram with this precise instruction has never come to light. The exhaustive investigations of Alberto María Carreño, published in 1958, indicate that there was a telegram from Díaz ordering the governor to 'shoot all the officers and every tenth member of the crew', but made it clear that this referred only to those who were openly implicated in the conspiracy. Mier y Terán's victims, however, included only two of the conspirators. Clearly, his actions exceeded his instructions.[47] Díaz subsequently sought to distance himself from the excesses committed by Mier y Terán, but he refrained from any direct criticism of the governor. Mier y Terán was, however, forced to resign the governorship of Veracruz in 1880, and was subsequently tried (but acquitted) by the National Congress.

The summary execution of political opponents in Veracruz attracted only limited comment in the contemporary press. In fact, José Valadés argues persuasively that the Veracruz 'massacre' only became significant during the final years of the regime when authoritarian practices and overt repression re-emerged as a reflection of its inner turmoil. According to Valadés, the Veracruz incident emerged, in other words, from 'the fantastic political literature of the last years of the Porfirian regime'.[48]

In the short term, the incident appeared to do little to promote internal political peace. There were two further minor *pronunciamientos* (by General Manuel Márquez de León in Sinaloa and General Jesús Ramírez in Baja California) and a more serious rebellion in Tepic (by General Miguel Negrete) in 1879 which challenged the survival of the regime and necessitated the organisation of a show of force.[49] The subsequent military campaign during the first months of 1880 was successful in restoring the authority of the Díaz administration in the north. The decision to give the command of the campaign to General Manuel González was certainly providential in promoting his subsequent candidacy for the presidency the following year.

. . .

THE ELECTIONS OF 1880

The year 1879 was one of considerable political manoeuvring in preparation for the major political event of the first Díaz administration – the presidential elections of 1880. Although anti-re-electionism (*no re-elección*) had been a major plank of the *tuxtepecano* programme, and although the constitutional amendment to forbid presidential re-election had been promulgated in May 1877, there was nevertheless still a good deal of speculation as to whether Díaz would revert to traditional *caudillista* practice and present himself as a candidate. This speculation was fuelled by Díaz's characteristic and calculated reticence, and his disingenuous claim that he did not want to prejudice the outcome of the electoral process.

Díaz's re-election had been proposed publicly by the state legislature of Morelos in 1879, which tabled a constitutional amendment. Privately, the idea had been proposed by many others. For example, the governor of Oaxaca, Francisco Meixueiro, wrote to Díaz's in October 1879 to suggest that the President should continue in office. Díaz's response reflected the current political uncertainties, but indicated that he was determined to stick to *tuxtepecano* principles and that he had no intention of seeking re-election:

> I know that you are very much in favour of a prorogation [of the period of office], in order to resolve the serious difficulties which have presented themselves in achieving a peaceful transfer of power in order to comply with the new constitutional principle of no re-election. I am grateful for the honour which your considerations bestow on me, but the means are not in accordance with the pre-scriptions of the Constitution, and, even if they are founded in serious concerns, or plausible excuses could be found, or constitutional justification could be provided, I could never personally accept them. For this reason it is necessary to find another solution which will provide a satisfactory outcome to further the cause of peace and the establishment of institutions.[50]

By the end of 1879, there was no shortage aspirants to succeed Díaz as President. This situation reflected the profound divisions which had emerged in the *tuxtepecano* camp after 1876. Ironically, as subsequent apologists for the regime were keen to point out, political factionalism appeared to have been actively stimulated by the commitment to the principle of 'no re-election', as political manoeuvring among potential successors became more intense. Following intense press speculation, the names of Ignacio Vallarta, Vicente Riva Palacio, Generals Trinidad García de la Cadena and Gerónimo Treviño all emerged as possible contenders.

By the beginning of 1880, however, two leading candidates had emerged: the 'civilian' candidate, Justo Benítez, the key figure in the *tuxtepecano* movement and Díaz's closest political advisor since the 1850s, and the 'military' candidate and another of Díaz's *compadres*, General Manuel González. Benítez campaigned under the banner of the *Partido Liberal Constitucionalista*, promising to uphold and protect the provisions of the Constitution of 1857, while González's programme emphasised a distinctly developmentalist platform – fiscal and economic reform, material progress ('work ought to be the gospel of the people') and, as was to be expected from the ex-Minister of War, reform and modernisation of the armed forces.[51]

Although Díaz's official pronouncements refused to give his blessing to either candidate, his support for González was well known. González wrote to Díaz in April 1880, for example, to thank him for 'the favours you have shown me in improving my circumstances'.[52] The elections themselves (the primary elections in June selected the electors, who then cast their votes in a secondary ballot in July) passed off peacefully, despite widespread fears of 'revolutionary disturbances'. When the votes of the electoral college were counted, González (11,528 votes) emerged the victor over Benítez (1,368). There was, however, evidence of fraudulent electoral practice. In Sonora, for example, military commander José G. Carbó entrusted the electors' ballot papers to González himself, asking him to ensure that they arrived at their destination through 'safe means'. When the votes were counted, all 224 votes had been cast in favour of González.[53]

In the formal report (*Memoria*) which Díaz delivered at the end of November 1880, the day before handing over of power to his successor, he claimed that the greatest achievement of his first term of office was the establishment of domestic political peace. Despite the obvious evidence to the contrary, he stated that 'Peace is a fact in the entire Republic, and has been so over the last four years.' He went on to assert that the principle of no re-election was 'the essence and triumph' of the Tuxtepec Revolution and that the constitutional amendment, promulgated symbolically on 5 May (1877) to coincide with the anniversary of the battle of Puebla, was a sacred principle which he was honouring by standing down from power.

He also articulated another principle that would forever be associated with his regime: '*poca política y mucha administración*' (very little politics but a great deal of administration) – a preference for administration and good government over political factionalism and ideological conflict. As Díaz himself explained, 'for some time now, it has been accepted that the satisfaction of the country's most pressing needs lies in administration rather than in politics'.[54]

In spite of the self-congratulatory tone of the report, the soon-to-be ex-President frankly admitted that 'the most important acts of my administration are better measured by what has yet to be done, rather than by what has been done'.[55] In short, the central goals of the liberal project – the establishment of representative institutions, the promotion of material and social development, or, as José Valadés puts it, the creation of a state and the emergence of a nation – had been sketched out, but only in principle. It was up to his successor, temporarily at least, to carry the process forward.

. . .

THE PRESIDENCY OF MANUEL GONZÁLEZ, 1880–84

Many accounts of nineteenth-century Mexican history consider that Manuel González was a 'puppet' of Porfirio Díaz, not only because they were personal friends and *compadres*, but because his candidacy was clearly endorsed and supported by the ex-President. As evidence from their correspondence clearly indicates, González's loyalty to Díaz was genuine and profound. The implication has always been that González was a 'safe' candidate, a mere cipher or a man of straw, who would not only represent continuity with the first Díaz regime, but who would be more than willing to hand power back to his *compadre* at the end of his term of office. González's presidency is, therefore, most frequently referred to as an interregnum, a hiatus between Díaz's first and second periods of office. The perception of collusion appeared to have been confirmed when González appointed Díaz Minister for Development in his first cabinet, and by Díaz's simultaneous election to the Presidency of the Supreme Court, which, in accordance with the 1857 Constitution, gave the incumbent the presidential succession.[56]

A closer examination of both the candidacy and presidency of González suggests a modification of this interpretation. Although the candidacy of González was certainly favoured by Díaz for the reasons mentioned above, it was the turbulent political circumstances of 1879 and 1880 which determined his emergence as a front-runner. The persistence of internal political divisions and the evidence of conspiracy suggests that the candidate with the support of substantial sections of the military was the most appropriate, and González's successful military campaign in the north-east in 1879 and 1880 had confirmed that he enjoyed that support.

Once in power, González certainly pursued the same strategies identified with the Díaz regime – domestic political reconciliation, political centralisation and the strengthening of the executive, external diplomatic recognition, the development of infrastructural projects and the stimulation of foreign investment. But González was no mere imitator of Díaz. He should, in fact, be credited with more autonomy, innovation and dynamism in these fields than has been generally acknowledged.[57]

In domestic politics, González was able to assert his independence from Díaz in the nomination of candidates for political office, and even, on at least one occasion, to challenge the recommendations of his mentor.[58] He continued the process of extending the executive power of the presidency by openly intervening in regional politics of the states to quell political disturbances, for example in Jalisco, Durango and Zacatecas. In his pursuit of the reform of the military, he was able to reduce military expenditure and to initiate a process of professionalisation which had eluded his predecessor. In the field of international relations, the González administration was able to make notable progress in the negotiation of treaties with the USA to regulate the growing problems of smuggling, banditry and Indian raids which themselves reflected growing cross-border trade and exchange. He also defended national interests in the border disputes with Guatemala, resisting both Guatemalan territorial demands and US attempts to mediate.

González should also, according to his biographer, Dan Coerver, be credited with building solid foundations for the extension of economic links between Mexico and the USA which would accelerate rapidly after 1884.[59] Significantly, the first direct railway link between Mexico and the USA (the Central Mexican Railway from Mexico City to Paso del Norte (today Ciudad Juárez)) was inaugurated in 1884 under the González administration, a clear symbol of the 'railway fever' which would come to characterise the later Díaz era.[60]

The greatest innovation of the González presidency was undoubtedly the vigorous pursuit of an economic policy which sought to free the restrictions on capitalist development in Mexico by restructuring property rights and the regulation of commerce, developing an infrastructure of transportation, public works and banking services, and, above all, making Mexico attractive to foreign capital investment for the exploitation of its mineral and agricultural resources. In fact, it was during the González presidency that the foundations for the export-oriented development most closely associated with the Díaz era were laid. The rapid and even frenetic enthusiasm of the González administration for railway development and foreign investment was conspicuous. The immense profits which could be made from land privatisation and railway concessions were no doubt an added incentive. There is evidence that government ministers, speculators and concessionaries made substantial profits. González himself certainly profited, for example from conveyencing fees and land sales following his acquisition of the concession for the projected Mexican Eastern Railway which was to cross the extensive properties he owned in Tamaulipas.[61]

Charges of government corruption and favouritism increased towards the end González's period of office, and found fertile expression in the national press as the regime became increasingly criticised for its poor economic management, its inability to renegotiate the burden of external indebtedness and its general impotence in the wake of the extended financial crisis of 1883 and 1884. As foreign investment and government revenues fell, the González administration's expensive programme of state subsidy was exposed and its financial reforms, such as the introduction of nickel coinage, prompted public demonstrations and popular riots in Mexico City in 1884.

Díaz himself maintained a low-key role in the González administration. After six months as Minister of Development, he became deeply involved in the governorship elections in Oaxaca. Once his election as governor had been secured, after only a brief period in office he requested permission (*licencia*) from the state legislature for a temporary leave of absence. In 1883 he again sought a *licencia* in order to be able to represent Mexico at the New Orleans trade fair. The mounting public criticism of González clearly had beneficial consequences for Díaz's return to the presidency in 1884. Díaz made no secret of his willingness to seek re-election, despite his refusal to make any public statements on the matter. The re-election campaign had begun in 1883, with sections of the *porfirista* press making exaggerated claims that Díaz's re-election would represent the return of the 'Saviour of the Nation'.[62]

Daniel Cosío Villegas attributes Díaz's re-election in 1884 to two main factors. First, the absence of alternative candidates. If González harboured re-electionist aspirations, his growing unpopularity, fuelled by press attacks, had considerably weakened his chances. González himself had, in any event, ruled himself out of the race, and he had stated as early as 1882 that he believed 'the election of General Díaz would be convenient because I see no other man who possesses the virtues that he does, not only for maintaining peace in the Republic, but also for supporting its institutions'.[63] González's rivals for the presidency in 1880 (Justo Benítez, Vicente Riva Palacio, Manuel María de Zamacona, Ignacio Vallarta, Juan Méndez and Trinidad García de la Cadena) had all fallen out of favour with the González administration, and thus out of the political limelight.

Second, the campaign to re-elect Díaz had begun in earnest as early as nine months before the primary elections of June 1884, with the publication of six *porfirista* broadsheets in Mexico City and a further 16 throughout the Republic, and the simultaneous establishment of political clubs in keeping with the traditions of nineteenth-century electoral practice. The Catholic press was supportive, and although the independent liberal press highlighted the dangers of re-election, they could find no credible alternative. The fact that Díaz, with characteristic caution, had failed to declare his candidacy, thus avoiding the accusation that he was seeking to promote his own personal ambition, seemed not to hinder but to enhance his electoral success. It therefore came as no surprise that the Electoral Commission of the National Congress, entrusted with the scrutiny and assessment of the votes of the electoral colleges throughout the Republic, announced in September 1884 that Díaz had been elected with 85 per cent of the vote.[64]

Many of the mechanisms and practices adopted during the first term of office – the cultivation of deference, the widespread use of patronage, the preference for negotiation and the adoption of manipulation and coercion – remained constants through the Díaz era. As the Juárez and Lerdo administrations had endeavoured to do since 1867, the first Díaz administration continued in its attempts to fit the round peg of constitutional liberalism into the square hole of personalist tradition and practice. Nevertheless, after Díaz's second re-election in 1884, there was a noticeable shift in political practice towards the consolidation of an unassailable personal authority. In pursuit of the maintenance of political peace, the central tenets of nineteenth-century liberalism, including the hitherto sacred principle of no-re-election, were increasingly marginalised, although never entirely abandoned. As a result, rather than attempting to maintain the pragmatic balance between the regime's constitutionalist roots and Mexico's authoritarian political traditions, the Díaz regime after 1884 became increasingly committed to a brand of elite or patriarchal liberalism in order to sustain a period of political peace which was to last for the next 20 years.

. . .

NOTES AND REFERENCES

1. Quoted in C. Beals, *Porfirio Díaz: Dictator of Mexico*, Philadelphia, PA, 1932, p.191.
2. C. Hale, *The Transformation of Liberalism in Late Nineteenth-Century Mexico*, Princeton, NJ, 1989, pp.27–63.
3. D. Cosío Villegas (ed.), *Historia Moderna de México* (hereafter *HMM*), 10 vols, Mexico City, 1955–72, Vol. X, p.854 suggests that the influence of the *científicos*, especially outside Mexico City, has been much exaggerated. This certainly merits further research.
4. Porfirio Díaz Archive, CPD:LVI:f.1065/2643.
5. CPD:LVI:f.1315.
6. The increasing adoption of the technology of the age, especially the telegraph and the typewriter, made little difference to the character of the correspondence, although it clearly made a difference to its volume. The Díaz archive contains more than one million items of correspondence for the period 1867–1915.
7. J.F. Iturribarría, *Porfirio Díaz ante la historia*, Mexico City, 1967, p.13.
8. CPD:L41:Vol./*Tomo* (hereafter T)3:f.102, Díaz to Gillow, 20 December 1884. For an exploration of the personal attributes and 'charisma' required of a classic *caudillo*, see E. Wolf and E. Hansen, '*Caudillo* Politics: A Structural Analysis', *Comparative Studies in Society and History*, 9(2), 1967.
9. For this and many other examples, see Cosío Villegas, *HMM*, Vol. X, p.98 and *passim*.
10. Mauricio Cavazos to Díaz, 1 February 1898, CPD:L23:C3:f.1395.
11. Manuel González to Díaz, 31 October 1867, CPD:L42:f.797. Díaz devotes a chapter of his memoirs to the early career of González, whose

change of allegiance from the conservative cause in the Wars of the Reforma to the struggle against the French invasion in 1862 is attributed by Díaz to González's patriotism. Díaz, *Memorias*, Vol. I, p.153. During the siege of Puebla in March and April 1863, he was appointed Díaz's Chief of Staff.

12. Díaz to González, 2 April 1885, CPD:L41:T1:f.406.
13. Porfirio to Félix Díaz, 27 November 1867, CPD:L42:f.896.
14. Díaz to Francisco Uriarte, 1881, CPD:L6:f.2711.
15. Díaz to Pacheco 10/12/1884 CPD:L41:I:f.027.
16. Gamboa, cited in E. Krauze, *Porfirio Díaz: Místico de la Autoridad*, Mexico City, 1987, p.104.
17. F. Bulnes, *El Verdadero Díaz y la Revolución*, Mexico City, 1921, p.39.
18. F. Bulnes, 'Rectificaciones y Aclaraciones a las *Memorias* del General Díaz', in Gonzálex Navarro (ed.), *Memorias de Porfirio Díaz*, 2 vols, Mexico City, 1994, Vol. 2, pp.247–325.
19. Díaz to Martín González, 18 June 1894, CPD:L11:17:ff.55–59.
20. CPD:L5:f.1719 and CPD:L36:f.2608.
21. CPD:L6:f.1968.
22. CPD:L36:f.2704.
23. CPD:L5:f.2556.
24. CPD:L5:ff.237/4636.
25. R. Falcón, 'Force and the Search for Consent: The Role of the *Jefaturas Políticas* of Coahuila in National State Formation', in G. Joseph and D. Nugent (eds), *Everyday Forms of State Formation: Revolution and the Negotiation of Rule in Modern Mexico*, Durham, NC, 1994, pp.107–34.
26. The following appointments were made: Protasio Tagle, Interior; Justo Benítez, Treasury; Ignacio Ramírez, Justice and Education; Vicente Riva Palacio, Development; General Pedro Ogazón, War; Ignacio Vallarta, Foreign Affairs.
27. A. Annino, 'Nuevas Perspectivas para una Vieja Pregunta', in A. Annino and R. Buve (eds), *El Liberalismo en México*, Hamburg, 1993, pp.5–13.
28. W. Pansters, 'Theorizing Political Culture in Modern Mexico', in W. Pansters (ed.), *Citizens of the Pyramid: Essays on Mexican Political Culture*, Amsterdam, 1997, pp.1–37.
29. J. Valadés, *El Porfirismo: Historia de un Régimen*, 3 vols, Mexico City, 1941, Vol. I, p.21.
30. Ibid., Vol. I, pp.22–3.
31. See, for example, the correspondence with his acolytes in Oaxaca over the list of candidates for the state legislature elections in 1881; CPD:L6:f.0805.
32. Jefe Político of Tlaxiaco to Díaz, CPD:LI:f.047.
33. Secretaría de la Cámara de Diputados, 9 July 1878, CPD:L1:f.0116.
34. R. Falcón, 'Force and the Search for Consent', p.109.
35. Díaz to Manuel Ramírez, 31 January 1880, CPD:L5C1:I:f.0394.

36. Díaz to Márquez, 16 February 1885, CPD:L41:T1:f.270.
37. Díaz to Reyes, 13 February 1885, CPD:L41:T1:f.256. The relationship between Díaz and Reyes is further discussed in Chapters 5 and 8.
38. T. Benjamin and W. McNellie, *Other Mexicos: Essays on Regional Mexican History 1876–1911*, Albuquerque, NM, 1984.
39. E. Bertola, 'La designazione dei candidati elettorali: la costruzione di un compromesso nel Messico Porfirista', *Quarderni Storici*, 3, 1988, pp.929–39.
40. G.P.C. Thomson, 'Porfirio Díaz, y el Ocaso de la Montaña, 1879–1892: El Fin del Liberalismo Popular en la Sierra de Puebla', in R. Falcón and R. Buve (eds), *Don Porfirio Presidente, Nunca Omnipotente*, Mexico City, 1998, pp.361–82.
41. Díaz's favourite military strategy had always been that of the *guerrilla*, which Díaz openly admitted required the blatant use of deception (*amago*). In one example, in December 1865, he apparently spread the rumour that he was ill, thus enticing the enemy to attack. Before they could do so, Díaz claims that he was able to launch a successful pre-emptive strike. Díaz, *Memorias*, Vol. I, p.239.
42. CPD:L41:ff.0734/0887.
43. Quoted in Valadés, *El Porfirismo*, Vol. I, p.130.
44. Ibid., Vol. I, pp.137–42.
45. Valadés suggests that Díaz did not doubt Mier y Terán's loyalties, but rather his abilities. Ibid., Vol I, p.146.
46. J. Seward, 'The Veracruz Massacre of 1879', *The Americas*, 32(4), 1976, pp.585–96. There is also a suggestion of personal conflict between Mier y Terán and two of the 'conspirators', Valadés, *El Porfirismo*, Vol. I, p.148.
47. A.M. Carreño, *Archivo del General Porfirio Díaz*, Vol. XXV, pp.34–5.
48. Valadés, *El Porfirismo*, Vol. I, p.151.
49. Cosío Villegas, *HMM*, Vol. IX, pp.181–4.
50. Díaz to Meixueiro, 31 October 1879, CPD:L4:C1:f.0160.
51. Valadés, *El Porfirismo*, Vol. I, p.44.
52. González to Díaz 19 April 1880, CPD:L5:f.0988; Enrique Krauze claims that González thus became the first '*tapado*' (a candidate selected in secret by the outgoing President) in the history Mexican presidential elections, a practice that became standard in post-Revolutionary Mexico. Krauze, *Porfirio Díaz*, pp.35–7.
53. Carbó to González, 24 August 1880, CPD:L5:f.1233.
54. Cosío Villegas indicates that the phrase belonged to Ignacio Vallarta, not to Díaz. See *HMM*, Vol. IX, p.xx.
55. P. Díaz, *Informe que en el último dia de su Período Constitucional da a sus Compatriotas el Presidente de los Estados-Unidos Mexicanos Porfirio Díaz*, Mexico City, 1880.
56. J.F. Iturribarría, *Porfirio Díaz*, p.47.

57. D. Coerver, *The Porfirian Interregnum: The Presidency of Manuel González of Mexico 1880–1884*, Fort Worth, TX, 1979; a more balanced interpretation was foreshadowed by Cosío Villegas in his *HMM*, Vol. IX, pp.575–798.

58. Coerver, *Interregnum*, p.55; interestingly, the clash of opinions resulted from the fate of Luis Mier y Terán, the notorious author of the Veracruz 'massacre' of 1879. Díaz wanted Mier y Terán to be elected as a senator from Veracruz, but González refused.

59. Coerver, *Interregnum*, pp.60–121, 123–81; for a detailed examination of increasing cross-border contacts in Sonora and Arizona, see Miguel Tinker Salas, *In the Shadow of the Eagles: Sonora and the Transformation of the Border during the Porfiriato*, Berkeley, CA, 1997. The opening of González's private papers at the Iberoamerican University in Mexico City in 1994 has stimulated further research on the González presidency.

60. G. José Valenzuela, *Los Ferrocarriles y el General Manuel González*, Mexico City, 1994, p.9. Economic development in the Díaz era is the subject of Chapter 7.

61. G. José, *Ferrocarriles*, p.15.

62. Cosío Villegas, *HMM*, Vol. IX, pp.740–58.

63. Coerver, *Interregnum*, p.302.

64. Cosío Villegas, *HMM*, Vol. IX, p.756. Díaz had obtained 15,766 votes out of a possible total of 18,530. 187 votes had been cast for a range of other individuals – 31 for Ramón Corona, 26 for Ignacio Manuel Altamirano, and 17 for Vicente Riva Palacio, none of whom, it must be emphasised, were official candidates.

Chapter 5

THE CONSOLIDATION OF POWER: PATRIARCHAL LIBERALISM, 1884–1911

Poca política, mucha administración. (Ignacio Vallarta)[1]

Porfirio Díaz's first re-election to the presidency in 1884 marked a significant watershed in the political evolution of the regime. As a foretaste of what was to come, the election was uncontested, with Díaz the only candidate. Thereafter, it is possible to identify a dual process of consolidation and transformation of the Díaz regime. While many of the mechanisms and tactics of Porfirian political pragmatism continued to be employed in the attempt to mediate and manage factional divisions, the personal and patriarchal authority of the President at the apex of the hierarchy of power became gradually consolidated and increasingly uncontested.

In accordance with the regime's adherence to liberal constitutionalism, the process of consolidation was legitimised by two amendments to the Constitution of 1857. The first, in 1887, permitted consecutive re-election, and thus allowed Díaz's second re-election in 1888. The second, in 1890, removed all restriction on future re-election to public office and allowed Díaz's third re-election in 1892 and gave legal endorsement to the fourth, fifth, sixth and seventh re-elections in 1896, 1900, 1906 and 1910. But although constitutional liberalism continued to provide the framework for the regime, its content was progressively ignored in practice. As José Valadés remarked many years ago, the regime increasingly lacked any coherent doctrine, other than that of subordination to the will of the patriarch. The regime was thus able to be, simultaneously and without contradiction, liberal and conservative, pro-foreign and nationalist, Masonic and confessional. The essential prerequisite was that each faction or interest group, irrespective of ideology, must be prepared to recognise and submit themselves to the authority of the President.[2]

As a consequence, the authority of Don Porfirio became gradually unassailable and 'necessary' (in the words of Daniel Cosío Villegas, Díaz became *El Necesario*, the Indispensable). He became the patriarch of the nation and the custodian and arbiter of the rules of conduct of Mexican political life. This meant not only the assertion of personal authority over the institutions which governed the conduct of politics (the cabinet, both houses of Congress, the state governors, the state legislatures, the regional *jefes políticos*), but over the institutions which had played a decisive role in nineteenth-century Mexican politics – above all, the army, the church and the press. The evolution of a cult of personality around the figure of Don Porfirio was an integral part of this gradual accretion of power.

Although the regime became increasingly centralised and authoritarian, there were, nevertheless, important constraints on presidential authority. In other words, the political control enjoyed by Díaz was never as absolute as his critics have argued, since the process of centralisation and consolidation was always contested, challenged and resisted at a variety of levels. Political factionalism and dissidence were, therefore, a constant feature of the Díaz era. At the national level, at the level of 'high' politics, 'pure' (*puro*) or radical liberals (also referred to in the contemporary press as 'jacobins' – *jacobinos*) who sought to uphold both the Constitution of 1857 and the *tuxtepecano* principle of no re-election, argued with moderate liberals and, increasingly, with the growing influence of the conservative or 'developmentalist' liberals, who became known after 1893 as the *científicos*. Although the *científicos* had reservations about the strengthening of presidential and executive authority which successive re-election implied, they were, nevertheless, generally supportive of the regime.

At a regional level, the conduct of elections provided a platform for the activities of anti-re-electionist and other opposition groups, and acted as a political barometer to test the standing of the regime. This would become particularly clear in the 1892 elections, when the controversial removal of all restrictions on re-election to political office prompted a wave of anti-re-electionist protest in various states (particularly in the northern states of Tamaulipas, Coahuila and Nuevo León). At the same time, the regime consistently faced outbreaks of popular protest in rural areas, most notably between 1891 and 1893, but in some cases – such as those of the *maya* in

Yucatán and the *yaqui* in Sonora – on a consistent basis throughout the lifetime of the regime.[3]

It is clear, therefore, that the projection by the apologists of the Díaz era as one of untroubled political peace or *pax porfiriana* requires serious revision. The extent of local political conflicts and the pattern of local political practice in this period have only begun to emerge in recent years, and they will become even clearer when more local (or 'microhistorical') studies become available. When they do, they are likely to reveal with greater clarity the astonishing heterogeneity of Porfirian Mexico, and the limited scope of central authority. Given the extent of both factional and regional conflict, the achievement of the regime in maintaining central authority and in managing and diffusing factional divisions was all the more remarkable. It is important to reiterate the fact that the degree of political stability achieved by the Díaz regime between 1884 and 1906 was unparalleled in Mexico's independent history.

. . .

POLITICAL PRACTICE AFTER 1884

Two central themes emerge in the conduct of Porfirian politics after 1884. The first is the gradual alteration of the management of *camarilla* (factional) politics. Díaz's loyalty to the *camarilla* associated with the Plan of Tuxtepec in 1876 (whose members were known as *tuxtepecanos*) was gradually transformed after 1884 into the management of competing factions by playing them off against each other, and ensuring that each faction recognised the authority of the President and his role as arbiter. The second, overlapping theme is the progressive subordination of all political actors (from members of the cabinet to regional *jefes políticos*) to the patriarchal authority of the *caudillo*. This represented authoritarianism by stealth within the framework of liberal constitutionalism. It can perhaps best be described as a form of patriarchal or elite liberalism.

The exercise of this brand of patriarchal liberalism was at the heart of the process of political consolidation in Mexico after 1884, but it led at the same time to what Cosío Villegas describes as the 'petrifaction' of politics, and to the preference for the administration of politics rather than the open or democratic practice of political debate and electoral competition. This has given rise to the much-quoted and appropriate dictum, first articulated by Ignacio Vallarta

(President of the Supreme Court in the first Díaz administration) and subsequently used to describe the nature of Porfirian politics in this period – '*poca política, mucha administración*' (very little politics, but a great deal of administration).[4]

As indicated in Chapter 2, *camarilla* politics, which had found fertile expression in the struggles between *juaristas*, *lerdistas* and *porfiristas* during the Restored Republic, had played a vital role in the development of political loyalties among the group of *tuxtepecanos* who had assisted Díaz in his achievement of presidential office in 1876. Accordingly, during his first administration, Díaz had made appointments to the cabinet, to state governorships and to the vital role of regional military commanders from among the ranks of his *tuxtepecano* allies, who were linked to Díaz by ties of *compadrazgo*, freemasonry and shared military or political experience. The most prominent members of this group included Justo Benítez, Protasio Tagle, Luís Mier y Terán (all of whom were fellow *oaxaqueños* and Masons) Carlos Pacheco, and Manuel González.

The appointments made after his first re-election in 1884, by contrast, showed a marked preference for the representation of different factions. In the new cabinet, for example, Ignacio Mariscal, former Mexican Minister in London, who was now appointed Secretary for Foreign Relations, had been a *lerdista* prior to 1876; Matías Romero, a former *juarista*, was confirmed as Mexican Minister in Washington; Manuel Dublán, the new Minister of Finance (*Hacienda*) had been a minister in the cabinet of the Emperor Maximilian. A further indication of a change of direction for the post-1884 administration was the appointment of the young positivist Joaquín Baranda to the Ministry of Justice, a post he had also occupied under the presidency of Manuel González. It is perhaps significant of the prevailing ethos of factional re-accommodation that the only remaining *tuxtepecano* representative in the new cabinet was Carlos Pacheco, the former governor of Chihuahua who became Minister of Development (*Fomento*).[5] While these appointments represented a spirit of 'reconciliation' within the Díaz regime after 1884, they should also be understood as part of an evolving strategy to gain greater control over the management of *camarillas*.

The most influential figure in the new cabinet was Manuel Romero Rubio, the Minister of the Interior (*Gobernación*) and another former *lerdista*. Significantly, Romero since 1881 had also been Díaz's father-in-law, following Porfirio's marriage to Carmen Romero Rubio.[6] This second marriage has always itself been interpreted as a further example of the spirit of political reconciliation, since it represented not only the unification of *lerdistas* and *porfiristas*, but also of the liberal Díaz regime with the Catholic Church. This was because Doña Carmen, or Carmelita as she was popularly known, was renowned for her piety. Even more significantly, the wedding ceremony had been performed by Archbishop Pelagio Antonio de Labastida y Dávalos, who had been an outspoken opponent of liberal anti-clericalism and an apologist for the conservative and imperial cause. Less frequently commented upon is the fact the couple met in the residence of the first US Minister to Mexico, John Foster, following the resumption of diplomatic relations between Mexico and the USA in 1878. Foster himself certainly regarded this event as symbolic of the dramatic improvements in US–Mexican relations under Díaz.[7] Doña Carmen is also given credit for tutoring her husband in the etiquette of 'polite' society, and giving greater formality to his dress, speech and table manners, and discouraging him from his habits of shouting, and even, it appears, of spitting on the floor. Francisco Bulnes later described Díaz's personal transformation after his marriage to Carmelita as a process of the 'aristocratization of Caesar'.[8]

Díaz's principal political objective was to establish himself as the mediator and arbiter between rival factions or *camarillas*. For this strategy to succeed, patronage was extended in order to control, or at the very least to supervise, the process of political nominations to both elected and non-elected posts at all levels, and thereby to manage both the core of the political process and the trajectory of individual careers. Manuel Romero Rubio played a vital role in this process until his death in 1895. Thereafter the role of principal advisor was taken up by Finance Minister José Yves Limantour. The central pillars of the strategy were, first, the streamlining of the process of electoral manipulation and, secondly, the removal of the restrictions on re-election, not only of the President, but for all elected (and non-elected) posts.

. . .

ELECTIONS AND RE-ELECTIONS

In his analysis of Porfirian political practice, Cosío Villegas provides ample evidence of the extent of electoral manipulation during the high tide of the Díaz regime. In the case of the election of representatives (*diputados*) to the National Congress, whenever the period of elections approached, Díaz, following consultation with Romero Rubio or, subsequently, with Limantour, would negotiate with the governor over the names of candidates who should be 'elected' as *diputados* to represent the state in the National Congress. The governor would then communicate the list to the *jefes políticos* in the electoral districts, who, in turn, forwarded the names to the *presidentes municipales* (municipal presidents). Once the 'elections' had taken place, the process of notification was repeated in reverse. The final stage was the publication of the results in the official journal of the Congress (*Diario de los Debates de la Cámara de Diputados*). While the process was by no means identical or straightforward in every case, the pattern and the vocabulary adopted in its implementation (citing, without fail, that the elections had been conducted on the basis of a 'strict adherence to constitutional principle') was remarkably similar throughout the Republic.[9]

This standardisation, or what François-Xavier Guerra describes as the 'bureaucratisation' of the electoral process, was further exemplified by the second part of the strategy – the successive re-election of office-holders, which ensured continuity and removed the possibility of electoral competition and, thus, of potential conflict.[10] Given the regime's adherence to 'legalism' and constitutionalism, re-election could only be legitimised by constitutional amendment. Díaz was anxious to avoid accusations of electoral manipulation, and made sure that the initiative did not emanate from the presidential office but from regional state legislatures, only subsequently to be later ratified by the National Congress.

The principle of re-election was established by the extension granted for one extra term of office, approved in 1887, from an initiative which originated in the state legislature of Puebla. This allowed Díaz to be re-elected in 1888 for a third four-year term. The ultimate prize of permanent and unrestricted re-election was achieved only in 1890, following a proposal initially put forward by the state legislature of Guerrero. In both cases, the process of constitutional change was slow and subject to widespread comment, criticism and speculation in the independent press. When the votes were finally taken in Congress, however, they were approved with an overwhelming majority.[11]

As Jan Bazant has pointed out, the effectiveness of the process of political consolidation under Díaz is also partly attributable to the slow pace of its implementation. He argues that the gradual accumulation of power by Díaz stands in marked contrast to the intemperate and hasty accumulation of power by those who have been vilified, along with Díaz, as the chief villains of Mexico's nineteenth-century history – Agustín de Iturbide and Antonio López de Santa Anna. Both had sought to elevate themselves to positions of supreme authority (Emperor in the case of Iturbide and Perpetual Dictator in the case of Santa Anna) after much shorter periods in power.[12]

Díaz further distinguished himself from his predecessors in his deliberate and calculated detachment, and his public reluctance to accept, let alone to promote, his own candidacy. In his speech to the members of the Morelos Political Club, organised in Mexico City to campaign for Díaz's controversial re-election in 1892, he emphasised both his studied humility, and his adherence to constitutional legality:

> I do not expect, gentlemen, much less allow myself to presume that my fellow citizens will honour me with an electoral majority once again. I feel quite satisfied that I have fulfilled the sovereign mandate over two consecutive constitutional periods. But I would never fail to obey if another period were imposed upon me legally.[13]

The effectiveness of the strategy can also be gauged not only by Díaz's own successive re-elections, but by the increasing longevity in power of cabinet ministers, congressmen, senators and state governors after 1892. The most striking example is the successive re-election of representatives in the National Congress (both *diputados* and *senadores*). In the congressional elections of 1896, for example, only 35 of a total of 258 *diputados* who had occupied their seats in 1892 failed to be re-elected. It has also been estimated that 86 per cent of the *diputados* elected in 1910 had occupied their elected posts since at least 1902.[14] There were cases of individuals being elected to more than one post – as, for example, in the case of *tuxtepecano* Genaro Raigosa, who in 1892 was elected to serve as the *diputado* for Mexico State and as a reserve senator (*senador suplente*) for two different states, Colima and Chihuahua. There were also cases where *diputados* were elected repeatedly for successive terms of office, such as the case of the maverick intellectual Francisco Bulnes, who was re-elected no fewer that 15 times between 1880 and 1910.

The fact that Bulnes was supposedly 'elected' to represent the federal territory of Baja California, which he appears never to have visited in his lifetime, illustrates another feature of Porfirian electoral politics – that of 'carpetbagging', whereby individuals were 'elected' to represent areas where they had no independent political base, and where they were consequently no more than nominees, elected on the basis of patronage. Another of Díaz's preferred tactics was to use his close associates from his native state of Oaxaca as trusted appointees who would be guaranteed to maintain their loyalty. In 1886, for example, of the total of 227 deputies in the Congress, no fewer than 62 were from Oaxaca.

The combination of permanent re-election of Díaz's ageing nominees and the progressive emasculation of the role of Congress in the wake of the concentration of power in the hands of the executive, leads Cosío Villegas to conclude dryly that Congress under the Díaz regime came to resemble a gerontocracy, 'a museum of natural history' rather than a democratically elected or a representative parliament. For Bulnes, despite the fact that he was a member of the Congress himself, the majority of his fellow deputies and senators were, he claimed, 'mindless dummies'.[15]

In the case of state governors, the incidence of re-election is highly revealing. A significant and ever-increasing number of governors occupied their posts on a more or less permanent basis after the constitutional amendment of 1892, until they were removed by either their own mortality, by the force of the anti-re-electionist movement in 1909, or by the Revolution of 1910. Joaquín Obregón González, for example, was governor of Guanajuato for 17 years between 1892 and 1909; Abraham Bandala was governor of Tabasco for 15 years from 1895 to 1910; Teodoro Dehesa was governor of Veracruz for 18 years between 1892 and 1910; Mucio P. Martínez was governor of Puebla for 17 years between 1893 and 1910; and Francisco Cañedo was also governor in Sinaloa for 17 years between 1892 and his death in 1909.[16]

Permanent reinstatement to political office nevertheless represented potential dangers to the regime. By removing all pretence of competition in the conduct of elections at the national and state levels, the regime became increasingly concerned about generating tangible evidence of popular approval and endorsement for what became an increasingly meaningless political ritual of uncontested elections, the outcome of which was never in any doubt. This led to a paradox in the conduct of Porfirian politics. The more the personal authority of Díaz became undisputed, the more necessary it became to seek alternative means of endorsement and legitimisation.

As a result, there was a notable tendency to pay more careful attention to what would be recognised today as the strategies of modern political mobilisation. Some of the strategies adopted – the formation of political clubs in support of specific candidates at both state and national levels prior to elections, and the publication of special, limited edition newspapers to support their campaigns – had been a consistent feature of post-independence electoral politics in Mexico. After 1890, the regime gave these practices new impetus and improved organisation.[17]

Other strategies adopted by the regime after 1888 were new, such as the organisation of public meetings and National Conventions which would draw up manifestos and plans of action, the endorsement of candidates by private business interests, the publication of electoral propaganda and even the attempt to gauge public opinion by means of a referendum or plebiscite. In 1892, for example, Díaz's candidacy received the open public endorsement of a non-political organisation, the Commercial, Manufacturing and Farming Confederation of the Mexican Republic.

The regime also experimented with new types of targeted political propaganda. The Central Re-electionist Convention, for example, campaigning for Díaz's fourth re-election in 1896, produced and distributed 18,500 leaflets, each of which, thoughtfully, carried a portrait of Díaz, no doubt to remind the electors in each of the 227 electoral districts throughout the Republic, if such a reminder were necessary, of who the candidate seeking re-election was. Prior to the 1900 presidential elections, the National Porfirian Circle organised a plebiscite in which 350,000 ballot papers were produced and distributed to all state governors. While the conduct of the plebiscite undoubtedly exposed the type of electoral manipulation which was common to the vast majority of elections in Porfirian Mexico, and while the results surprised nobody in returning an overwhelming endorsement for the incumbent President, this was nevertheless a significant innovation in Mexican electoral politics.[18]

Although it might be possible to argue that successive re-election to political office represented a process of consolidation and centralisation, it is important not to forget its limitations, or to overstate either its scope or its homogenisation. The repeated re-election of state governors, for example, even though they were also always manipulated and endorsed by Díaz, did not necessarily mean that he was able to bend local politics entirely to his will.

. . .
DÍAZ AND THE GOVERNORS

The criteria for the selection of state governors was an area to which Díaz devoted special attention, given their crucial importance within the political system as the key mediators between national and state power. In his choice of candidates, Díaz had to act with extreme sensitivity in order to judge the particular configuration of local circumstances. Given the weakness of the central state, the traditions of federal autonomy and the variable power base of local factions, circumspection, accurate information and good judgement were vital in order to avoid potential threats to presidential authority. In the first instance, governors were drawn, especially in the early years of the regime, from among those regional leaders whose authority derived from a local power base, and who were consequently rewarded for joining Díaz's coalition of Tuxtepec.

Such was the case of Gerónimo Treviño, whose loyalty to Díaz in 1871 and 1876 was vital in securing the frontier states (Coahuila, Chihuahua and Nuevo León) for the Tuxtepec campaign. Díaz was initially obliged to allow Treviño considerable leeway in maintaining both his own fiefdom or *cacicazgo* as well as the authority of central government in these key states, turning a blind eye to Treviño's accumulation of a personal fortune from the control of cross-border trade with the USA. Nevertheless, the independence of regional *caciques* was clearly an obstacle to the establishment of presidential authority, and the suppression of the Treviño *cacicazgo* became a priority during the second Díaz administration. It took Díaz, with the loyal assistance of Bernardo Reyes, two years to achieve, between 1885 and 1887. The 'victory' was symbolised by the election of a 'neutral' candidate (Lázaro Garza Ayala) as governor of Nuevo León in 1887.[19]

The second group from which governors were recruited were those governors whose authority and standing within their native states was confirmed by Díaz's support and sponsorship. This long list included, for example, Francisco Cañedo of Sinaloa, governor from 1892 until the Revolution of 1910, and Carlos Díez Gutiérrez, governor of San Luís Potosí from 1889 until his death in 1898.[20] A third group consisted of those whose military and political services were rewarded by nominations to governorship positions; this group included Luis Mier y Terán, whose loyalty was rewarded by his nomination to the governorship of Veracruz (1876–79) and, sub-sequently, to that of his native Oaxaca (1883–88).

A fourth group consisted of those loyal, trustworthy and experi-enced individuals (whom Guerra calls 'the President's Men'), who were used by Díaz as independent 'compromise' candidates to settle electoral disputes which erupted in certain states between opposing factions. Such was the case of Rosendo Márquez in Puebla, who was brought in to mediate the long-standing conflicts and rivalries of the highlands (*Montaña*) and the lowlands (*Llanura)* as governor in 1884. Another example was the case of Lauro Carillo, a native of Sonora who was nominated to serve as governor of Chihuahua (1892–97) in order to mediate between, and ultimately to neutralise, the local conflicts between the powerful Terrazas family and the sup-porters of Díaz's close *tuxtepecano* ally, Carlos Pacheco.[21]

Some governors clearly manifested a degree of deference, devo-tion and subordination to the President which bordered on the slavish and the sycophantic. Díaz's authority was treated virtually as divine law within their jurisdiction. For example, one of Díaz's most loyal servants and *compadres* from Oaxaca, Albino Zertuche, was 'elected' governor of his native state in 1888. Zertuche's ex-planation of his election showed not only the extent of deference to Díaz, but also unwittingly revealed the nature of the authority which the *caudillo* was able to exercise: 'General Díaz was kind enough to nominate me as official candidate for the governorship of the state [of Oaxaca], and he, in turn, elected me unanimously.'[22] Governor Mucio Martínez of Puebla (1893–1910), in a similar expression of extreme deference, implored the President on one occasion to 'believe me, sir, that everything I have ever done . . . has never had any other motivation other than my unbreakable and steadfast determination to serve you'.[23]

On the other hand, it is apparent that other governors, who were no less loyal to the President, were able to retain a degree of auto-nomy in the government of their respective states, on the basis of their firm control of local politics and their commitment to the modernising ethos of the Porfiriato. The case of Governor Próspero Cahuantzi of the state of Tlaxcala in central Mexico is perhaps a typical example. Cahuantzi, a native of Tlaxcala, was a loyal *tuxtepecano* and a former subordinate of Díaz during the War of the French Intervention. He was first elected to the governorship in 1885. As a result of his administrative abilities and the maintenance of a critical degree of independence from the *hacendado* elite within the state, Cahuantzi was able to maintain a delicate but precarious balance between the interests and aspirations of the *hacendados* and rural *caciques* in the implementation of the Porfirian project of political order and material progress.

As a reward for maintaining an important, but never absolute, degree of political peace within the state, Cahuantzi obtained Díaz's approval for six successive re-elections to the governorship. Díaz's positive and public endorsement of Cahuantzi during the campaign to promote his sixth re-election in 1908 was a classic example of Porfirian political discourse, combining respect for the constitutional sovereignty of the people, but clearly indicating at the same time the importance within the Porfirian system of the President's personal support: 'provided the will of the majority of the people of Tlaxcala does not oppose the re-election of the candidate [Cahuantzi], proposed by farmers and industrialists in the state, I will support them in their proposal'.[24]

The case which perhaps best exemplifies the limitations of presidential authority was Díaz's relationship with Bernardo Reyes, who became governor of Nuevo León in 1885. Born in 1850, and therefore 20 years younger than Díaz, and one of the youngest members of the Porfirian inner circle, Reyes was a member of one of the most prominent political families of Jalisco. His father was a National Guard captain and *jefe político*, and his cousins were Pedro Ogazón (governor of Jalisco and Minister of War under Juárez and Díaz's first Minister of War in 1876–77) and Ignacio Vallarta (another former governor of Jalisco, Minister of the Interior (*Gobernación*) and President of the Supreme Court).

Reyes's early prominence was due to his highly successful military career. A volunteer at the age of 14 in 1864, he had remained loyal to Juárez during Díaz's Rebellion of La Noria but had transferred his loyalties to Díaz after 1876. As military commander of the region, he became Díaz's 'proconsul' in the northern states of San Luís Potosí, Sonora, Sinaloa and Baja California, in the military campaigns against the *apache*, the *yaqui* and the *cacicazgos* of Generals Naranjo and Treviño, which were consistent obstacles to the consolidation of Díaz's power in the region. As reward for his services, and as a recognition of his administrative and political abilities, Reyes became governor of Nuevo León in 1885.[25]

Although Reyes was intensely loyal to the President, Díaz was nevertheless always circumspect in his dealings with Reyes, whose power base in the north of Mexico and his support within the military made him one of the two most prominent political figures of the late Porfiriato (the other was Finance Minister Limantour). At the same time, Reyes's prominence and popularity made him a potentially dangerous rival. In his correspondence with Reyes, Díaz clearly recognised the limitations of his own authority and the autonomy which Reyes enjoyed in the region under his jurisdiction. For example, Díaz's response to a request in 1890 from Reyes for clarification over rumours of a change in government policy, Díaz replied:

> If there had been a change of policy which would have affected your region, I would have contacted you so that we could have worked it out [*confeccionaramos*] together, because, in general, and with regard to federal politics, although I have the information and sufficient authority to proceed on my own, I would be very exposed, and would commit a number of mistakes if I judged myself competent to manage local politics, which is always the most troublesome . . . [remember that] neither you nor I are infallible.[26]

There were, therefore, important constraints on the exercise of central authority during the period of consolidation after 1884. Nevertheless, while Díaz was always suspicious of potential rivals, he was always prepared to use their talents in the pursuit of his objectives. He therefore took full advantage of Reyes's administrative talents and military skills as part of his campaign to neutralise another of the potential threats to his authority – the military.

. . .

THE MILITARY

The military played a crucial role in nineteenth-century Mexican politics. In the face of external and domestic threats to the new Republic after independence in 1821, the need to maintain expenditure on the regular army had indebted, and consequently undermined, the authority of successive governments between 1821 and 1855. In the 1820s, for example, military expenditure accounted for nearly three-quarters of national revenue. It was hardly surprising, under these circumstances, that military officers had dominated the presidency for more than a generation until the ascendancy of Benito Juárez and liberal civilian government in the 1850s. The very weakness of the state and the fragmentation of central authority had

allowed the creation of personal fiefdoms by regional military commanders largely beyond the control of central government. This
degree of autonomy had allowed the construction of regional alliances which had been at the root of many of the *pronunciamientos*
(military coups) regularly launched against central government.

The military in nineteenth-century Mexico was also rent by internal divisions. Regular army officers tended to support centralism
and the protection of corporate privilege. In general, they advocated
centralised government and the maintenance of the favoured status
of military personnel as a corporation with special legal privileges
(*fueros*). This made conservative regular army officers the natural
allies of clerical efforts to resist secularisation and the eradication
of colonial institutions. This, in turn, explains the adoption of the
anti-liberal rallying cry of *religión y fueros* which characterised many
nineteenth-century *pronunciamientos.* Federalists and liberals, by contrast, sought to remove military privilege and to challenge centralist
tendencies through the creation of locally-accountable militia to
defend regional and state interests. The liberal Constitution of 1857
represented the crystallisation of the attack on corprorate privilege
and political centralisation, and stimulated a predictably hostile response from regular army officers.

The subsequent decade of internecine struggle between 1857 and
1867 dealt a serious blow to the status and structure of the old
regular army, and gave a corresponding boost to local militia and
National Guard units which were crucial to the victory of the liberal
cause. But the persistent fragility of the state, and of civilian government, did not permit the eradication of the autonomy of regional
military commanders or the propensity to military *pronunciamiento*.

Díaz's own military career and political experience had made him
acutely conscious of the potential disruption to political peace which
military autonomy represented. In his pursuit of civilian political
consolidation, he was determined to emasculate this powerful threat
to the survival of his regime. Two central strategies were adopted:
first, the demobilisation of the National Guard, which, with its nominal roll of 70,000 troops in 1876, outnumbered the regular army by
a ratio of three to one; and, second, the professionalisation of the
regular army itself, and a substantial reduction in the numbers of
officers and troops on active service.

As indicated in previous chapters, Díaz's service in the National
Guard had been an important source of his own power, as was
demonstrated by the fact that most of the military commanders who

had supported the Tuxtepec campaign had been, as he had, National Guard commanders. It was also, however, the institution which had acted as the principal source of strength in the maintenance of regional *cacicazgos* throughout Mexico during the turbulent years of the 1860s and 1870s, which Díaz was now determined to break. The strategy adopted between 1879 and 1893 consisted of gradually and selectively disbanding the National Guard units, or transferring their former members (*milicianos*) to the regular army, either to the regular (*permanente*) or to the reserve (*auxiliar*) units.[27] It was, inevitably, a complex and slow process, and one requiring tact and sensitivity. In some areas, the measure provoked serious resistance since it not only threatened the survival of local autonomy, but also deprived all *milicianos* of their right to be exempt from taxation.

In the case of the Sierra Norte in Puebla, for example, Guy Thomson has shown that the negotiations between Díaz, Governor Rosendo Márquez and the local *cacique* Juan Francisco Lucas were approached with great caution in order to avoid provoking a potential *serrano* rebellion. The autonomy which stemmed from the local control of the National Guard had been the basis of popular support for the liberal cause in the region, and had been the mainstay of Lucas's power. The forced demobilisation of veteran National Guardsmen in the region in 1888 effectively destroyed the Lucas *cacicazgo*, and thus demonstrated the importance of National Guard demobilisation in the process of political consolidation and centralisation practised by Díaz after 1884.[28]

The second strategy pursued by the regime was the professionalisation of the regular army, with the intention of inculcating a professional *esprit de corps* among army officers which would discourage them from intervening in national politics. This was a strategy adopted by all civilian governments in Latin America during the course of the nineteenth century.[29]

In the case of Mexico, professionalisation had been envisaged since the establishment of the *Colegio Militar* in 1841 but, as Alicia Hernández Chávez has argued, it had been seriously hampered by a series of factors. First, the combination of persistent civil conflict and government bankruptcy in the early post-independence years militated against long-term solutions. Second, the struggles of the 1850s and 1860s not only further depleted the resources available to the state, but had isolated Mexico from the principal sources of weapons technology and expertise, and credit, especially after the severance of diplomatic relations with France and Britain in 1862.

Third, once diplomatic relations were restored (with France in 1880 and with Britain in 1884), the administrations of both Díaz and Manuel González preferred to channel foreign investment into infrastructural and economic development, and not into military rearmament.[30]

Although the *Colegio Militar* had been reopened for the professional training of regular army officers in 1869, professionalisation was only begun in earnest in the decade of the 1880s. In keeping with the spirit of reconciliation of factions which characterised the Díaz regime, Díaz's former adversary, General Sóstenes Rocha, who had crushed the Rebellion of La Noria in 1871, was appointed as Director in 1880. Rocha was responsible for a thorough overhaul of the education and training of officers, as well as a restructuring and formalisation of the basis of promotion, now based upon merit and success at passing examinations rather than on seniority.

At the same time, employment opportunities for the newly-qualified officers declined in the wake of a dramatic reduction in the size of the officer corps, by as much as 70 per cent in the case of officers between the rank of colonel and general in the auxiliary forces. The reduction was most severe in the reserve or auxiliary sector, which constituted two-thirds of the total corps, but the cut-backs also affected regular or permanent officers.[31]

A second wave of restructuring, modernisation and professionalisation of the armed forces followed the appointment of Bernardo Reyes as Minister of War in 1900. Reyes is credited with the improvement of the quality of the armaments and supplies, and the provision of a new military code of conduct, but his most important innovation was the organisation of a civilian Second Reserve, a 20,000-strong volunteer army of patriotic citizens (including many future revolutionaries in 1910, such as Francisco Madero) who could be called upon to defend the *patria* in times of need. The parallels with the National Guard and the potential political risks of civilian mobilisation under the control of a charismatic and popular Minister of War, were all too apparent to Díaz, and he acted swiftly. In 1902, Reyes was demoted from the Ministry of War and the Second Reserve was disbanded.

The results of professionalisation were decidedly mixed. In political terms, the reduction in the numbers of officers, and their professionalisation, certainly affected their direct participation in politics and the appointment of military officers to political posts. In 1889, for example, only eight states were governed by civilians, the

21 remaining governors being generals (including those of the Federal District and the federal territory of Baja California). By 1903, in contrast, the position had been reversed, with only eight states in the hands of governors who held military rank. In addition, Díaz was always careful in his appointments of military commanders to the ten military zones throughout the Republic, to avoid the possibility of collusion or conspiracy between regional military *jefes* and state governors. And, as Cosío Villegas points out, the consolidation of political peace throughout the Republic was a powerful deterrent in itself to military intervention.[32]

But the political emasculation of the officer corps was also matched by the reduction in the effectiveness of the federal army as a fighting force. Between 1880 and 1910 the size of the army had been reduced by over 25 per cent, with a reduction in senior officers of nearly 50 per cent. In addition, the new professional graduates of the revamped *Colegio Militar* still had to contend with the favouritism shown in making senior appointments to loyal acolytes of the President. With the disappearance of the National Guard and the disbandment of Reyes's Second Reserve in 1902, there was little support for an increasingly depleted and demoralised army.

Even the effectiveness of the paramilitary support offered by the *Rurales* (Rural Police Force), accountable to the Ministry of the Interior, in policing rural unrest, appears to have been strictly limited. The reputation of the *Rurales* for efficiency, effectiveness and brutality in both contemporary accounts and in the popular imagination was, in fact, much exaggerated. During the course of the Porfiriato, the *Rurales* consisted of only eight corps of 200 men each or, in other words, a total of 1,600 men, concentrated in the states around the capital city. In the opinion of Alicia Hernández Chávez, they acted mainly as a source of information on local 'dissident' activities and were incapable of facing, let alone resisting, any serious rebellion. Paul Vanderwood estimates a higher total of 2,500 *Rurales*, but emphasises their lack of equipment and training, and their general incompetence. For Vanderwood, their contemporary reputation for striking fear and trepidation into the hearts of Mexico's rural inhabitants, and inspiring purple prose by foreign visitors was far more important than their effectiveness as a police force.[33]

In short, the extent of the demoralisation of the troops and the officer corps in the federal army, who could no longer rely on the support of the disbanded National Guard or Second Reserve units, would become fully apparent when the regime was faced with a series of local insurrections during the early phase of the Revolution in 1910 and 1911. Nevertheless, from the perspective of the regime, Díaz's control over the army was comprehensive, and he proved to be the most effective of all of Mexico's nineteenth-century presidents in undermining the culture of the military *pronunciamiento* and in preventing the intervention of the military in politics. He enjoyed more mixed success, however, in subordinating another of the major institutions of nineteenth-century Mexico – the Catholic Church.

. . .

THE CHURCH

Relations between church and state had been central to the evolution of Mexican political life since independence. Despite the fact that post-independence Mexico was essentially a Catholic Republic, church–state conflict remained at the centre of all the major political upheavals faced by Mexico as an independent nation after 1821. The Mexican Church, with its ten dioceses, over 1,000 parishes, 300 convents and monasteries and around 700 priests, had emerged battered and bruised from the independence struggle. Its capital and property were under threat of confiscation and privatisation, and its monopoly of social and cultural influence, and its monopoly over public and private morality, was challenged by the liberal advocacy of secularisation and religious toleration. Although the Constitution of 1824 recognised Catholicism as the official religion of the state (and rejected religious toleration), and had maintained the Church's legal privileges (*fueros*), its economic, social and educational status increasingly came under liberal and Masonic attacks on the colonial legacy of corporate privilege and power.

The Revolution of Ayutla in 1854 represented a watershed in church–state relations, allowing Mexican liberalism finally to impose a liberal constitution on what was an overwhelmingly Catholic country. The package of reforms associated with the Reforma (particularly the *Ley Juárez* and the *Ley Lerdo*) abolished the Church's legal autonomy and immunity, and forced the sale of its property. The 1857 Constitution incorporated these provisions, and included further measures to curb the influence of the Church in education and to prevent the clergy from election to Congress. The hostile reaction of Mexican bishops and clergy (and of the Vatican) prompted civil war, which further radicalised the liberal attack on the Church

– the Reform decrees of 1859 and 1860 formally nationalised Church property, suppressed the religious orders, secularised the education system, established the civil registration of births, marriages and deaths, and established freedom of religion.

The implementation of the liberal anticlerical programme was a much more complex and protracted process, however, and it was far from complete by the time of Díaz's accession to power in 1876. Despite the 'triumph' of liberalism and the restoration of the Republic in 1867, there was considerable cultural and political resistance to secularisation, not only from conservatives and Catholics, but also from within the ranks of the Liberal Party, with the moderate wing rejecting the radical enthusiasms of the *puros*. Apart from the differences over national policy, the reality of political decentralisation also meant that there was marked regional variation in the implementation of the Reform Laws, with the interpretation of secularisation in the hands of state officials, each with their own prejudices, loyalties and affiliations.

The issue had become sensitive again during the presidency of Lerdo de Tejada (1872–76). The formal incorporation of the Reform Laws into the Constitution in 1873 had provoked widespread opposition within the Church, and had provoked popular unrest and rebellion, especially in the Bajío region of north-west central Mexico. The church–state issue was, therefore, very much alive when Díaz came to power in 1876, and one which continued to stir the blood of political conflict and controversy. The aim of the regime was, as in the case of the military, to subordinate the Church to Díaz's political authority. This required the maintenance of a delicate balance between official avoidance of any major concessions over the basic principles of the Reform Laws, while in practice turning a blind eye to multiple violations of both the spirit and letter of the Constitution.

As indicated in Chapter 2, Díaz's political roots were in freemasonry and radical liberalism. Like his predecessor Benito Juárez, his *compadre* and presidential successor Manuel González, and the generation of liberals affiliated to the Masonic lodges during the Reforma and the Restored Republic, he shared an antipathy to the corporate power of the Mexican Church and actively endorsed the policy of secularisation of social and political institutions.[34] In terms of the spectrum of liberal politics, Díaz had initially emerged after 1867 as an advocate of radical or 'jacobin' policies. The policies pursued during the *tuxtepecano* years reflected his radical 'jacobin' affiliations.

In one of its first acts, the Díaz government ordered in November 1876 that all property in the hands of corporations, including Church property (i.e. all property which had escaped the provisions of the *Ley Lerdo* of 1856) should be handed over to the municipal authorities, with the proceeds of any sale to be devoted equally to educational and charitable activities. Further measures confirmed the early regime's endorsement of radical anti-clericalism – freedom of religion, marriage as a civil contract and a confirmation of the prohibition of the clerical acquisition of property.[35]

The radicalism of this early legislation was both deceptive and short-lived. It was out of keeping with Díaz's personal beliefs and his preferred strategy of reconciliation. Díaz made no secret of his own personal faith, nor of his opposition to the religious conflict which had led to what he described in 1880, in a reference to the Wars of the Reforma, as 'those turbulent scenes of former times'. He was thus able to separate his private beliefs from his public obligations, to advocate the practice of Catholicism in the private sphere, but to enforce the Reform Laws in the public arena. In this way he sought to appeal to Catholic conservatives and at the same time to appease liberal anti-clericals. As he explained to his 'distinguished and faithful' friend, the Archbishop of Oaxaca, Eulogio Gillow: 'As Porfirio Díaz, in private and as head of a family, I am a Roman and Apostolic Catholic; as Head of State I profess no religion, because the law does not permit me to do so.'[36]

The ultimate goal, which took priority over all other personal, religious or ideological considerations, was the establishment of political peace and the consolidation of Díaz's personal authority. Provided that the Church accepted his authority, Díaz was prepared to be conciliatory and not to implement the letter of the law. He provided Archbishop Gillow with an explanation of the essence of his reconciliation policy:

> With peace assured in the Republic, and independence established between church and state, there is no longer any motive for precautions or hostility against the Catholic Church, as long as it limits itself to the legitimate objects of its ministry, without trying to meddle in political matters.[37]

There were occasions, however, when Díaz, confronted with evidence of the open abuse of the Reform Laws, allowed the language of delicate diplomacy to slip and his liberal and Masonic affiliations, and perhaps his anticlerical proclivities, to rise to the surface. He wrote, for example, with a combination of sarcasm and exasperation to the governor of Yucatán, General Guillermo Palomino, in 1889, instructing him to keep a close watch on the Bishop of Yucatán, who had instructed local priests to threaten all those who failed to pay tithes to the Church with excommunication. He advised the governor to use the law if necessary, but to use alternative methods of diffusing the tension if he deemed it appropriate. He also took the opportunity to poke fun at the inhabitants of Yucatán, who were renowned for their broad, angular foreheads:

> Despite the fact that the bishop is an educated man, and sound in other respects, nevertheless he is still a bishop . . . as soon as the first case [of law-breaking] occurs, you should impose the sentences which common law dictates in cases of disturbances of the public peace; assuming, that is, that you consider that the behaviour of the bishop and the priests has alarmed Yucatecan consciences; but if you consider that their consciences are as broad as their foreheads . . . then it would be better to discredit ecclesiastical fury by allowing it full vent so that by openly brandishing their weapons they will end up by blunting them . . . we can also help them out in the newspapers which are friendly to the government, which will treat these matters through comedy and caricature.[38]

Crucial to the success of the reconciliation policy was the relationship which Díaz cultivated with leading representatives of the Church hierarchy, and especially his close relationship with Eulogio Gillow, whom Díaz had supported in his nomination as Archbishop of Oaxaca in 1891. Son of a Liverpool merchant who had made his fortune and acquired, through marriage, extensive property in the state of Puebla, and of an aristocratic Spanish mother (the Marquesa de Selva Nevada), Gillow had been educated in the Jesuit College of Stonyhurst in England, and subsequently in Rome, where he had entered the personal service of Pope Pius IX. Gillow had returned to Mexico in the 1870s to pursue his farming and business interests, and had met Díaz in 1877 at an exhibition in Puebla to promote foreign investment in Mexico.

Gillow has been credited above all for acting as an intermediary between Díaz and the head of the Mexican Church, Archbishop Pelagio Antonio de Labastida y Dávalos, who had been a vehement critic of liberalism and the Reforma. Labastida had been President of the Junta of Notables which had invited Maximilian to Mexico in

1863, and subsequently of the Regency Council. He had been exiled following the restoration of the Republic in 1867, but returned to Mexico at the invitation of Benito Juárez in 1871. According to Gillow in his memoirs, the reconciliation between President Díaz and Archbishop Labastida, as representatives respectively of state and church, was represented by the marriage of Díaz to Carmen Romero Rubio in 1881. Gillow acted as intermediary in persuading Labastida to perform the ceremony. As a further symbol of reconciliation, Díaz attended the funeral of Labastida in 1891.[39]

Gillow was an active advocate of Catholic revivalism within Porfirian Mexico, as well as a supporter of agricultural modernisation. As a modernising *hacendado* he was active in the Mexican Agricultural Society, building a hydroelectric plant, telegraph and telephone lines and importing the latest developments in farm machinery. As Archbishop of Oaxaca, he built and restored churches, built schools and asylums, and built himself a sumptuous residence in Oaxaca City. Gillow also achieved literary immortality when the English writer D.H. Lawrence chose him as the model for his character Bishop Severn in his novel *The Plumed Serpent*, published in 1926.[40]

While the cultivation of personal relationships with members of the Church hierarchy was important in maintaining the policy of reconciliation, it is vital to emphasise that the policy was successful also because it mirrored a process of internal reform which the Mexican Church had been undergoing since 1867. This was reflected in a progressive withdrawal from conflict in the public political sphere, and a greater concentration on internal, passive resistance and institutional reorganisation.[41]

As part of the process of re-evaluation and reorientation, Manuel Ceballos Ramírez has identified the establishment of much closer links between the Mexican Church and the Vatican, especially during the pontificate of Leo XIII (1878–1903). The Pope's encyclical *Rerum Novarum* of 1891 outlined a form of 'social catholicism', urging Catholics to campaign against the social vices (corruption, alcoholism, prostitution) identified as the consequences of liberal secularisation and industrial capitalism. As a result of the concern for social issues, over 40 Catholic labour organisations were established in Mexico between 1874 and 1902, culminating in the institutionalisation of disparate organisations into the Catholic Workers Union (*Unión Católica Obrera*) in 1908.[42]

As Karl Schmitt has noted, there is ample evidence of far-reaching changes in attitudes on the part of the ecclesiastical hierarchy during the Porfiriato, without which reconciliation could not have been achieved. The Catholic position on the oath to the Constitution, for example, changed from absolute condemnation to permission without reservation. Catholics generally acquiesced in the regime's insistence on prohibiting the Church's ownership of property. The vehement opposition to the liberal law on civil registry of marriages was transformed into a compromise in practice by permitting the civil ceremony to take place after the religious service.

Areas of conflict undoubtedly remained, particularly over the creation of a secular state school system and the banning of religious education in state schools. But even here, the early prohibitions imposed upon parents forbidding them to send their children to state schools became more relaxed in practice, provided that Catholic instruction could be maintained in private. The attempt to impose restrictions on the use of clerical garb and on the ringing of church bells in public religious ceremonies (such as the celebration of Holy Week) did lead to conflicts with local authorities in some cases.[43] Occasional popular unrest was also fuelled by intemperate editorials in both the Catholic and the liberal press, which never ceased to berate one another.[44]

Nevertheless, the co operation of the hierarchy of the Catholic Church with the overall strategy of reconciliation is clearly indicated by the recommendations of the Fifth Provincial Council of Mexican Bishops in 1896, which required all members of the Catholic Church to 'urge and promote obedience to the civil authorities' and forbade any involvement, under any circumstances, in political matters, while not relinquishing Catholic doctrine:

> Although the absolute separation of church and state is deplorable, ecclesiastics must behave respectfully to the civil authorities, and, without prejudicing the right to truth and justice, and preserving the prescriptions of the Church, they will provide appropriate assistance whenever it is requested.[45]

A further indication of church–state reconciliation was the appointment of Nicolás Averardi as the emissary from the Vatican to Mexico in 1896. His arrival prompted heated exchanges between the Catholic and liberal press over the imminence of a Concordat between the Mexican state and the Vatican. This was firmly denied by the Díaz regime, which explained the acceptance of his appointment in terms of the government's commitment to religious freedom and on condition that his mission's purpose was 'strictly and simply ecclesiastical'.

The regime also demonstrated its sensitivity to the popular cult of the Virgin of Guadalupe, an important symbol not only of popular religiosity but also of Mexican identity, by providing a guard of honour for the official coronation of the image of the Virgin on 12 October 1895.[46] The Díaz regime was thus able to provide official endorsement of the cult and of public displays of religiosity in general, while emphasising its primary concern – the preservation of order and the subordination of the Church to civil authority in general, and to the personal authority of Díaz in particular.

One of the most vexed and confrontational issues within church–state relations during the Porfiriato, especially at a local and popular level, was the question of religious toleration and the support from the government, and from local authorities, for the expansion of the activities of Protestant and non-Catholic organisations. The spread of non-Catholic religious organisations during the Porfiriato has become an important focus of recent research. The encouragement provided by Masons and liberals for such organisations stemmed from a dual concern: on the one hand, to break the religious monopoly of the Roman Catholic Church and, on the other, to gain the confidence of North American investors, and thus to stimulate the influx of foreign capital, which was one the regime's principal economic objectives. As a result, while the regime was seeking simultaneously to appease both anticlerical liberals, the Church hierarchy and the mass of practising Catholics, Díaz, like his predecessors Juárez and Lerdo, sought actively to encourage the spread of Protestant communities, and of other churches (such as the Mormons) mainly from the USA, who were seeking to expand their missionary activities throughout Mexico after the 1870s.

Díaz certainly gave his personal endorsement to the strategy. He courted controversy, especially in the Catholic press, by attending the inauguration of a Protestant church in 1885. He also granted private audiences to representatives of various Protestant denominations, as well as those from other churches in the USA, and encouraged their missionary and colonisation programmes. In the case of the Mormon Church, for example, one of the 'apostles' sent to resurrect the Mexican Mission in 1901, John Henry Smith, described how he was received with open arms by the President. Smith subsequently described Díaz as the Mormon's 'greatest benefactor . . . no more heroic man stands on God's green earth . . . than the man who stands at the head of the government of Mexico'.[47]

According to Jean-Pierre Bastian, by 1892, at the height of the expansion of Protestant societies in Mexico, there were approximately 469 Protestant congregations, with in excess of 100,000 members, including railroad and textile workers, schoolteachers and *rancheros* (small landowners), concentrated in major urban centres and those areas where the economic transformation of the Porfiriato was most profound, especially the urban centres which were products of the development of the railways or of mining (in San Luis Potosí, Zacatecas and the Sierra Madre Occidental, for example). Ironically, in the light of the regime's encouragement of their activities, Protestant congregations were to become an important focus of political opposition to the regime after 1900. They criticised the regime's conciliation of the Catholic Church, its suppression of labour organisations and its failure to uphold citizens' rights, especially with regard to the legitimacy of elections. Many Protestant pastors would join the ranks of the Mexican Liberal Party, and played a prominent role in the Revolution of 1910.[48]

Despite the dangers inherent in the regime's pursuit of a dual strategy of Catholic reconciliation and Protestant proselytism, the strategy undoubtedly contributed to the consolidation of the regime before 1900. It cannot be argued, however, that church–state conflict was ever resolved during the Porfiriato. There remained many inconsistencies and laxities in the application of the Reform Laws by the national government and by local authorities. There were also plenty of cases of acts of both subtle and blatant clerical defiance of civil authority. There is also ample evidence that the confrontational rhetoric of the Reform era continued to resurface in both the Catholic and the liberal press.

Conversely, there were regional examples of intimate collaboration between Porfirian state governors and members of the Church hierarchy in an active promotion of integrated programmes of social and economic modernisation. Such was apparently the case of the *Alianza Progresista* (Progressive Alliance) between *científico* Governor Olegario Molina (1902–10) and Bishop Martín Tritshler of Yucatán, who jointly sought to combine positivist economic modernisation with social Catholicism, through a collaborative programme of improvement in the social infrastructure through the construction of railways, schools and churches.[49]

In short, the priorities of the Catholic Church during the Porfiriato gradually shifted away from open political conflict towards institutional and social reform. In its turn, the regime was able to make minor concessions and, above all, to relax the application of the law, without conceding any major questions of liberal principle, or amending the Constitution. Most importantly, as far as the regime was concerned, the Church became resigned to the acceptance of the legal authority of the state and of the personal authority of Porfirio Díaz.

. . .

THE PRESS

Control and censorship of the press, the principal vehicle for political debate in Porfirian Mexico, was an important part of the strategy of consolidation of power under the Díaz regime. The manner in which the Díaz regime dealt with the press, however, was another example of the subtleties and complexities which characterised the regime – in other words, a blend of authoritarianism and conciliation, manipulation and concession.

The most detailed examination of the press during the Díaz era are the two volumes of Cosío Villegas's *Historia Moderna* which deal with the political life of the Porfiriato. His account is itself largely based upon press sources. He is at pains to illustrate the authoritarianism of the regime, in its increasing contempt for the press, and the recourse to censorship, the imprisonment of journalists, and even, on very rare occasions, their assassination or mysterious disappearance. He nevertheless tacitly recognises that blanket censorship and the suppression of dissident voices – practices now commonly associated with dictatorial regimes in Latin America in the late twentieth century – were never part of the Díaz strategy. The independent, opposition press was silenced, but never, it appears, for very long. Dissident voices were constantly heard and opposition papers continued to publish. But, at the same time, editors and journalists were hounded and imprisoned with notable regularity – so much so that one journalist apparently suggested that a special Club for Imprisoned Journalists be established at the Belén prison in Mexico City.[50]

Contrary to what might be expected under an authoritarian state, the number of newspapers and journals published during the Díaz era did not diminish but actually increased. Cosío Villegas indicates that during the Lerdo administration (1872–76), there were nine major newspapers in circulation, seven of which were opposition papers, and only two of which were pro-government. Following Díaz's first re-election in 1884, there were still six opposition papers, but many more pro-government publications – a total of apparently 24 daily newspapers throughout the Republic, 17 of which were published in Mexico City. Taking into account the number of special or occasional publications – especially those which were produced in order to support a political candidacy, which would then disappear following the elections – the total number of publications in circulation in 1888 reached 227, which prompts Cosío Villegas to describe this period as 'the zenith of Mexican journalism'. By 1889 the total number of publications had reached 385, and by 1898, a total of 531.

Circulation of the most influential daily papers, however, remained small. The main pro-government daily, which received an important but undisclosed level of government subsidy, was *El Partido Liberal*, begun in 1885, with a circulation of no more than 1,000 in the 1880s. This was substantially less than the circulation of the main independent daily, *El Monitor Republicano* (estimated at 7,000) and the Catholic papers *El Tiempo* (4,000), *El Nacional* (3,000) and *La Voz de México* (2,500). Unfortunately, there is little information about the constituency of the reading public, or an analysis of the political influence which these papers enjoyed. It is nevertheless apparent that the political influence of opposition newspapers was of major concern to the regime, given the evidence of growing efforts after 1884 to censor their output.

Cosío Villegas indicates that the roots of Porfirian censorship of the press dated from the amendment to Article 7 of the 1857 Constitution, which was approved by Congress during the presidency of Manuel González in 1883. Article 7 was, in essence, a declaration of the right to freedom of expression and, in particular, to guarantee the absolute 'freedom of the press, only to be limited by respect for private life, public morality and public order'. Any contraventions of press freedom (referred to as *delitos de prensa* or 'press crimes'), including accusations of slander or defamation of character against public officials, would be tried by two separate popular courts (*jurados populares*). The amendment passed in 1883 did not seek to change the declaration of rights to freedom of speech, but to transfer the prosecution of press infringements from popular courts to the ordinary courts (*tribunales comunes*), whose presiding judges were nominated by the Minister of Justice and, therefore, by implication, more directly open to political interference.[51]

Cosío Villegas cites innumerable examples of the frequent and repeated arrest and imprisonment (usually for periods of between three and six months) of editors and journalists of the independent press after 1884. There were even unexplained cases of the murder of journalists (such as the editor of the provincial liberal newspaper *El Explorador*, Luís González, in 1885). However, murder and assassination were far from frequent and they were certainly never part of a general strategy of press control. In fact, the absence of any coherent or co-ordinated strategy is apparent, and Cosío Villegas exonerates Díaz himself from any complicity, suggesting that 'although he tolerated persecutions [of the press], he did not initiate them, much less pursue them'. The blame, for Cosío Villegas, lay principally with the local judicial authorities.[52]

It would be disingenuous, however, to suggest that the President's views on the proper conduct of the press were insignificant in determining government policy. In official pronouncements, Díaz emphasised that his government was a sincere advocate of press freedom, but that it was also obliged, 'however reluctantly', to enforce the law. As ever, Díaz himself remained cautious and circumspect, frequently hiding behind the official, constitutional constraints on the authority of the President by claiming that the executive was not able to interfere with the functioning of the judiciary. But it is also clear that he advocated a characteristic combination of flattery, persuasion and intimidation in dealing with the press.

Díaz's public pronouncements frequently sought to flatter, famously on one occasion eulogising the press as 'the brains of the Republic', but also indulging in the language of patriotic rhetoric to remind journalists of their responsibility 'to defend, in good faith, that which is good for the country, which is, consequently, also of indisputable importance for the government'. By contrast, his private statements were more candid. He advised Carlos Díez Gutiérrez, the governor of San Luís Potosí (from 1884 until his death in 1898), who had written complaining about the editorials of the local broadsheet *El Estandarte*, to exercise a subtle but persistent persecution of critical journalists:

> My opinion, which I offer to you in a friendly manner, is that better results would be obtained if those who feel themselves to have grievances [against journalists] should pursue them, even if this means a

period of two or three months imprisonment; . . . if this period of
confinement fails to silence them, the accusations and sentences should
be repeated and increased until they are sedated in two or three years.
This is an unpleasant and tiring exercise for you: but you can be sure
that the accused will tire of it sooner than you.[53]

The fate of one of the more critical of the liberal Mexico City
newspapers, *El Diario del Hogar*, first published in 1881, and that of
its editor, Filomeno Mata, one of the most well-known opposition
journalists of the era, serve as an indication of the regime's treatment of political dissent. Mata had been a loyal *tuxtepecano* and
continued to represent the views of *puro* or 'jacobin' liberalism,
above all in his consistent opposition to re-election. Mata had supported the first re-election of Díaz in 1884, since it had been legitimised by the interregnum of Manuel González, but he was much
more vocal in his opposition to the second re-election in 1888, as a
result of which he was imprisoned for the first time in 1889. Significantly, Mata refused to blame Díaz himself, whom he praised for
'all the sacrifices he has made to achieve the freedom of the press'
but attacked instead what he referred to as the 'capricious, obstinate
and sinister party of [those who advocated] re-election'.

Mata became an even more outspoken critic of permanent re-
election, especially during the debates which preceded the constitutional amendment of 1890. He not only urged Díaz to resign his
candidacy, but published a satirical poem which lampooned Díaz as
'Don Perpétuo', a caricature which stuck in the popular imagination, but clearly annoyed the President. As a consequence, Cosío
Villegas estimates that *El Diario del Hogar* was subjected to an average of four prosecutions a year between 1885 and 1890, and that
Mata himself spent a total of 47 days in prison in 1890 alone. He
was imprisoned again in 1891 and 1892 and, even though he resigned as editor in 1892, the persecutions continued. In 1899 Mata
continued to publish editorials which argued for a free vote and to
make open accusations of electoral fraud which he had personally
witnessed. In 1900 he demonstrated his continuing resistance to
permanent re-election by refusing to allow a contribution from *El
Diario del Hogar* to the publication of a commemorative volume in
honour of Díaz's fifth re-election in 1900.

In 1901, Mata was the subject of further persecution for allowing
what later became the most famous of anti-re-electionist newspapers,
Regeneración, to be printed on his presses. This resulted in the

enforced closure of his printing business in June 1901. In 1907 Mata once again resumed the editorship of *El Diario del Hogar* and, again, his printing equipment was confiscated by the judicial author- ities. It was not surprising, given his life-long commitment to radical liberalism, that Mata should join the growing anti-re-electionist campaign as Secretary (along with Félix Palavicini and the young José Vasconcelos) to the Anti-Re-electionist Centre which was estab- lished in June 1909 (of which Emilio Vásquez was President and Francisco Madero Vice-President). What was more surprising, and more difficult to explain, was that following this litany of arbitrary and frequent persecution over a period of more than 20 years, Mata continued to show a remarkable degree of deference to Díaz. In 1911 he plaintively urged the President to 'please tell me if my work in journalism is not helpful to the progress of the country, since I want to make a contribution, in my small sphere of influence, to the noble ideals which you are carrying out with such dedication'.[54]

It is interesting to speculate here that, despite the increasing criticism levelled by anti-re-electionists against the regime in a grow- ing number of opposition newspapers after 1904, the personal author- ity of the President continued to remain strong, and the level of deference and of personal popular support was still remarkably high. This was perhaps due, in no small measure, to the success of the campaign to create a cult of personality, to which the Porfirian press had made an important contribution.

. . .

THE CULT OF PERSONALITY

As has been indicated above, the cultivation of deference to the patriarchal figure of Porfirio Díaz was a central goal of the regime, and one of its defining characteristics. It was also an essential com- ponent of a deliberate strategy to establish Díaz as the uncontested (and incontestable) source of political legitimacy and authority. Dur- ing the lifetime of the regime, the cultivation of deference became increasingly channelled into an official campaign to forge a cult of personality around the figure of Díaz, in order to add his name to the pantheon of republican patriotic heroes and to identify him with the destiny of the nation.

One of the fundamental goals of the liberal project in nineteenth- century Mexico was to weave liberal discourses of patriotism and republicanism into civic ceremony and to promote the notion of citizenship, and thus to permeate the consciousness of all 'Mexicans'. At a national level, the evidence of liberal nation-building accumulated on an incremental scale throughout the Porfiriato. It was to be found in the regime's preoccupations with domestic and scientific progress through the pursuit of a broad range of activities and initiatives in industry, sanitation, public hygiene, mental health, and even the cult of the bicycle and the efficiency of the postal service.[55]

The adoption of these projects gave Mexico international respectability and identified it firmly with the cosmopolitan and industrial culture of the late nineteenth-century western, capitalist world. They helped to establish a positive (and positivist) self-image of a modern, progressive, strong and sovereign nation with a positive future as a major centre of industrial growth and an axis of international trade. Díaz increasingly saw himself as leading a nation which had emerged from shaky foundations in 1876 finally to conquer the demons of post-independence Mexican history – political instability, economic stagnation, cultural backwardness and a profound absence of social cohesion or integration, or of national identity.

In constructing the nation, the Díaz regime not only became engaged in numerous public and civic works projects, but also in writing the history of the *patria* through the construction of national monuments, as well as the invention of civic ceremony and patriotic ritual.[56] The culmination of this process would be the series of activities and events which the regime planned in order to commemorate the centenary of Mexican independence in 1910. At the centre of the celebrations, although he specifically (and significantly) refused to allow any personal monument or statue to be erected, was the figure of Porfirio Díaz, whose career was projected as a reflection of the painful development of the nation since 1855. From a youthful and vigorous *mestizo* radical, following his first involvement in the Revolution of Ayutla, to the dynamic classical republican hero of the Wars of the Reforma and French Intervention, to the statuesque patriotic *criollo*, the patriarch of the nation.[57]

There had been indications long before his accession to the presidency that Porfirio Díaz was aware of the political importance of patriotic ritual. Following the fall of Mexico City to liberal forces in July 1867, not only did Díaz personally supervise the fabrication of a huge national flag to fly symbolically over the National Palace, but also ensured that the unveiling was delayed until President Juárez was able to preside personally over the public ceremony, thus re-establishing not only the personal authority of Juárez, but also that of the liberal republic.[58]

After 1876, the commemoration of Díaz's military exploits rapidly became incorporated into the public calendar of patriotic ritual, and made a significant contribution to the development of a cult of personality. The public celebration of Díaz's participation in the Republic's most famous military victories (5 May 1862 and 2 April 1867) therefore not only established them as landmarks in the evolution of the liberal republican state, but also served to establish Díaz as a classical republican nation-builder, a member of the pantheon of liberal heroes who had contributed to the creation of the *patria*.[59]

Daniel Cosío Villegas identified the first stirrings of a cult of personality in Díaz's second administration (1884–88), as a reflection of the need to prepare the nation for immediate re-election. As a result, in 1886 an organisation called the Society of Friends of the President was established, with the express purpose of 'considering, discussing and organising the appropriate celebrations of General Díaz's birthday'. Following the award by the Spanish government of the Military Merit Cross in 1888, *El Partido Liberal*, which became the principal vehicle for official pro-Díaz propaganda, described the figure of the President as not just a head of state, but 'the incarnation of the Mexican Nation'. This theme was subsequently elaborated by the National Porfirian Circle, the organisation established to promote Díaz's repeated candidacies, to such an extent that parallels (and distinctly mixed metaphors) were drawn between the physical appearance of the President and the geographical landmarks of the nation: 'General Díaz, with his head covered with snow, like the volcano Popocatépetl which stands prominently in our Central Plain . . . is the lighthouse of our organisation.'[60]

Another example of the evolving cult was the inauguration in August 1887 of the statue of Cuauhtemoc (Cuauhtemotzín), the symbol of Aztec resistance to the Spanish invasion, which still stands in the Paseo de la Reforma at the heart of Mexico City. In his inaugural address, the archaeologist and dramatist Alfredo Chavero compared the resistance of Cuauhtemoc to European invasion with the liberation of Mexico City by patriotic forces under Díaz in 1867:

Mr. President: more than three and a half centuries ago the great Cuauhtemotzín fell, as did the city, into the hands of Hernando Cortés, captain of the Austrian emperor Charles V, and it is twenty

Qw==

years since you recovered the city from one of the descendants of
Charles V himself (Prince Khevenhüller), after a bloody struggle.
You have revenged Cuauhtemoc! It is your right to unveil his statue![61]

Following the second re-election, the cult of personality continued to be promoted at a number of levels, especially in the context of preparations for the crucial elections of 1892. The *Junta
Central Porfirista* was established in 1891, followed by the 'voluntary'
organisations such as the *Círculo de Amigos de General Díaz*, which
organised annual processions of students, workers and *funcionarios*
(civil servants) on the anniversary of the battle of Puebla (5 May).
Motions were passed by all state legislatures awarding Díaz the title
of *benemérito* or 'distinguished citizen', and the state of Morelos
initiated in 1890 the practice of ordering that a portrait of the
President be hung in all public offices within the state, a practice
which has been repeated ever since.

The cult reached its height in the 1890s and 1900s, when Díaz was
fêted with ever more lavish praise, and awarded an increasing number
of honorary degrees (such as an honorary doctorate in laws from the
University of Pennsylvania) and various medals and honours from a
succession of foreign states (such as the Grand Cross of the Orders
of Charles III and Isabel la Católica from Spain, of the Order of
the Bath from the UK, and the Legion d'Honneur from France).[62]
As indicated in Chapter 2, following a campaign sustained by the
'Circle of the Friends of the President', the annual celebration of
his birthday (15 September) became combined in 1897 with the
celebrations to mark the independence of Mexico from Spain (16
September). Thereafter, Díaz was obliged to receive a long line of
admirers from the afternoon of 15 September until he launched the
grito at 11:00 pm, thus commemorating the call to independence
issued by Miguel Hidalgo in 1810, thereby establishing a permanent
link between Díaz's personal life and the destiny of the nation.

. . .

¿PAX PORFIRIANA?

The collective impact of the various strategies and manipulations
adopted by Díaz and his apologists in domestic politics after 1884
produced two decades of unprecedented political peace. This has

always been the mantra of the regime's apologists, and the principal *raison d'être* of the regime in its last years, and it was by no means a negligible achievement, certainly by comparison with the degree of political turbulence experienced in Mexico since 1821. Even those historians who have criticised the regime for its serial abuse of constitutional norms and its increasing authoritarianism have acknowledged its achievements in the avoidance of revolution and military *pronunciamiento*. Cosío Villegas, for example, one of the regime's most consistent critics, grudgingly asserts that, until the last years of the Porfiriato, 'there can be no doubt that the central course of Mexican life progressed with tranquillity and confidence'.[63]

Nevertheless, the description of the Díaz regime at its height as a haven of *pax porfiriana* is less than accurate. As part of the process of political consolidation, the regime faced a number of serious challenges. First, from regional *cacicazgos* or personal fiefdoms which had strongly resisted central authority (for example, those of Gerónimo Treviño in Nuevo León and García de la Cadena in Zacatecas, which preoccupied the regime throughout 1884 and 1885). Second, from those dissident voices at both the national and regional levels who challenged the principle of permanent re-election. These included those who speculated over the suitability of either Manuel González or Manuel Romero Rubio replacing Díaz in the elections of 1888; those who, more significantly, supported the efforts of the Liberal Union in an unsuccessful attempt to place constraints on the authority of the executive prior to the establishment of permanent re-election in 1892; those who gave support to the abortive rebellion of Catarino Garza on the Sonora–Arizona border in 1891; or those in Mexico City who supported the maverick candidacy of writer and astrologer Nicolás Zúñiga y Miranda in the elections of 1896 and 1900. Díaz also survived a serious attempt to assassinate him during the Independence celebrations in September 1897.[64]

The third source of resistance to the *pax porfiriana* came from those communities, many of which had consistently resisted the encroachment of the central state, but whose livelihood, security and autonomy were now threatened by the regional impact of the Porfirian process of economic modernisation. Popular rebellions developed, most notably in rural communities in Guerrero, Yucatán, Sonora and Chihuahua, especially between 1891 and 1893, thus contributing to the political uncertainties surrounding Díaz's third re-election. Although these were a combination of 'traditional' *campesino* rebellions against the abuses of local authorities, *hacendados* or *caciques*, they also reflected new grievances, such as land usurpation and the imposition of additional taxation.

Despite their local significance and intensity, they remained localised rebellions, with no co-ordinated national leadership, and they were ultimately suppressed with relative ease, in some cases with violence, and in others by means of negotiation and amnesty, depending on the configuration of local circumstances.[65] Much less subtle means of repression were adopted in the suppression of persistent indigenous rebellions of the *maya* in Yucatán, and the *yaqui* in Sonora, which pre-dated the Díaz era. In the case of the *yaqui*, the regime's policy fluctuated between military campaigns (1886), negotiated treaties (1897) and the encouragement of agricultural modernisation with the privatisation of over half a million acres in the Yaqui Valley (1894). The persistence of *yaqui* guerrilla resistance, however, ultimately led to a draconian policy of forced deportation of entire communities to the *henequén haciendas* of Yucatán imposed by state and central government after 1902.[66]

Perhaps the most significant rebellion in this period, and one which would have serious political repercussions for the regime, occurred in the *pueblo* of Tomochic in western Chihuahua in 1891. Here the inhabitants rebelled against the local *jefe político* and the threat of the *leva* (compulsory military draft), but the uprising took on religious overtones, since the inhabitants were followers of the spiritist cult of Santa Teresa de Cabora. Religious inspiration helped the rebels to subject the federal forces to humiliating defeat and to nearly 500 casualties before they were brutally massacred. The subsequent public outcry was loud and long-lasting, and Tomochic would become an important symbol of popular rebellion during the Revolution of 1910.[67]

Despite the multiple and sometimes serious disruptions to the *pax porfiriana*, political dissidence and popular discontent were largely contained before 1906. The tactics and strategies employed in the control of dissidence ranged from the arbitrary and excessive use of force (which characterised the suppression of the *maya* and the *yaqui*, and the rebellion of Tomochic in Chihuahua in 1891), to the use of caricature and ridicule (as in the case of the religious zeal of the Bishop of Yucatán in 1890). Dissidence and dissonance were certainly never curtailed, however, and the instances of more overt repression carried with them longer-term consequences which would revisit the regime during its last decade in power, and would expose the fragile base on which political control ultimately rested.

. . .

NOTES AND REFERENCES

1. D. Cosío Villegas (ed.), *Historia Moderna de México* (hereafter *HMM*), 10 vols, Mexico City, 1955–72, Vol. IX, p.xx.
2. J. Valadés, *El Porfirismo: Historia de un Régimen*, 3 vols, Mexico City, 1941, Vol. II, pp.145–6.
3. F. Katz and J. Dale Lloyd (eds), *Porfirio Díaz Frente al Descontento Popular Regional (1891–1893)*, Mexico City, 1986.
4. Cosío Villegas, *HMM*, Vol. X, p.xx.
5. Ibid., pp.11–16.
6. Díaz's first wife, his niece Delfina, had died in 1880 following the still-birth of their seventh child.
7. J. Foster, *Diplomatic Memoirs*, 2 vols, Boston, MA, 1910, Vol. I, p.99.
8. J.F. Iturribarría, *Porfirio Díaz ante la Historia*, Mexico City, 1967, pp.103–7.
9. Cosío Villegas uses the example of correspondence between Díaz and the governor of Puebla between 1884 and 1893, Rosendo Márquez; *La Constitución de 1857 y sus críticos*, 2nd edn, Mexico City, 1973, pp.130–1.
10. F.X. Guerra, *México: Del Antiguo Régimen a la Revolución*, 2 vols, Mexico City, 1988, Vol. I, pp.59–125.
11. Cosío Villegas, *HMM*, Vol. X, pp.293, 648.
12. J. Bazant, *A Concise History of Mexico*, Cambridge, 1977, p.103.
13. Cosío Villegas, *HMM*, Vol. X, p.599.
14. Guerra, *México: Del Antiguo Régimen*, Vol. I, pp.111–13.
15. F. Bulnes, *El Verdadero Díaz y la Revolución*, Mexico City, 1921, pp.181–2, 360.
16. Cosío Villegas, *HMM*, Vol. X, pp.491–3; Xavier-Guerra has produced a table which illustrates this pattern. See *México: Del Antiguo Régimen*, Vol. II, Anexo III, Cuadro AIII.2.
17. Cosío Villegas, *HMM*, Vol. X, pp.595–623.
18. The parallels with the modern electoral activities of the Revolutionary Institutional Party in contemporary Mexico are apparent; see R. Camp, *Politics in Mexico*, Oxford, 1993, pp.55–73.
19. Cosío Villegas, *HMM*, Vol. X, pp.110–24.
20. Ibid., pp.483–5, 445.
21. For the politics of Chihuahua during the Porfiriato, see M. Wasserman, *Capitalists, Caciques, and Revolution: The Native Elite and Foreign Enterprise in Chihuahua, Mexico 1854–1911*, Chapel Hill, NC, 1984.
22. Cosío Villegas, *HMM*, Vol. X, p.98.

23. Ibid., p.449.
24. R. Rendón, *El Prosperato: Tlaxcala de 1885 a 1911*, Mexico City, 1993, p.65.
25. Guerra, *México: Del Antiguo Régimen*, Vol. I, pp.90–1.
26. Díaz to Reyes, 20 March 1890, CPD:L41:C17:f.68.
27. A. Hernández Chávez, 'Origen y ocaso del ejército porfiriano', *Historia Mexicana*, Vol. XXXVII, 1988, pp.257–97.
28. G.P.C. Thomson, *Patriotism, Politics and Popular Liberalism in Nineteenth-Century Mexico: Juan Francisco Lucas and the Puebla Sierra*, Wilmington, DE, 1999, pp.230–60.
29. The parallel process in the rest of Latin America is described in B. Loveman and T. Davies, Jnr (eds), *The Politics of Anti-Politics: The Military in Latin America*, 3rd edn, Wilmington, DE, 1997.
30. Hernández Chávez, 'Origen y ocaso', pp.260–1.
31. J.R. Kelley, 'The Education and Training of Porfirian Officers', *Military Affairs*, 39(3), 1975, pp.124–8.
32. Cosío Villegas, *HMM*, Vol. X, pp.425–6.
33. P. Vanderwood, *Disorder and Progress: Bandits, Police and Mexican Development*, Tuscaloosa, NB, 1981, pp.119–38.
34. Guerra, *México: Del Antiguo Régimen*, Vol. II, pp.165–70.
35. D. Coerver, 'From Confrontation to Conciliation: Church–State Relations in Mexico 1867–1884', *Journal of Church and State*, 32(1), 1990, pp.65–80.
36. Quoted in M. Bazant, *Historia de la Educación Durante el Porfiriato*, Mexico City, 1993, p.161. Despite this public declaration, Díaz never regularly attended mass, except for the annual festival of Covadonga celebrated in the Church of Santo Domingo in Oaxaca. See M. González Navarro, *HMM*, Vol. IV, p.480.
37. Quoted in R. Conger, 'Porfirio Díaz and the Church Hierarchy, 1876–1911', PhD dissertation, University of New Mexico, Albuquerque, 1985.
38. Díaz to Palomino, 30 January 1889, CPD:L41:C7:T15:f.0058.
39. J.F. Iturribarría, 'La política de conciliación del General Díaz y el Arzobispo Gillow', *Historia Mexicana*, Vol. XIV, 1964, pp.81–101.
40. R. Parmenter, *Lawrence in Oaxaca: A Quest for the Novelist in Mexico*, Layton, UT, 1984.
41. M. Olimón Nolasco, 'Proyecto de Reforma de la Iglesia en Mexico 1867–1875', in A. Matute, E. Trejo and B. Connaughton (eds), *Estado, Iglesia, y Sociedad en Mexico, Siglo XIX*, Mexico City, 1995, pp.267–92.
42. M. Ceballos Ramírez, 'Las Organizaciones Laborales Católicas a Finales del Siglo XIX', in Matute *et al.*, *Estado, Iglesia y Sociedad*, pp.367–98.
43. K.M. Schmitt, 'Catholic Adjustment to the Secular State: The Case of Mexico 1876–1911', *Catholic Historical Review*, 48(2), 1962, pp.182–204; also 'The Díaz Conciliation Policy on State and Local Levels', *Hispanic American Historical Review*, 40(4), 1960, pp.513–32.

44. C. Dumas, 'El Discurso de Oposición en la Prensa Clerical Conservadora en la Época de Porfirio Díaz', *Historia Mexicana*, Vol. XXXVII, 1989, pp.243–57.
45. Quoted in Valadés, *El Porfirismo*, Vol. II, pp.204–5.
46. M. González Navaro, *HMM*, Vol. IV, p.469.
47. F. LaMond Tullis, 'Re-opening the Mexican Mission in 1901', *Brigham Young University Studies*, 22(4), 1982, p.445.
48. Jean-Pierre Bastian, *Los Disidentes, Sociedades Protestantes y Revolución en México*, Mexico City, 1989; J. Valadés, *El Porfirismo*, Vol. II, p.211.
49. F. Savarino, 'Religión y Sociedad en Yucatán durante el Porfiriato', *Historia Mexicana*, Vol. XLVI, 1997, pp.617–52.
50. Cosío Villegas, *HMM*, Vol. X, p.236.
51. Cosío Villegas, *HMM*, Vol. IX, p.728.
52. Cosío Villegas, *HMM*, Vol. X, pp.257–8.
53. Ibid., Vol. X, p.258.
54. Ibid., Vol. X, pp.389, 410, 533–4, 559, 593, 647.
55. W. Beezley, *Judas at the Jockey Club and Other Episodes of Porfirian Mexico*, University of Nebraska, Lincoln, 1987.
56. P. Nora, 'Between Memory and History: *Les Lieux de Mémoire*', *Representations*, 26, 1989, pp.7–25.
57. M. Tenorio Trillo, '1910 Mexico City: Space and Nation in the City of the Centenario', *Journal of Latin American Studies*, 28(1), 1996, pp.75–104.
58. Díaz, *Memorias*, Vol. II, pp.124–5.
59. The fifth of May is still today a public holiday in Mexico, which is testimony to its enduring popular impact since the late nineteenth century.
60. Cosío Villegas, *HMM*, Vol. X, p.166.
61. Cited in Díaz, *Memorias*, Vol. II, p.108. Public ritual was also adopted as a further means of promoting political reconciliation. Prince Khevenhüller was invited to Mexico in 1901 to receive a commemorative medal of the Virgin of Guadalupe from his former adversary, and he was invited to inaugurate a commemorative chapel in Querétaro.
62. The full list of national and international honours (including awards from Sweden, Norway, Portugal, Japan, Italy, Belgium, Prussia, Austria-Hungary, Persia, Germany, the Netherlands, Russia and China) can be found in A.M. Carreño, *Archivo del General Porfirio Díaz*, 30 vols, Mexico City, 1947–51, Vol. 3, pp.153–4.
63. Cosío Villegas, *HMM*, Vol. X, p.677.
64. W. Beezley, 'Mexican Sartre on the Zócalo: Nicolás Zúñiga y Miranda', in W. Beezley and J. Ewell (eds), *The Human Tradition in Latin America: The Nineteenth Century*, Wilmington, DE, 1989, pp.204–14.
65. F. Katz and J. Dale Lloyd (eds), *Porfirio Díaz Frente al Descontento Popular Regional (1891–1893)*, Mexico City, 1986.

66. E. Hu Dehart, 'Development and Rural Rebellion: Pacification of the Yaquis in the late Porfiriato', *Hispanic American Historical Review*, 54(1), 1974, pp.72–93.

67. P. Vanderwood, *The Power of God against the Guns of the Government: Religious Upheaval in Mexico at the Turn of the Nineteenth Century*, Stanford, CA, 1998.

Chapter 6

DIPLOMACY, FOREIGN POLICY AND INTERNATIONAL RELATIONS, 1876–1911

Pobre México: tan lejos de Dios y tan cerca de los Estados Unidos

('Poor Mexico: so far from God, and so close to the United States')
(Porfirio Díaz (attr.))

Dio a su patria derrotero,
y viril la engrandeció;
pero el gran Hombre murió
por su amor al extranjero

('He gave his country a purpose,
and made it grow virile and strong,
but the great Man died
because of his love for all things foreign') (Popular refrain, Mexico
1908)[1]

There are few areas within the historiography of the Díaz regime which require greater revision than those of international relations and foreign policy. *Anti-porfirista* historiography has argued that, in its drive to obtain international recognition and, above all, to secure the foreign investment which its economic policy required to fuel economic development, the Díaz regime betrayed the interests of the nation, throwing its arms open to rapacious foreign entrepreneurs who exploited the country's resources. Mexico's political and economic sovereignty were, it is argued, seriously abused in the process.

Applying a similar logic, if the Revolutionary governments which followed the collapse of the Díaz regime in 1911 have been perceived as promoting nationalism and restoring a commitment to the protection of national sovereignty, then, by contrast, the Díaz regime must have represented the opposite – the wilful neglect and, even worse, the surrender of sovereignty, with multiple favours bestowed upon foreign entrepreneurs, and only neglect, repression and suffering for the native Mexican population. As a result, it became commonplace to describe Mexico in the Díaz era as the 'mother of foreigners, and stepmother to Mexicans'.

Recent historiography has gone some way to restoring a more balanced and nuanced view, one which sees foreign policy from the perspective of the nineteenth century, not through the prism of the Revolution.[2] Porfirian foreign policy can only be understood, first, in terms of the legacy of the painful experiences Mexico had undergone since independence, and, secondly, in relation to the policy objectives of all liberal governments in Mexico after 1855.

During the first 50 years of its life as an independent nation, there had been a number of serious external threats to Mexican sovereignty. Post-colonial retribution – from Spain in 1829 – and neo-colonial ambition – from the USA in 1847–48 and France between 1862 and 1867 – had all threatened Mexico's survival as an independent nation, and had made all nineteenth-century governments acutely aware of the external threats to national self-determination. At the same time, external threats had played an important role in galvanising popular resistance in support of the *patria* and, consequently, in developing a sense of national identity and consciousness.

Liberal policy after 1855, therefore, linked diplomatic recognition and the development of economic links to the burgeoning North Atlantic economy, with the consolidation of a fragile national state and the project of state- and nation-building. Mid- and late nineteenth-century liberals of the Reforma and Porfiriato were therefore faced with the difficult task of protecting national sovereignty at the same time as opening up national frontiers to foreign capital, investment and colonisation. They saw these goals as complementary rather than contradictory.

The repercussions of this strategy for domestic policy during the Díaz era were clear: the pursuit of an unchallenged political peace ('order') became an absolute priority; and the creation of a legislative and institutional environment conducive to entrepreneurial activity, and attractive above all to foreign investors and immigrants, was a prerequisite of national development ('progress'). Two further initial observations need to made: first, that this precarious and fragile balance of interests was successfully maintained for most of the lifetime of the regime; and, second, that international diplomacy and foreign investment made a significant contribution to the political stability of the Díaz era. The situation changed significantly, however, after 1898.

. . .

THE PARAMETERS OF FOREIGN POLICY

The Díaz regime inevitably had to adapt its foreign policy in response to changing internal and external circumstances. Three periods can be identified, which correspond broadly to the chronological framework which has already been identified in preceding chapters for the politics of the regime. In the *tuxtepecano* phase (1876–1884), foreign policy concentrated on ensuring the survival of the regime, particularly in the light of the initial hostility of the USA. Tensions ran high, and prevented diplomatic recognition of the Díaz government until 1878. In spite of Díaz's initial inclination to adopt the xenophobic rhetoric of 'jacobin' nationalism, the early regime largely continued the policy of the Juárez and Lerdo administrations, eschewing the restoration of diplomatic relations with the European powers, or the pursuit of closer relations with Mexico's sister republics in Latin America, in favour of the pursuit of a 'special relationship' with the United States of America.[3]

Simultaneously, the regime began to address the principal obstacles to the restoration of relations with the major European powers. These were, first, Mexico's persistent default of debt repayments and, second, the introduction of fiscal and regulatory reforms which would attract foreign investment. During the presidency of Manuel González, in particular, negotiations with European bondholders of the Mexican debt were intensified, and the legislative assault upon what were essentially colonial restrictions on subsoil rights in the granting of mining concessions and foreign ownership of property was initiated.

During the phase of consolidation of the regime following Díaz's first re-election in 1884, the diplomatic and commercial offensive towards the USA was maintained, under the direction and guidance of Matías Romero, who had been reappointed as Minister plenipotentiary to Washington in 1882. Romero had always been a tireless and enthusiastic advocate of closer ties between Mexico and the

USA, and had proved to be a capable and successful advocate of the cause of the Juárez government as Mexican Minister in Washington in a difficult and delicate period between 1863 and 1868.[4]

At the same time, the regime began to pursue the renewal of diplomatic and commercial relations with Mexico's European adversaries – Great Britain, France and Spain. This was partly to tap into additional sources of overseas investment, but also, significantly, to ensure that European capital would act as a counterbalance to excessive dependence on US capital. The constant fear expressed by many of the Porfirian political elite, and particularly by the *científicos* during the 1890s and 1900s, was the same fear articulated by Mexican conservatives throughout the nineteenth century – that Mexico was in danger of being swallowed by the monstrous 'Caliban' of the USA, devouring the *patria* in the name of Anglo-Saxon, Protestant and materialist imperialism.

The pro-European strategy found a powerful advocate in Ignacio Mariscal, who had been Minister of Justice under Juárez (1868–69) and Díaz (1879–80), and Minister of Foreign Relations under Manuel González (1880–84). Mariscal was reappointed to the Ministry of Foreign Relations by Díaz in 1885 – a post he would hold until his death in 1910. Mariscal remained deeply suspicious of the threat to Mexican interests which close ties with the USA represented, and he therefore acted as a counterweight within the inner circle of the Díaz regime to the pro-US enthusiasms of Romero.

The central strategy of the Díaz regime during the period 1884–1900 was therefore to maintain a delicate balancing act between the protection and strengthening of Mexican sovereignty in the international arena and the enticement of foreign investment and colonisation to exploit the country's abundant natural resources. Despite its many trials and tribulations, outlined in more detail below, it was a policy which was pursued with considerable success. The Díaz regime was able, in fact, to mount an effective challenge to increasing signs of aggressive intervention into the political and economic affairs of the Caribbean and Central America from the USA in this period.

For example, Mexico, in league with the other Latin American delegates at the first Inter-American Conference held in Washington in 1889, was able to defeat a proposal from the USA for a hemispheric customs union which would have given US trade and investment in Latin America significant advantages over their European competitors.[5] And the Mexican government, in defence of what became known as the 'Díaz Doctrine', openly rejected the assumption within US foreign policy in the 1890s that the USA was to be the sole guardian and defender of the American continent against European intrusion. The Díaz regime argued instead that all Latin American nations should share a collective responsibility in hemispheric defence of Latin American sovereignty.

The delicate balancing act was progressively undermined after 1898, however, for three principal reasons. First, as indicated, the growing intensity of US strategic, commercial and diplomatic ambitions in the Caribbean and Central America (as demonstrated in Cuba and Puerto Rico in 1898, and Panama after 1903) made the attempt to reconcile the accommodation of US interests and the protection of Mexican and Latin American sovereignty increasingly difficult to achieve. Second, the rapid influx of overseas capital to Mexico in the 1880s and 1890s stimulated real fears within the regime of a loss of economic sovereignty and of foreign (mainly US) control of key sectors of the national economy. Third, the death of Matías Romero in 1898, who had, ironically, in that same year been appointed as Mexico's first Ambassador to the USA – Mexico was the first country in Latin America to achieve this status – deprived the regime of a respected pro-US voice and of the skills of an experienced mediator just at the time when US–Mexican relations were entering a very difficult phase.

As a result, especially following the events in Cuba after 1898, the regime was increasingly unable to maintain an effective challenge to the ambitions of the USA to increase its commercial, strategic and economic presence in Central America and the Caribbean. The regime's freedom to manoeuvre and the balancing act which had been maintained for so long were undermined and ultimately destroyed. The regime proved ultimately unable to square the circle of contradictions in its foreign policy, or to reconcile the expression of private fears of US aggression with public declarations of cordial co-operation. After 1907, the regime became increasingly paralysed by the fear of upsetting US investors, especially in the aftermath of the economic and financial crisis of that year. During the final months of the regime, relations between the Mexican and US governments reached their lowest point since 1877, and the Porfirian political elite was unable to convince either the growing tide of opposition or critics within its own ranks that it was protecting national interests. In short, the failures of foreign policy mirrored, and contributed to, the political failures in the domestic sphere.

. . .
DÍAZ AND FOREIGN POLICY

Díaz's personal contribution to the conduct of foreign policy was significant. His official diplomatic discourse was always characteristically discrete, and emphasised cordiality and the need for dialogue. In private, he continued to harbour anti-imperialist suspicions, particularly of the USA. Fundamentally, Díaz strove constantly to reconcile the interests of Mexican nationalism and the protection of sovereignty with a positive endorsement of improved international communications, trade and diplomatic relations.

During the early years of his presidency, he continued to espouse the rhetoric of radical, 'jacobin', nationalism in associating liberalism with patriotism and the defence of national interests, and in resisting the 'sale of Mexico to the foreigner'. As the (reformed) Plan of Tuxtepec had stated in 1876: 'We do not deserve the name of Mexican citizens, or even of men, if we continue to consent to be governed by those who are stealing our future and selling us to foreign interests.'[6]

Nevertheless, Díaz's official public rhetoric was tempered by his pragmatism and *realpolitik*, and in his close personal dealings with foreign diplomats, overseas investors and foreign businessmen. Even before he came to power, for example, during his preparations for the Tuxtepec Revolution during his stay in Brownsville, Texas, in early 1876, there is clear evidence that Díaz received arms, supplies, troops and money (an estimated US$130,000) from south-west Texas merchants and landowners, in return for a pledge that he would adopt 'energetic measures' to prevent future raids by Mexicans into Texas, and increase communications and trade between Mexico and Texas.[7]

The favourable treatment of overseas businessmen and foreign investors became central to the character, structure and development of the Díaz regime. The strategy had important political repercussions. First, the types of business practice adopted by the regime can be seen as an integral feature of what William Schell describes as a form of 'tributary capitalism' which operated during the Porfiriato in the absence of more formal, regulatory institutions. Foreign entrepreneurs thus formed a powerful and significant pro-Díaz *camarilla* within the structure of Porfirian politics.[8] Second, Díaz's role as patron, benefactor and intermediary between foreign entrepreneurs and local elites was clearly another example of the way in which patronage was used to instil personal loyalty to Díaz and to the regime.

The accusations frequently levelled at the regime in *anti-porfirista* historiography imply that, through his close personal dealings with US and European businessmen, Díaz was betraying national interests. The strategy clearly conformed, however, to one of the central goals of the regime, which it shared with the previous liberal regimes of Juárez and Lerdo – the promotion of economic development, which, according to the regime, could be achieved only by attracting foreign capital and therefore protecting the interests of overseas investors. As far as the Díaz regime was concerned, the promotion of national interests could be enhanced only by extending links with overseas investors. And it was also the case that the influence of those foreigners interested in the exploitation of Mexican resources had a positive impact on ending diplomatic hostility and improving diplomatic relations.

The sympathetic (and self-interested) voices of US entrepreneurs, for example, proved to be effective in putting pressure on Washington to alter the aggressive stance it had demonstrated towards the first Díaz administration by delaying full diplomatic recognition until May 1878. Pressure from British business interests was also influential in ending the diplomatic *impasse* between Britain and Mexico, which had lasted from 1867 until 1884.

In 1883, Díaz had an opportunity to consolidate and extend his personal relationship with prominent US businessmen during a two-month tour of the USA in his official capacity as Commissioner General of the Mexican delegation at the New Orleans World Fair, to be held in 1884. The New Orleans fair was Mexico's first major participation in the large number of International Fairs which were held in Europe and the Americas in the late nineteenth century (Philadelphia in 1876, Buenos Aires in 1883, Berlin in 1883, Paris in 1899 and 1900, St Louis in 1904).[9] Díaz's acceptance of this commission was a clear indication of his commitment to the promotion of Mexico's image as a modern, progressive and sovereign nation anxious to diversify its international links in order to exploit its full economic potential.[10]

The trip had also been inspired by personal considerations. Díaz had recently married Carmen Romero Rubio, and thus the trip was a *luna de miel* (honeymoon) – albeit a rather unusual one. He had also accepted the invitation offered by General Gerónimo Treviño to be godfather (*padrino*) to his son. The fact that Treviño's wife was the daughter of US General Edward Ord, the commander of US troops in Texas, and Treviño's adversary during the border clashes of 1877 (see below), meant that the marriage and the baptism were interpreted in some quarters as the dawning of a new era in US–Mexican relations.[11]

Accompanied by his new wife and his close associate the English-speaking Monsignor Eulogio Gillow, Díaz also visited St Louis, Chicago, Washington, Boston and New York. Through the agency of Matías Romero and his American wife, Díaz was introduced to a number of powerful individuals such as railway 'magnate' Jay Gould, and former President Ulysses S. Grant. In fact, Díaz, Grant and Gould were already business partners, along with Romero, Ignacio Mariscal and businessmen and politicians from Oaxaca, Miguel Castro, Fidencio Hernández and Francisco Meixueiro, in the ill-fated Mexican Southern Railway Company, which had been formed in 1880 in order to link the cites of Puebla and Oaxaca.[12]

In his farewell speech in New York, Díaz provided a characteristic example of Porfirian diplomatic discourse. He praised the material, intellectual and spiritual development of the USA, emphasising the progress made in education (both schools and universities), the press, religious tolerance and welfare provision. He concluded, with classic republican and anti-European rhetoric:

> I wish the great American people health and prosperity . . . your country has achieved first place among all nations . . . and, through the splendour of its civilisation based upon peace, it will eclipse the false sparkle of ancient empires based upon war.[13]

Another example of official Porfirian diplomatic discourse was the speech made by Díaz at the ceremony to mark the arrival in 1897 of General Powell Clayton, the first US Ambassador to Mexico. It was significant that the ceremony should also commemorate the 50th anniversary of the 'Boy Heroes' (*Niños Héroes*), the cadets who died in the heroic but vain struggle to save Mexico City from the invading US army in 1847. Ambassador Clayton made a significant symbolic gesture of co-operation by laying a wreath on the graves of the cadets who had died fighting the Yankee invader. President Díaz responded:

> Great is the admiration that your country inspires among the Mexican people, who have taken it for a model for their political institutions,

and who are attempting to imitate it in the development of their natural resources.[14]

Public expressions of republican empathy and co-operation, and the cultivation of personal relations with prominent US businessmen and politicians stands in marked contrast, however, to Díaz's more private ambivalence, fears and suspicions of the threat posed by the USA to Mexican sovereignty. There are examples from his private correspondence where remnants of his 'jacobin' nationalism can be detected. He wrote, for example, to Carlos Rivas, Senator for Tamaulipas, in 1890 to reassure the state's citizens that, in spite of the encouragements offered to US land colonisation companies, both their own and the nation's interests would continue to be safeguarded by the government. The residents were fearful that public lands would be sold to North Americans:

> You can assure the people of Tamaulipas that the government does not prefer *gringos*, and that it only awards them concessions provided that, some considerable time after the laws have been in force, there are no Mexicans who show themselves willing to take advantage of the benefits.[15]

Díaz was also privately wary of the threat to Mexico's economic sovereignty through an excessive dependence on US capital. In 1889, for example, he advised Ramón Corral, the influential entrepreneur and governor of Sonora (and Vice-President after 1904), who was seeking funds for his latest enterprise: 'I would recommend you to favour European capital in order to balance it with American capital, since there is already a good deal of the latter in Mexico.'[16]

Díaz's dual strategy of balancing US and European interests served the regime well until the end of the 1890s. After 1898 it became increasingly difficult to sustain.

. . .

MEXICO AND THE USA

Diplomatic relations between Mexico and the USA during the Porfiriato were more tense than has generally been supposed. Tensions ran particularly high during the period 1876–78 and deteriorated again after the events in Cuba in 1898. By comparison with the history of US–Mexican relations over the previous half-century, however, they constituted a distinct improvement.

Mexico had suffered acutely from the territorial ambitions of her northern neighbour since the achievement of independence. The incorporation of the Mexican province of Texas into the USA in 1845 was followed by Mexico's defeat in the war of 1846–47, culminating in the devastating loss of one half of Mexican territory to the USA according to the terms of the Treaty of Guadalupe Hidalgo in 1848. The acquisition by the USA of the former Mexican province of California strengthened the pressure on Mexico to concede territorial or transit rights across the Isthmus of Tehuantepec, as one of the three proposed sites for an inter-oceanic canal or railway (the other sites were Nicaragua and Panama, where the canal was eventually built in 1914). In 1853 the US government acquired La Mesilla (the northern part of Sonora and Chihuahua) in return for US$10 million as part of the Gadsden purchase.[17]

Mexico had also had to suffer numerous filibusters by private citizens of the USA in the 1850s. William Walker had attempted to 'conquer' Lower (Baja) California and Sonora in 1853, and Sam Houston had hatched an abortive plot to establish a protectorate in northern Mexico in 1859.[18] US–Mexican relations improved considerably during the Reforma, as a result of the assistance given to Juárez during the liberal struggles against Mexican conservatives and French invaders between 1859 and 1867. Nevertheless, the turbulent history of US–Mexican relations left a powerful legacy of distrust of US intentions for all subsequent Mexican governments, including that of Porfirio Díaz.

The pursuit of closer diplomatic, commercial and political links with Mexico's predatory northern neighbour faced a number of difficulties after 1867. The perennial issues were cross-border banditry, raids from indigenous communities in Chihuahua and Coahuila on properties across the US frontier, *apache* raids on properties in Sonora, forced loans levied on US citizens in Mexico, the smuggling of imported European goods into Texas, and the indemnification of the property of US citizens in Mexico which had been affected by the political disturbances of the Wars of the Reforma and French Intervention.[19]

In addition, there were substantial political barriers on both sides of the border to closer 'fraternal' co-operation. In private correspondence, and in the press, there were mutual expressions of indifference, ignorance, suspicion or outright hostility. There were, for example, frequent denunciations in the Mexican (particularly the Catholic) press of the inevitable consequence of closer links, which would signify the 'peaceful conquest' (*conquista pacífica*) of Mexico by the USA. Concern over the potential threat to Mexican sovereignty had led to the Lerdo administration's failure to endorse a series of projected railway schemes which sought to link Mexico with the US border.[20]

Following the Revolution of Tuxtepec in 1876, a serious diplomatic conflict developed which denied the Díaz regime formal recognition from Washington. The Díaz regime responded, first, by calling for presidential elections in 1877 in order to confirm its legitimacy, and, second, by paying the first instalment of the 'American debt', despite the precariousness of its finances. The extent of the debt had been fixed by the Joint Claims Commission, which had been created in 1868, but whose verdict had not been delivered until 1877. Díaz fulfilled both of these requirements, but formal recognition was denied on the basis that serious security issues on the border had not been resolved.

Relations deteriorated to such a point that there was a real danger of clashes between US and Mexican troops as a result of the order given in June 1877 to General Edward Ord in San Antonio to pursue bandits across the Rio Grande. In response, Díaz despatched troops under the command of Gerónimo Treviño, with orders to repel any 'invasion' of Mexican territory by US troops. The issue had been complicated by the electoral scandal in the USA which had led to the disputed election victory of Republican President Rutherford Hayes in 1877 and the consequent desire to divert public attention in the USA away from domestic politics towards the conflict with Mexico. Eventually, the combination of pressure from the House Foreign Affairs Committee of the US Congress, and from the business consortium which had signed a concession with the Díaz government for the construction of a railway from El Paso, Texas, to Mexico City, convinced the Hayes administration formally to recognise the Díaz regime in April 1878.[21] Once formal *de jure* recognition had been obtained, the obstacles to the surveying of suitable routes and to the issue of railway concessions fell away. As a result, diplomatic relations increasingly took second place to the implementation of a new regulatory environment to facilitate railway construction, mining, cross-border trade and the rapid penetration of US capital, particularly during the government of Manuel González.[22]

By the end of the 1880s the true character of US–Mexican relations was determined less by the health of diplomatic exchanges than by the rapid rise of cross-border trade, stimulated and symbolised above all by the construction of railway lines which linked Mexico City with the southern USA. The border region in particular was, as a consequence, rapidly transformed from unregulated frontier into an international border.[23] In 1885 it was reported to the US Senate that US exports to Mexico had overtaken exports from both Britain and France for the first time (whereas in South America US exports represented less than one-third of British, and less than one-half of French exports). As Paolo Riguzzi has explained, after 1884 these closer links began to have a significant impact on economic, social and cultural life on both sides of the frontier:

> From the definition and control of the borders, to the access to rivers on the frontier for the purposes of irrigation, from extradition treaties to literary copyright, from industrial patents to postal communications ... areas of progressive interdependence, and of permanent inter-change were developed.[24]

The assumption of many accounts is that US–Mexican relations after 1884 were cordial and conflict-free.[25] On the surface, burgeoning commercial relations and the maintenance of cordial diplomatic discourse suggested widespread consensus and co-operation. In the private correspondence of the inner circle of the regime, however, there was persistent and serious concern at the growing manifestations of territorial, diplomatic and economic aggression from north of the border. Their fears were not without foundation. The late nineteenth century has been long identified as an era of 'militant spread-eagleism' – a period in which US strategic and commercial ambitions in the Caribbean and Central America were transformed into a confident and aggressive assertion of US hegemony.

An important indicator of the restructuring of geo-political relations in the Caribbean was the conflict between Britain, the USA and Venezuela over the disputed territorial boundaries between British Guyana and Venezuela in 1896. Despite some sabre-rattling and the delivery of an ultimatum to the government of Venezuela, Britain refrained from direct intervention, being more concerned with the events in southern Africa which foreshadowed the second Boer War (1899–1902). The incident demonstrated, first, that Britain was increasingly prepared to recognise the Caribbean as a predominantly

US sphere of influence, and second, that the USA was anxious to redefine the Monroe Doctrine and to assert the right to intervene in the protection of US strategic and commercial interests, and the policing of regional conflicts. This redefinition would be more fully and notoriously expressed in the Platt Amendment to the Cuban Constitution in 1901 and the Roosevelt Corollary in 1904. The former gave the USA the right to intervene in Cuban affairs in order to safeguard US interests, and the latter justified the intervention of US troops to settle internal conflicts of the sovereign states of Hispanic America. The attempt to redefine the role and responsibility of the USA in the Caribbean led directly to the articulation of the Díaz Doctrine, an alternative interpretation of the Monroe Doctrine from a Pan-American perspective.

The Díaz Doctrine

By the end of the nineteenth century, the USA appeared to be ready to assume the status and responsibilities of a colonial power, as the war with Spain over Cuba in 1898, and the subsequent occupation of the island, indicated. The Cuban crisis, along with a series of conflicts within the Caribbean region during the 1890s and 1900s, therefore represented a watershed in the geo-politics of the Caribbean and Central America, and had serious repercussions for US–Mexican relations.[26]

Díaz was far from silent in the face of the growing threat to the political sovereignty of Mexico and Latin America represented by US activities and ambitions in the Caribbean region in the 1890s. In a revealing letter in 1896 to one of his long-term political allies, former deputy and later senator for the state of Jalisco, Alfonso Lancaster Jones, Díaz explained his views on the realities of foreign policy, and of US–Latin American relations. The tone is characteristically ironic and cynical, and reflects the frustrations in resisting the presumptions of the US government (described sarcastically, but significantly, as 'our officious protector'):

> The Monroe Doctrine has neither the significance which American statesmen have attributed to it through their loose interpretation, nor should it be accorded respect by the Hispanic-American Republics, unless it is under the auspices of a treaty which, without damaging the rights of the European powers, prescribes reciprocal rights and duties in the spirit of absolute sovereignty for all. I doubt that the US is seeking such an outcome, since it would grant them equal status with all of the signatories of this type of Alliance; but, I repeat, that

only in the manner stated above could we Latin Americans accept what our officious protector has so 'generously' offered us.[27]

There was, nevertheless, a notable reluctance in Mexican government circles to trumpet this alternative Díaz Doctrine. In the same letter, Díaz expressed a characteristic preference for discretion, always aware of the dangers implicit in antagonising the USA. Nevertheless, Díaz's reputation as a defender of the political sovereignty of Latin American nations certainly did not go unnoticed within Latin America and the Caribbean, even if it escaped the attention of *anti-porfirista* historiography. His articulation of widely-expressed fears explains the decision of Cuban patriot and revolutionary José Martí to visit Mexico in July 1894 as part of preparations for the liberation of Cuba, and his decision to seek the personal support of Díaz for his cause.

The tone adopted in Martí's letter to Díaz requesting a 'conversation' with the President was in keeping with the radicalisation of Martí's political thought after 1889, which transformed his early enthusiasm for the 'bold ingenuity' of the USA, its achievements in industry, commerce and education, into a realisation that political independence for Cuba meant not only the rejection of Spanish sovereignty, but also a challenge to the strategic and territorial ambitions of the USA.[28] Martí's letter expressed admiration for Díaz's 'profound and constructive wisdom', his 'passionate suffering for the freedom of the [American] continent, and unity he has given to his people'. He urged Díaz to assist his struggle to support the liberation of Cuba from Spain, but at the same time to avoid Cuba's falling into the 'disastrous dominion' of the USA, which he described as a 'hostile republic'.[29] There were clear and obvious parallels between Martí's views and the Díaz Doctrine over the urgency of protecting the sovereignty of Hispanic America against the threat of the USA.

According to Federico Gamboa, Martí obtained both political and financial support from Díaz, although, given the delicacy of US–Mexican relations, there was certainly never any official declaration of Mexican support for the Cuban patriotic cause.[30] In fact, there is evidence that the Díaz government was attempting to play a double game, by tacitly supporting the cause of Cuban independence while at the same time eliciting the support of the Spanish government in resisting US ambitions by reassuring them of Mexican support for the maintenance of Spanish sovereignty in Cuba. For example, Foreign Relations Minister Ignacio Mariscal informed Madrid in 1895 that he had 'absolute faith in the victory of Spanish arms'.[31] During

1896 and 1897, as tensions continued to mount, the Díaz government attempted in vain to offer its services as a mediator between the Cuban patriots and the Spanish government, but its overtures were rejected by both Washington and Madrid. Once hostilities between Spain and the USA broke out in 1898, the official Mexican position remained one of strict neutrality, but this failed to hide the weakness of the Mexican position, and the fact that the strategy of maintaining the precarious balance of interests had been seriously undermined.

Prominent members of the Porfirian inner circle expressed their profound, but increasingly impotent, consternation over the territorial and commercial ambitions of the USA and the vulnerability of Mexico's position. Prominent *científico* and Finance Minister José Yves Limantour wrote to Matías Romero in Washington, expressing his fears that, 'given the political, economic, and geographic conditions of our country in relation to those of the United States, we must be very careful not to provide our neighbours with any opportunity for giving full vent to their ambitions'.[32]

Similar fears were manifest again during the Panamanian Revolution of 1903, when the USA supported the cause of Panamanian independence from Colombia in return for Panamanian acceptance of the USA's acquisition of sovereignty over the future route of the Panama Canal. As in the Cuban conflict, Mexico maintained strict neutrality, but showed more concern than any other Latin American nation over the threat to hemispheric political sovereignty. Mexico formally recognised the independent state of Panama in 1904, but as the US Ambassador (Powell Clayton) himself reported, 'the Mexican government regards the matter unfavourably'. Ignacio Mariscal openly expressed the view that events in Panama constituted 'a very serious political development'.[33]

There are further examples after 1900 where the protection of Mexico's economic and political sovereignty clashed with the interests of the USA. In the 1890s, as will be shown in Chapter 7, the Díaz regime's economic strategy continued to promote external links in the search for new export markets and sources of investment, but simultaneously sought to exercise a much greater degree of state control and intervention in the regulation of key sectors of the economy. This policy was most clearly expressed in the strategy to 'mexicanise' the railways in 1908, and in the massive state subsidy provided for reconstruction of the Tehuantepec National Railway (1896–1907), linking the Atlantic with the Pacific. US control over this vital inter-oceanic route had been, as indicated earlier, one of the central goals of US policy in the Caribbean.[34] It was, therefore, significant that the Mexican government should have chosen a British firm (that of Sir Weetman Pearson) as the contractor for the Tehuantepec concession. It was a decision which prompted an inevitably angry request from the USA to the Mexican government in 1902 as to why the USA had been 'so odiously excluded' from the Tehauntepec project.[35]

Towards the end of the decade both governments became embroiled in a dispute over landing rights for the US Navy at a coaling station in the Bahia Magdalena on Mexico's Pacific coast. These rights had previously been exercised by the US Navy, but the Díaz government after 1906 became increasingly reluctant to renew them. When the landing rights were finally renewed in 1907, the contract was limited to three years.[36]

Of more serious concern was the growing clash of interests in Central America. Porfirian foreign policy in Central America, following on from the policy adopted by its liberal predecessors, pursued a dual strategy which sought to contain both US and Guatemalan ambitions, and to enhance Mexico's political status in the region. Mexico's principal disputes with Guatemala centred on the contested sovereignty of the state of Chiapas, and on Guatemalan ambitions to unite the Central American states under its control. The conflicts had their origins in the early post-independence period, when the United Provinces of the Centre of America (*Provincias Unidas del Centro de América*) had broken away from the Mexican Empire of Agustín Iturbide in 1823.

In the 1880s both issues were resolved. Pressure to define the legitimate borders between Chiapas and Guatemala grew with the influx of foreign investment to exploit the region's potential for coffee cultivation, and in 1882 an agreement was signed between Guatemalan President Justo Rufino Barrios and President Manuel González. Barrios's subsequent attempt to create a Central American Union in 1885 was vigorously opposed by the Díaz regime (and by the Central American states of El Salvador, Costa Rica and Nicaragua), and Mexican troops were despatched to the border. War was avoided, however, and Barrios's death during the Guatemalan invasion of El Salvador put an end to Guatemala's pretensions.

From the 1890s, Mexican policy towards Guatemala and Central America became inevitably enmeshed with the increasingly ineffective attempts to resist US intervention in the region. Washington's strategy involved seeking the Mexican government's endorsement of

its policy of using direct military intervention in order to police conflicts in the region. Díaz enjoyed some success in resisting several
invitations from the government of President Theodore Roosevelt
to co-operate in 'peacekeeping' interventions with the USA, for
example in the Dominican Republic in 1904, refusing to play any
part in endorsing what became commonly known as Roosevelt's
'Big Stick' policy. Ultimately, the pursuit of the Díaz Doctrine in
Central America forced Mexico to confront Washington. In 1909,
following the resignation of the liberal nationalist José Santos Zelaya
in Nicaragua in the wake of a US-supported coup, the Díaz regime
offered sanctuary to Zelaya, and supported continued resistance to
the pro-US faction.[37]

Finally, as domestic political opposition to the Díaz regime
mounted in intensity across the north of Mexico in 1909 and 1910,
the Díaz regime became increasingly frustrated with the slow and
irregular prosecution by US authorities of the violations of neutrality laws by anti-Díaz conspirators and activists in the USA. On
the eve of the Revolution, it is possible to argue, therefore, that
US–Mexican relations had reached their lowest point since 1877.
Friedrich Katz, for example, has argued that both the US government and US business interests were hostile to the Díaz regime
by 1910, a factor which therefore played a significant role in the
demise of the regime.[38]

There appears to be little evidence, however, of active or direct
collusion from Washington in the downfall of the regime. Nevertheless, there certainly is evidence of increasing public criticism, and
of the growing opposition of prominent US business interests to the
clear favouritism shown by the regime to non-US companies in the
awarding of important government contracts (as was the case with
the contracts and concessions awarded to Sir Weetman Pearson in
railways and oil). The meeting between Presidents Díaz and Taft
on the Mexican border in October 1909, while ostensibly a manifestation of the health of US–Mexican relations, in fact masked serious
tensions between Mexico and her northern neighbour.[39]

. . .

MEXICO AND THE EUROPEAN POWERS

If US–Mexican relations during the final years of the Díaz era can
be described, at best, as cautious and ambivalent, and, at worst, as

increasingly conflictive, it could be argued that the reverse was true for Mexico's relations with the major European powers: Britain, France, Spain and Germany. Increasing *rapprochement* with Europe, however, contrasted sharply with the situation which had prevailed at the time of Díaz's accession to power in 1876.

During the early years of the regime, relations with Britain, Spain and France had faced serious obstacles. They had been hampered by the persistent failure to resolve the problem of debt obligations to overseas bondholders since the 1820s, and they had been severely damaged as a consequence of the French invasion and occupation of Mexico between 1862 and 1867. Thereafter, the renewal of diplomatic and commercial links was a slow process. By the mid-1880s these issues had been mostly settled, and diplomatic and commercial relations had been restored. Over the subsequent two decades, under the guidance of Minister of Foreign Relations Ignacio Mariscal, Mexico's diplomatic, commercial and financial links to Europe, and the number of Europeans and European businesses operating in Mexico, grew exponentially. The health of European–Mexican relations on the eve of the Revolution therefore contrasts sharply with the deterioration of US–Mexican relations in the same period.

The reasons for the increasing *rapprochement* with Europe were both economic and political. The economic strategy of the regime required capital investment and external links with the expanding international economy. But as US capital and investment began to flow at a rapid rate into Mexico after 1880, the Díaz regime became increasingly concerned with encouraging non-US sources of investment to act as a counterbalance to the threat which US interests posed to Mexico's economic and political sovereignty. By the end of the regime, particularly under the guidance and influence of the Europhile Minister of Finance, José Yves Limantour, the favouritism shown towards European, and particularly towards British, French and German investors, was unmistakable. Ultimately, the challenge mounted by Mexico and its European partners, whose own imperial rivalries were a notable feature of the late nineteenth-century world, failed to stem the tide of US hegemony in Central America and the Caribbean. And the carefully cultivated European diplomatic support for the regime was unable to prevent its rapid collapse in 1911.

Before 1876, Mexico's relations with the European powers had fluctuated considerably. Relations with Spain can best be described as turbulent and conflictive. Spain had failed to recognise or respect the independent status of her former colonies in the Americas, and maintained interventionist pretensions throughout the nineteenth century in an attempt to reassert Spanish power in the Americas (as demonstrated in the Dominican Republic in 1861).[40] Relations with France had also been determined by conflicts which arose over debt and imperial ambition. The negotiation of the Jecker bonds by the Conservative government in 1859, their subsequent repudiation by the Juárez government, combined with the ambitious plans of Emperor Napoleon III to add Mexico to France's imperial adventures in North Africa and Indo-China, were the fundamental causes of the French occupation of Mexico after 1862.[41]

In the case of Britain, the predominance in the early post-independence period of British mining investments, the importance to Mexican public finances of the tariffs paid on British imports, and the presence of British merchant houses, highlighted the significance of British–Mexican relations.[42] At the same time, Mexico's persistent and increasing indebtedness to British bondholders was a constant source of tension. There were two main groups of bondholders. First, and most significantly, the London bondholders who represented the loans made to Mexico in 1824 and 1825, and, second, the Convention bondholders whose claims for damages suffered before 1842 had been recognised by the Mexican government in 1851. The debt owed to British bondholders in total is estimated to have reached over 64 million *pesos* in 1862, out of a total debt of 81 million.[43]

The decision of the Juárez government in 1861 to suspend payment of the debt for two years, in order to divert the government's meagre funds into infrastructural development to repair the damage inflicted by civil war, prompted an inevitably hostile reaction from all of Mexico's overseas bondholders. In October 1861, Britain, Spain and France approved joint military intervention to put pressure on the Juárez government to rethink its decision. However, once the extent of French ambitions to proceed with a full-scale invasion became clear, Britain and Spain withdrew.

France's abortive imperial adventure in Mexico between 1862 and 1867 dramatically altered Mexico's relations with Europe. After 1867, relations with Britain, France and Spain were severed, and the subsequent blockage of Mexican access to European financial markets provided opportunities for commercial and diplomatic ties between Mexico and the USA to develop. Germany was also well-placed to take advantage of the downturn in British trade after 1867. By 1878 it is estimated that two-thirds of Mexico's export trade was controlled by German merchants from the Hanseatic cities of Hamburg, Bremen and Lübeck.[44]

Relations with both Spain and France had been partially restored by the Juárez government in 1871, but the issue of outstanding debt obligations continued to impede the resumption of British–Mexican links. As indicated above, the Díaz regime in its early years pursued the policy of the Juárez and Lerdo governments of giving priority to the strengthening of US–Mexican relations.

However, at the same time as overtures were being made to Washington and, above all, to US investors, there was an acute awareness of the need to encourage European influence as a counterbalance to excessive dependence upon the USA. In a significant letter from the Mexican envoy in France to Díaz as early as 1882, the urgency was made explicit: 'it is vital to re-establish our relations with England, because we must at all costs attempt to establish European influence as a counterbalance to American influence'.[45]

The resumption of financial, commercial and diplomatic relations with Britain, therefore, was a significant priority for the government of Manuel González after 1880. At the same time, pressure was brought to bear on the British government by both the London bondholders and by British business interests, supported by the Association of Chambers of Commerce of the United Kingdom, who argued in 1876 that the renewal of diplomatic relations would be of considerable benefit in assisting existing trade and in developing new commercial opportunities.

Although economic historians of British overseas interests have pointed out the reluctance of British diplomats in Latin America to intervene on behalf of British commercial interests, in the case of Mexico in the 1880s there was clearly a convergence of diplomatic and commercial concerns.[46] As a result, by the mid-1880s both of the outstanding disputes between the British and Mexican governments were settled – the 'English debt' and the diplomatic impasse since 1867 – and in 1884 formal diplomatic relations were resumed. From this point, although with an important hiatus in the early 1890s with the onset of the Baring crisis, British capital investment began to flow once again into Mexico and, according to the available statistics, began considerably to outstrip levels of French, Spanish and German investment, and even to rival levels of US investment.[47]

As the growing levels of European investment indicated, between 1884 and 1898 diplomatic relations in themselves became increasingly less important than personal and business relations which overseas investors developed with Mexican officials and politicians, including those with Díaz himself. The everyday work of European diplomatic missions in Mexico in this period related overwhelmingly to commercial matters, and to protecting the personal interests of the growing number of foreigners resident in Mexico. Ultimately, the health of Mexico's overseas relations must be judged by the collective impact of foreign investment on the Porfirian economy, which will be dealt with in the next chapter.

However, the political importance of diplomatic relations was highlighted again in relation to the Cuban crisis in 1898 and its aftermath. During the last decade of the regime there was a significant realignment of diplomatic priorities. Diplomatic overtures to all European diplomatic representatives notably increased in this period, as the Díaz government attempted to cement alliances which might challenge the growing power and influence of the USA. The overseas missions most affected by this shift were those of Spain and Germany.

As indicated above, Mexican relations with Spain were transformed during the Porfiriato. The main reason for the reversal of the antagonism which had characterised Spanish–Mexican relations throughout most of the nineteenth century was the assertion of US ambitions in the Caribbean and Central America in the 1890s, most specifically with regard to the Spanish colony of Cuba. This coincided with the final settlement of the terms and conditions of the repayment of outstanding debt to Spanish bondholders according to an agreement signed in 1894.[48] Improved trade and financial connections between Spain and Mexico were also the result of the efforts and energies of a small but very active group of Spanish entrepreneurs, merchants and financiers, most notably in Mexico City, Puebla and Monterrey.[49] The reinvigoration of Spanish–Mexican relations was also reflected in the promotion in government and intellectual circles in Spain of *hispanismo*, the notion of a common cultural, linguistic, religious and spiritual inheritance within the Hispanic world, as a challenge to the attempt by the USA to export its anglophone, Protestant and materialist vision of *panamericanismo* (Pan-Americanism) throughout the Americas.

In the late 1890s, therefore, there was a clear convergence of political, economic and cultural interests between Spain and Mexico. This was also the case of German–Mexican relations after 1898, although there was much less of a cultural dimension to the relationship. Friedrich Katz argues that German diplomatic priorities after 1898 were, first, to use Mexico as a pawn in developing tensions between Mexico and the USA as a means of challenging US hegemony in the region, while at the same time avoiding any direct confrontation with Washington. Every encouragement was given, therefore, to enhancing the commercial and financial penetration of the Mexican market from German merchants and banking houses (especially Bleichröder, and the Deutsche and Dresdner Banks), to take advantage of the preference during the late Díaz regime for European rather than US business ventures. Ultimately, the substantial German investments in railways and mining, which were planned in the wake of the recession in the USA in 1907, failed to come to fruition. Katz concludes that German influence in Porfirian Mexico was 'very far from being a series of successes', but that it was significant, if, ultimately, marginal.[50]

. . .

THE INTERNATIONAL IMAGE OF MEXICO IN THE *FIESTAS DEL CENTENARIO*, 1910

The state of Mexican diplomatic relations during the last decade of the regime is perhaps best reflected in the nature of the celebrations chosen by the regime to commemorate the centenary of Mexican independence in 1910. The *Fiestas del Centenario* were designed, above all, as a lavish celebration of the political, economic, cultural and diplomatic achievements of the regime. Simultaneously, of course, the *Fiestas* provided an obvious and glaring contrast with social and political shortcomings of Porfirian development, which became manifest so soon afterwards in the 1910 Revolution which began only two months later.

The participation of the diplomatic corps was vital to the celebrations, and every attention was paid to the comfort of visiting delegates in an attempt to impress overseas visitors with Mexico's 'progress' under Díaz. International conferences were organised, such as the Congress of Americanists, and delegates were taken to see the excavations being carried out at the archaeological site of Teotihuacán by the new International School of Archaeology and Ethnology, established in 1910.[51]

The monuments selected as part of the centenary commemorations are also worthy of note. US–Mexican relations were celebrated with the inauguration of a monument to George Washington. French culture and scientific achievement were commemorated with a monument to Louis Pasteur. The inauguration of a Japanese garden and a

Japanese exhibition reflected the growing relations between Mexico and Japan. In the military parade staged on 16 September, Mexican officers proudly displayed their new German spiked helmets, commissioned by the Germanophile former Minister of War, Bernardo Reyes (1900–02).[52] In a further demonstration of Mexico's international esteem, a significant part of the military parade was a homage to Mexico from representatives of the armed forces from both sides of the Atlantic: Brazil, Argentina, Germany and Spain. British–Mexican relations had already been celebrated during the lavish inauguration of the reconstructed trans-Isthmus Tehuantepec railway in 1907.

Most significantly of all, in the context of Mexico's international relations after 1898, there were a number of events which celebrated the renewed and reinvigorated cultural and political relations with Spain. For example, a foundation stone was laid for a monument to Isabella I of Spain (although it was never completed). In a heavily symbolic gesture of reconciliation, the head of the Spanish delegation to the centenary celebrations, the Marquis of Polavieja, made a ceremonial presentation to President Díaz of the uniform belonging to José María Morelos, one of the two key figures of the anti-Spanish insurgency of 1810 which had initiated the independence movement in Mexico.[53]

The contrast between the regime's portrayal of its achievements in the *Fiestas del Centenario* of 1910 and the social, economic and political realities of late Porfirian Mexico on the eve of the Revolution could not have been greater. Nonetheless, the maintenance of cordial (if progressively strained) diplomatic relations with the USA, and the restoration of diplomatic and commercial relations with Mexico's recent European adversaries, represented considerable triumphs for the Díaz regime. The regime's growing international respectability was a vital factor in consolidating domestic stability. Most significantly, the achievements of Mexican foreign policy had helped to restore Mexico's international credit, and to attract overseas investment, one of the central components of the regime's economic strategy. This is the subject of the next chapter.

. . .

NOTES AND REFERENCES

1. Quoted in D. Cosío Villegas (ed.), *Historia Moderna de México* (hereafter *HMM*), 10 vols, Mexico City, 1955–72, Vol. IV, p.159.

2. J. Buchenau, 'Inversión Extranjera y nacionalismo: lo paradójico de la política internacional de Porfirio Díaz', *Dimensión Antropológica*, 6, 1996, pp.7–24.

3. It is interesting to note that, in the absence of formal diplomatic relations with Britain and France, it fell to the US Minister in Mexico to act on their behalf: see John W. Foster (US Minister in Mexico, 1875–1880) *Diplomatic Memoirs*, 2 vols, Boston, MA, 1910, Vol. I, p.31.

4. H. Bernstein, *Matías Romero 1837–1898*, Mexico City, 1973.

5. J. Buchenau, *In the Shadow of the Giant: The Making of Mexico's Central America Policy, 1876 1930*, Tuscaloosa, AL, 1996, pp.39–40.

6. Plan of Tuxtepec reformed in Palo Alto, quoted in J. López-Portillo y Rojas, *Elevación y Caída de Porfirio Díaz*, Mexico City, 1921, p.107.

7. J. Hart, *Revolutionary Mexico: The Coming and Process of the Mexican Revolution*, Stanford, CA, 1987, pp.122–3.

8. W. Schell, 'American Investment in Tropical Mexico: Rubber Plantations, Fraud, and Dollar Diplomacy 1897–1913', *Business History Review*, 64, 1990, pp.218–54.

9. G. Yeager, 'Porfirian Commercial Propaganda: Mexico in the World Industrial Expositions', *The Americas*, 34(2), 1977, pp.230–43.

10. M. Tenorio Trillo, *Mexico at the World's Fairs: Crafting a Modern Nation*, Stanford, CA, 1996, pp.38–43.

11. D. Cosío Villegas, *The United States Versus Porfirio Díaz*, Lincoln, NB, 1963, pp.215–19.

12. The company had been established in 1880, but collapsed in 1884 before construction had begun. The Puebla–Oaxaca line was eventually built in 1892; O. Hardy, 'Ulysses S. Grant, President of the Mexican Southern Railroad', *Pacific Historical Review*, 26, 1955, pp.111–20; D.M. Pletcher, 'Ex-President Ulysses S. Grant', in *Rails, Mines, and Progress. Seven American Promoters in Mexico 1867–1911*, Ithaca, NY, 1958, pp.149–81.

13. *Recuerdos de un Viaje. En honor de la visita a los Estados Unidos del General Porfirio Díaz con sus compañeros en marzo y abril 1883*, St Louis, MO, 1883, p.48.

14. Quoted in N. Ray Gilmore, 'Mexico and the Spanish-American War', *Hispanic American Historical Review*, 43(4), 1963, pp.511–25.

15. *Gringo* is the less than complimentary term used by Mexicans to refer to the citizens of the United States; Porfirio Díaz to Carlos Rivas, 28 August 1890, CPD:L41:T1:f.246.

16. Porfirio Díaz to Ramón Corral, 12 March 1889, CPD:L41:T15:f.158.

17. W. La Feber, *Inevitable Revolutions: The United States and Central America*, New York, 1986.

18. W. Dirk Raat, *Mexico and the United States: Ambivalent Vistas*, Athens, GA, 1992, p.82.

19. Cosío Villegas, *The United States versus Porfirio Díaz*, p.229.

20. Hart, *Revolutionary Mexico*, p.109.
21. C. Hackett, 'The Recognition of the Díaz Government by the United States', *Southwestern Historical Quarterly*, XXVIII, 1925, pp.34–55.
22. Raat, *Mexico and the United States*, p.84.
23. M. Tinker Salas, *In the Shadow of the Eagles: Sonora and the Transformation of the Border during the Porfiriato*, Stanford, CA, 1997.
24. P. Riguzzi, 'México, Estados Unidos, y Gran Bretaña, 1867–1910: Una difícil relación triangular', *Historia Mexicana*, Vol. XLI, 1992, pp.365–437.
25. J. Zoraida Vázquez and L. Meyer, *Mexico Frente a Estados Unidos: Un ensayo histórico 1776–1988*, Mexico City, 1982, pp.89–112.
26. J. Smith, *The Spanish-American War: Conflict in the Caribbean and the Pacific, 1895–1902*, Harlow, 1994, p.216.
27. Díaz to Alfonso Lancaster Jones, 31 January 1896, CPD:L41:C8:T18: d.937.
28. J.M. Kirk, 'José Martí and the United States: A Further Interpretation', *Journal of Latin American Studies*, 9, 1977, pp.275–90. Martí was killed in action at the beginning of the second war of Cuban independence in 1895.
29. Martí to Díaz, 23 July 1894, CPD:L19:C21:f.10440.
30. Gamboa is quoted in R. de Armas, 'José Martí: el apoyo desde México', *Universidad de la Habana*, 219, 1983, pp.80–103.
31. A. Sánchez Andrés, 'La normalización de las relaciones entre España y México durante el Porfiriato (1876–1910)', *Historia Mexicana*, Vol. XLVIII, 1999, pp.731–66.
32. Quoted in Bernstein, *Matías Romero*, p.327.
33. C.J. Bartlett, 'Latin American Reactions to the Panamanian Revolution of 1903', *Hispanic American Historical Review*, 24(2), 1944, pp.342–51.
34. In pursuit of this strategy, the Hay–Ponceforte Treaty of 1901 between Britain and the USA had granted the USA exclusive rights to build and to control a canal in Nicaragua. See J. Smith, *Spanish-American War*, p.227.
35. J. Body to W. Pearson, 3 October 1902, in Science Museum Archive (SMA), Records of S. Pearson and Sons (PEA), Box A4.
36. D. Cosío Villegas, *HMM*, Vol. VI, 1963, pp.298–320.
37. Buchenau, *In the Shadow*, pp.80–108.
38. F. Katz, *La Guerra Secreta en México*, 2 vols, Mexico City, 1982, Vol. I, pp.40–6.
39. This has been a controversial issue: A. Knight, *The Mexican Revolution*, 2 vols, Cambridge, 1986, Vol. I, pp.184–6, rejects the notion of US influence (or '*gringo* connivance') in the overthrow of Díaz in 1910–11. In contrast, John Hart sees the Mexican Revolution as a war of popular, national liberation from *gringo* imperialism; see Hart, *Revolutionary Mexico*.

40. Sánchez, 'Normalización de las relaciones', p.732.
41. B. Hamnett, *Juárez*, Harlow, 1994, p.168.
42. L. Meyer, *Su Majestad Británica contra la Revolución Mexicana: El fin de un imperio informal 1900–1950*, Mexico City, 1991, p.51.
43. A. Tischendorf, *Great Britain and Mexico in the Era of Porfirio Díaz*, Duke, NC, 1961, pp.3–8.
44. Katz, *Guerra Secreta*, Vol. I, p.72.
45. Velasco to Porfirio Díaz, 19 December 1882, CPD:L17:f.119.
46. R. Miller, *Britain and Latin America in the Nineteenth and Twentieth Centuries*, Harlow, 1993
47. According to Nicolau D'Olwer, *HMM*, Vol. VIII, p.1154, US investment during the Porfiriato amounted to 1.3 billion *pesos*, compared to 989 million from British sources.
48. Sánchez, 'Normalización de las relaciones', p.760.
49. C. Lida, 'España y México: Relaciones Diplomáticas, Negocio y Finanzas en el Porfirato', *Historia Mexicana*, Vol. XLVIII, 1999, pp.719–30.
50. Katz, *Guerra Secreta*, Vol. I, p.93.
51. R. Godoy, 'Frans Boas and his Plans for an International School of American Archaeology and Ethnology in Mexico', *Journal of the Behavioural Sciences*, 13, 1977, pp.228–42.
52. W. Schiff, 'German Military Penetration into Mexico', *Hispanic American Historical Review*, 39(4), 1959, pp.568–79.
53. M. Tenorio Trillo, '1910 Mexico City: Space and Nation in the City of the Centenario', *Journal of Latin American Studies*, 28(1), 1996, p.101.

Chapter 7

PAYING FOR ORDER AND PROGRESS: ECONOMIC DEVELOPMENT, 1876–1911

If before I die morality is restored to our society and in public administration; if the poor find instruction and bread; if the rich have acquired enough confidence to invest their capital in national enterprises; if, from one end of the Republic to the other, the train, with its powerful voice awakens and mobilises all Mexicans, then my desires will have been satisfied. (Porfirio Díaz, 1880)[1]

In contrast to the divergent interpretations of Porfirian foreign policy, there has always been widespread consensus that the Díaz era was one of unprecedented economic transformation. The economic history of post-independence Mexico has identified two major periods of accelerated economic development since independence in 1821: first, the Díaz era; and, second, the era of post-Revolutionary industrialisation in the three decades after 1940 which are referred to as the 'Mexican Miracle'.[2] Most economic historians, whether they are partial or hostile to the Díaz regime would agree that the Mexican economy under Díaz made substantial, even dramatic, economic advances. Many of the obstacles to economic development which had plagued Mexico since independence in 1821 were progressively eradicated: the absence of integrated national markets, prohibitive internal tariffs, expensive and inadequate transportation, a weak state apparatus, a lack of codification or regulation of commerce, and a chronic shortage of investment.

The statistics of early nineteenth-century economic performance indicate the extent of the problems which the Díaz regime inherited in 1876. Following an economic boom at the end of the colonial period, it has been estimated that Mexico experienced a drop in per capita gross domestic product (GDP) of some 37 per cent between

1800 and 1860. In addition, in the view of John Coatsworth, until the 1880s, Mexican economic development continued to be constrained throughout the nineteenth century by 'a deficient institutional environment for entrepreneurial activity'.[3]

Following the achievement of independence, Mexico had sought to extend the scope of its international links but, at the same time, to protect its vulnerable national sovereignty from its predatory hemispheric and European enemies. Attempts to stimulate the export trade and to attract foreign investment before the 1860s had faced numerous obstacles. Civil war and foreign intervention, the decline of the mining industry, tariff impositions on the flow of inter-regional trade (represented by the *alcabala* or inter-state sales tax) and the lack of infrastructure and markets, all conspired to limit their expansion. The various schemes proposed by foreign entrepreneurs to exploit Mexico's abundant natural resources before the 1860s had mostly ended in failure, as had been demonstrated, for example, in the case of British mining ventures.[4] In addition, as indicated in the last chapter, those investors who had speculated in Mexican bonds had been faced with repeated suspensions of debt repayments.

During the first Díaz administration (1876–80), there were only a few indications of the transformations to come. It was during the presidency of Manuel González (1880–84) that the future direction of economic policy became clearer, with the rapid growth of trade and investment with the USA. After Díaz resumed power in 1884, the re-establishment of links with overseas bondholders and the extension of Mexico's external links with the international economy became the regime's primary economic goals, and its principal obsessions.

Porfirian economic performance must be seen in the broader context of developments in the global economy. The Díaz era in Mexico coincided with a period of notable expansion of world trade, as a consequence of which the economies of Latin America became increasingly incorporated into the international economy as exporters of raw materials and agricultural commodities, and importers of foreign capital and technology, and, in some spectacular cases (such as Argentina between 1880 and 1914), importers of labour.[5] International demand for raw materials had grown rapidly after 1850, as a direct result of the evolution of the industrial revolution in Europe and North America. Demographic growth, capital accumulation and changes in the technology of industrial and agricultural production in the North Atlantic economy had a dramatic effect on the capacity of the industrialised nations to export and import. The economic resources and raw materials of Latin America therefore became pro-gressively integrated into this growing international network.[6]

The bare statistics of Porfirian economic growth have been de-scribed as spectacular and even 'revolutionary.' During the Díaz era, railway mileage grew at an average annual rate of 12 per cent; indus-trial production rose by an annual rate of 6.5 per cent, mining by 7 per cent, exports by 6 per cent, and imports by 5 per cent. In 1901 Mexico produced some 8,000 barrels of oil, but by 1910 the figure had reached 8,000,000.[7]

If there is broad agreement on the statistics of economic growth, their impact and the political consequences for the regime are still controversial. There can be little doubt that the political advantages which accrued to the regime as a result of export-led economic growth made a significant contribution to its longevity. The estab-lishment of political 'peace' was deemed the essential prerequisite of nation-building and economic development, and justified the authori-tarian imposition of order in the name of progress as a necessary means to an end. The extension of communications (particularly the railway and telegraph) brought vast areas of Mexico into the political orbit of the capital, and thus contributed to the process of political centralisation. Improved lines of communication facilitated the deployment of troops to deal with any local or regional chal-lenge to central authority.

Despite the factional divisions within the liberal camp, there was broad consensus among the vast majority of nineteenth-century Mexican liberals that the best hope for national development rested on closer integration into the world economy. As foreign capital began to flow from the 1880s onwards, the fruits of that integration provided tangible evidence that the developmentalist strategy which the regime pursued was the appropriate formula. This was recog-nised even by the political opponents of the regime, most notably in the case of Francisco Madero, the leader of the Anti-Re-electionist Movement which brought down the regime in 1911, who balanced his critique of the regime's political authoritarianism with praise for its economic achievements.[8]

Economic development therefore tended to consolidate the loy-alty of the political elite, especially those individuals who were the direct recipients of government patronage in the distribution of concessions for a vast range of enterprises, or who acted as inter-mediaries for overseas speculators. In addition, the development of a state bureaucracy, the infrastructure of public works and the pace of urban development provided new opportunities for employment by the growing ranks of the middle-classes.

At the same time, however, the impact of rapid economic development undoubtedly had the potential to generate profound socio-economic conflict, and to disrupt the political peace of the Porfirian years. The benefits of economic expansion for the growing urban population and for the mass of the rural population were much less tangible, as the popular discontent which exploded in 1910 and 1911 indicated. Instead of providing increased demand for labour or new opportunities for employment, by 1910 there is evidence of stagnation in the labour market and rapid price increases which had outstripped wage rises. The impoverishment of factory workers, urban artisans and the mass of the rural population have been widely identified as root causes of popular discontent which erupted after 1910.[9]

Many of the criticisms of Porfirian economic performance have their roots in post-1960 structuralist and nationalist critiques of late nineteenth-century modernisation, which still enjoy a powerful residual influence in many general surveys of Mexican and Latin American economic history. Structuralists, most notably those who are (or were) proponents of the 'dependency' school, have long argued that the export model of growth was both structurally flawed and detrimental to national interests. The decline in the terms of trade or the relative value of commodity and raw materials exports in relation to manufactured imports was, it has been argued, a secular trend which, in the long term, disadvantaged raw materials producers and resulted in structural underdevelopment. Mexico, like her sister republics in Latin America, became locked into a cycle of monocultural (i.e. single-product) production and external dependency for markets, capital and technology, and was forced to follow slavishly the dictates of foreign interests and, in effect, to surrender its national resources for precious little in return. This process, it is argued, distorted national development and prevented the pursuit of any alternative model of development (such as, for example, the development of domestic manufacturing industry).

According to this line of argument, the social and political costs of the late nineteenth-century developmentalist project in Latin America were highly damaging. Economic and political power were concentrated in the hands of a minority elite, a 'comprador bourgeoisie', who were unable and unwilling to act in the national interest. The overall impact, it has been alleged, was impoverishment of the masses and a serious loss of economic and political sovereignty.

The recent work of economic historians of Latin America and Mexico has challenged a number of these assumptions and interpretations. Recent analysis has focused less on structuralist theory and far more on detailed empirical analysis of internal economic conditions and resources, and on the fate of individual enterprises. Recent research has emphasised, first, that the terms of trade did not always deteriorate and, indeed, that Latin America's raw materials exports in the nineteenth century enjoyed periods of 'comparative advantage' in world markets. Second, in some cases, and particularly in the case of Mexico, there has been growing recognition that, far from distorting the process of industrial development, the development of social infrastructure and the greater integration of regional and national markets laid the foundations for industrialisation in the twentieth century. Finally, in contrast to the portrayal of weak or supine national elites slavishly obeying the dictates of international capital, there is growing evidence that governments in Latin America (particularly in the largest countries in the region – Mexico, Brazil and Argentina) actively promoted national interests and the development of the nation-state by erecting tariff barriers and granting subsidies to support industrial development, and by regulating the activities of foreign capitalists in pursuit of developmentalist, nationalist goals.[10]

These recent interpretations are important for an understanding of the nature of economic policy in the Díaz era. As with all other interpretations of the Díaz era, there has been a strong tendency to view the substantial economic changes which took place during the course of the regime from the perspective of the Revolution. Because the popular grievances which sought expression during the decade after 1910 were inevitably connected to the socio-economic transformations which had occurred, there has been a strong temptation to emphasise the failures and weaknesses of export-led growth. But if the economic record of the Díaz regime is judged from the perspective of the nineteenth century, the achievements appear more substantial, and the conclusions rather different.

Another distortion which arises from the interpretation of economic performance from the perspective of the Revolution is the assumption that the interventionist, protectionist and nationalist economic policy pursued by post-Revolutionary governments was a reaction to, and a rejection of, Porfirian economic strategy, and therefore a product of the Revolution itself. It is now clear that such policies had become the economic priorities of the Díaz regime by the end of the 1890s. The major thrust of government policy, therefore, shifted incrementally towards state regulation of the economy, in order to maintain the protection of economic sovereignty.

. . .

THE EVOLUTION OF ECONOMIC POLICY

The report which Díaz presented to Congress in 1880 at the end of his first term of office clearly indicated the strategy and pre-occupations of the early years of the regime. The primary emphasis was on the achievement of internal peace, without which no long-lasting economic development could take place. No less significant was what the outgoing President referred to as the 'complete dis-organisation of public finances' which he had inherited in 1876, which made the renegotiation of the debt obligations with Mexico's international creditors and the settlement of claims for damages suffered by US nationals both urgent priorities.

The restoration of diplomatic relations and of Mexico's international reputation and credit-worthiness were therefore at the centre of Díaz's economic strategy. They were, however, by no means simple or straightforward tasks, as the previous chapter has indicated. Nevertheless, as discussed in the previous chapter, major breakthroughs were registered in the 1880s in the settlement of long-standing diplomatic disputes. At the same time, important first steps were taken in the development of a financial infrastructure. Crucial to this process were the development of a banking system and the evolution of stable domestic capital markets.

Carlos Marichal has argued that the traditional emphasis of economic historians of the Díaz era on the central role of foreign investment and railways has tended to underestimate the contribution made by the establishment of banks, financial institutions and domestic capital markets to economic development. It was precisely the absence throughout much of the nineteenth century of such institutions, or of a stable market for public securities and bonds (central to the development of industrial economies of Europe and the USA), which demonstrated the underdevelopment of the Mexican economy. Until the 1880s, the impoverishment and permanent indebtedness of successive governments, and the absence of political stability or codification of commerce and financial regulation, had allowed a small number of some 20 merchant houses and merchant financiers (*agiotistas*) to control a wide range of financial activities.

Agiotistas traded principally (and most profitably) in loans to bank-rupt governments, but they were also engaged in the import and export business, and in the mining and textile industries.[11]

Significant developments in the evolution of a financial infra-structure took place during the administration of President Manuel González (1880–84). The restoration of relations with France in 1880 was followed by the establishment of the *Banco Nacional Mexicano* in 1881, with French (as well as British and German) capital. This was only the second chartered bank to be established in Mexico, after the Bank of London and Mexico had received its charter in 1864. In 1884, the *Banco Nacional* merged with another recently-formed bank, the *Banco Mercantil*, to form the *Banco Nacional de México* (Banamex), which would play a crucial role in financing government projects, especially in funding the subsidies to railway companies which was so crucial to the development of the rail network.

A further important step forward was the successful renegotiation of the terms of the 'English debt', the long-standing obligations to English bondholders, which had been left unresolved since the suspension of British–Mexican diplomatic relations in 1862. The negotiations were led by Manuel Dublán, whom Díaz appointed as Finance Minister in his second administration in 1884, a post he held until his death in 1891. Diplomatic relations with Britain were restored in 1884, and Dublán was able to reach an agreement in 1886 to reduce the total of the London debt, which UK bond-holders had calculated at £23 million, to less than £15 million. Dublán was subsequently able to negotiate a significant loan with European banks for a nominal sum of £10.5 million, which was used to re-deem the outstanding bonds of the London debt. Further loans were raised (£2.7 million in 1889, £6 million in 1890) to finance government subsidies to railway companies and to raise funds for the Díaz government's most important, and most expensive, infra-structural project – the construction of a railway across the Isthmus of Tehuantepec.[12]

Although Mexico's total foreign public debt continued to rise in subsequent years (from a total of an estimated 52 million *pesos* in 1884 to 441 million *pesos* in 1910), it was more than compensated for by the overall expansion of the economy, as measured by the rise in foreign investment (which reached a total of approximately US$1.4 billion by 1911) and by the rapid expansion of the banking network (with over 30 chartered banks with total assets of over 1,116 million *pesos*).[13]

The success in persuading foreign entrepreneurs and financiers to invest in Mexico was assisted by the active promotion outside Mexico of the country's abundant natural resources and enormous economic potential. After 1876, under the guidance of the Minister of *Fomento* (Development), Carlos Pacheco (1881–91), the Díaz and González administrations committed substantial resources to enhancing Mexico's international image as a nation fully committed to material progress and the application of science.[14] The regime spent, for example, close to US$700,000 on its representation at the World Columbian Exhibition of 1892, and more than US$400,000 on the Paris World Fair in 1889. Scientific and commercial catalogues describing Mexico as a model of stability and prosperity and legal haven for foreign entrepreneurs were freely and generously distributed, and visitors were entertained by bull-fights, archaeological displays and even the marching band of the Mexican Eighth Cavalry. Self-promotion did not end there, since *Fomento* also sponsored permanent 'commercial museums' to promote contacts between Mexican producers and foreign merchants in Yokohama, Philadelphia, New York, Cardiff, Liverpool, Milan, Paris, Vienna and Berlin.[15]

There can be doubt that Díaz was personally committed to the developmentalist vision of Mexico as a beacon of 'modernity' whose future prosperity lay in the systematic and scientific exploitation of its extensive, but under-utilised resources. As indicated above, he was, for example, actively involved in the campaign, acting as Chief Commissioner in Mexico's delegation to the New Orleans Exhibition of 1884. But in the conduct of economic policy in general, and the detailed negotiations with Mexico's international creditors, Díaz was more than happy to delegate to his subordinates. He was fortunate in being able to take advantage of the loyal and virtually uninterrupted services of two Ministers of Finance after his first re-election in 1884: Manuel Dublán (1884–91) and José Yves Limantour (1893–1911).

Dublán's stewardship of the Treasury set the tone for the economic strategy pursued by the regime. The drive to attract foreign investment was enhanced by the Commercial Code of 1884, which sought to regulate and to centralise the granting of concessions to domestic and foreign enterprise, and to establish clear rules for the functioning of banks and financial institutions. Dublán's tenure of office was punctuated by periodical economic fluctuations and damaged by a severe economic crisis in 1891. Dublán died soon after, to be replaced as Finance Minister, briefly, by Matías Romero, and then, in 1893, by José Yves Limantour. It is Limantour who has been credited with taking Mexico's financial management and economic strategy to new and unprecedented heights.

Limantour's central strategy, and his principal achievement, was the stabilisation of Mexico's public finances. In his own words, his principal concerns were, in order of priority, first, to achieve a balanced budget and to eliminate the permanent fiscal deficit which all nineteenth-century Mexican governments had endured; second, the prudent management of Mexico's public debt; third, the abolition of restrictions on trade and, specifically, the abolition of the *alcabala*. Finally, Limantour sought tighter regulation and government control over the growing number of financial institutions.[16]

Limantour's strategy was, in its own terms, strikingly successful. In 1896, he provided Mexico with a balanced budget and the first ever surplus on the public account since Mexico achieved the status of an independent nation in 1821. Budget surpluses were registered every subsequent year until the Revolution. While Mexico's public debt continued to grow, Limantour's cautious management allowed Mexico to obtain ever more favourable terms of credit, with rates of interest on new loans reduced to only 4 per cent in 1910. This meant that, although public debt continued to grow at an unprecedented rate, the burden of debt servicing was reduced from 38 per cent of government income in 1895 to less than 5 per cent in 1910.[17] In addition, the *alcabala* was abolished in 1896, a reform which had a positive impact on levels of domestic trade. The Banking Code of 1897 tightened up the regulations governing the functioning of banks operating in Mexico. The growth of banking institutions accelerated rapidly, with over 20 chartered and many more private banks, trusts and insurance companies becoming registered between 1897 and 1910.

As the Díaz era entered its final decade, North American and European investors continued to invest ever higher sums in Mexico. Over half the entire overseas investment portfolio of the USA before 1910 was directed south of the border, and the list of investors reads like a Who's Who of late nineteenth-century international corporate capitalism: Guggenheim, Speyer, J.P. Morgan, Bleichroeder, Rockefeller. This list not only indicated the importance of Mexico as a target for foreign investment (second only in Spanish America to Argentina in this period), but also indicated the changing composition of the foreign investors in the 1890s. Whereas many of those who participated in the early phase of investments in the 1880s were small investors (both domestic and foreign), by the 1900s large-scale corporate financiers and financial institutions predominated.[18]

The perceived threat that Mexico's developing infrastructure of railways and public utilities, its financial institutions and its leading industrial enterprises might be absorbed by US trusts or monopolies, or that its expanding export trade might become entirely dependent upon the US market, was of considerable concern to Limantour.[19] The threat to economic sovereignty mirrored the threat to Mexican and Central American political sovereignty represented by increasingly overt US aggression in the Caribbean after 1896, as examined in the previous chapter.

As a result, Limantour adopted a series of interventionist measures in pursuit of a strategy of national development under the control of the state. In effect, long before the Revolution, the Mexican state had begun to exert a much greater degree of control and regulation of the economy, and had obtained a controlling interest in the infrastructure of public works. The policy was costly, and necessitated the negotiation of a series of foreign loans and domestic bond issues, but it was largely successful, and by 1910 the state had become a majority shareholder in a number of enterprises which had hitherto been private companies. The most important and significant example of this process was the acquisition of a controlling interest in two-thirds of the railway network with the formation of the National Railways of Mexico (*Ferrocarriles Nacionales de México*) in 1907. The 'mexicanisation' of the railways was highly significant, not only because of their economic and strategic importance, but also because of their symbolic value as an emblem of both Porfirian modernisation and national development.[20]

Limantour's last significant policy initiative was the monetary reform of 1905 and the adoption of the gold standard, which was designed primarily to stabilise the Mexican *peso*. The decision was prompted by the long-term fall in the international price of silver which had followed on from the adoption of the gold standard in the USA in the 1870s. Countries like Mexico, and her sister republics in Latin America which continued to operate on the silver standard, saw a prolonged depreciation of their currencies. Nevertheless, the devaluation of the silver *peso* had brought certain benefits to some sectors of the economy. It had helped to stimulate the export trade and had encouraged the development of industry on the basis of import substitution, given the correspondingly high cost of manufactured imports. However, those merchants who paid for foreign imports in silver were at a distinct disadvantage. The main loser was the government, which had to make payments from public funds in order to meet their debt repayments. Limantour therefore converted to the gold standard in order to protect the *peso* and stabilise the exchange rate in 1905.[21]

The impact of the adoption of the gold standard was distinctly mixed. Government finances continued to be healthy, with a budget surplus of 74 million *pesos* registered in 1910, but there were more disturbing trends in other sectors of the economy. The timing was certainly unfortunate. While the gold standard should have encouraged long-term stability in international trade and investment, its implementation coincided with an economic crisis in the USA in 1907, the effects of which were rapidly transported to Mexico. Foreign investment, the lubricant of Porfirian economic expansion, suffered a dramatic downturn. Domestic bank credit within Mexico dried up, and those who had benefited from the rapid expansion of credit facilities under the regime – whether they were miners, merchants, industrialists or *hacendados* – faced bankruptcy, and a number of businesses closed.[22] Although the economy had begun to show signs of recovery by 1910, the confidence in the economic stability of the regime among those who had been its major beneficiaries had been seriously damaged. This situation clearly contributed to the political difficulties faced by the regime after 1908.

. . .

INDICATORS OF PROGRESS

As a consequence of expanding world trade, growing international confidence in Mexico and the regime's own profound commitment to progress, the Mexican economy was transformed during the Díaz era. Five areas in particular merit more detailed examination. First, there was steady demographic growth, but with only a small increase in the rate of urbanisation. Second, dramatic improvements were registered in transportation and infrastructure, most significantly with the exponential growth of the railway network. Third, both domestic and overseas trade expanded, especially with the resurgence of mining and, during the final years of the regime, the development of the oil industry. Fourth, there was a notable expansion and diversification of industrial production (in iron and steel, textiles, paper, glass, beer, tobacco) stimulated by fiscal and legislative incentives and the introduction of new technology and new power and energy sources. Finally, Mexico's extremely diverse rural economy was subjected to new stimulants and pressures as a result of the drive towards land privatisation and the expansion of commercial agriculture.

Demographic trends

The population of Mexico grew slowly and unevenly throughout the nineteenth century, with a notable acceleration during the Díaz era. In the aftermath of independence in 1825, the total population was estimated at 6.2 million. On the eve of the Tuxtepec Rebellion (1875), the population had risen to 8.3 million. By the end of the Porfiriato (1910), the 1875 figure had almost doubled, to 15.1 million, representing an average annual growth rate of 1.7 per cent, in comparison with a growth rate of 0.6 per cent for the period 1825–75.

The distribution of population growth was uneven, however, and demonstrates considerable regional variation. While each of the states and federal territories increased its population between 1875 and 1910, growth rates varied considerably, with the highest increases (of between 130 and 370 per cent) in the Atlantic Border states (Tabasco, Veracruz, Tamaulipas), along with the northern states of Nuevo León, Coahuila, Guanajuato and the territory of Baja California. Other states registered growth rates of between 50 and 70 per cent (such as Yucatán, Puebla, Morelos and Jalisco).

The absence of statistics prevents a more rigorous analysis of demographic trends. Although the Mexican Society of Geography and Statistics had been established in 1833, and the Department of *Fomento* in 1835, no national census was produced until 1857. The first modern census was carried out by the *Dirección General de Estadística* (a subdivision of *Fomento*) in 1895, and repeated in 1900 and 1910. These surveys indicate that certain social indicators, such as rates of birth and mortality and life expectancy, changed surprisingly little over the course of the Díaz era, despite the regime's much-vaunted claims of material and social progress. The rate of mortality, for example, was 34 per thousand in 1895, and 33 per thousand in 1910, and life expectancy remained unchanged at 29 years.

The available statistics also demonstrate that the rate of urbanisation was also very slow during the Díaz era, and remained virtually static throughout the nineteenth century. The four largest cities (Mexico City, Guadalajara, Puebla and Monterrey) constituted

4 per cent of the total population in 1823, rising only to 5 per cent by 1895. Even Mexico City, whose population grew from 165,000 in 1823 (2.6 per cent of the total) to 471,000 by 1910, still represented only 3.1 per cent of the total population.[23]

Mexico, in common with the majority of Latin (and North) American countries in the late nineteenth century, attempted to stimulate population growth through the active promotion of colonisation programmes to encourage foreign settlers to exploit the country's untapped resources in the vast areas of unoccupied or sparsely occupied lands. Here the Díaz regime followed the precedent set by the Juárez government with the *tierras baldías* (unoccupied lands) decree of 1863, which had ordered the alienation and occupation of all lands which had yet to be put to productive use. The Law of 1883 encouraged private companies to survey unused public lands by granting them as much as one-third of the lands surveyed as payment and, initially, obliged all survey companies to promote colonisation, although this latter condition was subsequently dropped.[24]

However, despite the generous terms and conditions offered to prospective colonists, the regime's colonisation strategy was a resounding failure in demographic, economic and political terms. By 1910, it is estimated that only 116,527 foreign settlers, less than 1 per cent of the total population, had established themselves i Mexico. The strategy was clearly much less successful than that of Mexico's continental neighbours. The millions of emigrants who sought to flee the harsh economic conditions in Europe at the end of the nineteenth century by crossing the Atlantic clearly preferred the attractions of Argentina, Brazil and the USA.

It is also important to note that many of those who did migrate to Mexico during the Díaz era were, in fact, Mexicans living in the USA, who were given more generous free land grants and tax exemptions than non-Mexicans. By 1887, a total of 14 colonies had been established, with a total of 2,704 non-Mexican immigrants, while Mexican 'repatriates' represented more than twice as many. By the end of the Porfiriato, a total of 60 colonies had been established – 16 by the government, and 44 by private colonisation companies. Of these, 18 (eight public and ten private) colonisation schemes (i.e. nearly one-third) recruited settlers of Mexican origin. The 20 Anglo-American colonies accounted for nearly half of the 'private' colonies but, significantly, given the nationalist preoccupations of the regime, not one of the government-sponsored colonies was Anglo-American.[25]

The economic contribution of these 'foreign' colonies (if they deserve to be called foreign) is difficult to assess. The most prosperous appears to have been the government-sponsored Colonia Tecate, on the northern frontier of Baja California, with a population of 158 men and women whose mixed agricultural and livestock production was valued by the Ministry of *Fomento* in 1907 at 158,000 *pesos*. It is apparent, however, that many of the remaining colonies failed to attract settlers, and even those that did struggled to survive.[26]

In political terms, despite the repeated failures of the colonisation projects, the release of large tracts of land to overseas colonisers and speculators laid the regime open to the charge of betraying national interests and the wilful surrender of national patrimony and sovereignty. Growing political pressure led to a significant revision of policy regarding the survey and sale of public lands after 1900. The legislation was fundamentally revised in 1902, and no longer permitted either foreigners or private survey companies to obtain public lands. Even more notable was the fact that the distribution of *terrenos baldíos* was abandoned entirely in 1909.[27]

Transportation and infrastructure

One of the frequently stated objectives of all nineteenth-century Mexican governments had been the urgent need to improve the transport and communications networks as a prerequisite of economic development and nation-building. However, the frequency of these declarations was matched only by the number of problems which had to be overcome. The mountainous terrain, the absence of navigable rivers, the deterioration of the colonial road network, banditry, political conflict and heavy taxation (road tolls, transit licences and the inter-state sales tax or *alcabala*) were frequently cited as the principal obstacles.

It has been estimated that, in 1877, only half of Mexico's 8,700 kilometres of federal 'highways' were suitable for wheeled traffic. As a consequence, most journeys were still undertaken either on foot, by mule or donkey, or occasionally, and only by the very wealthy, by stagecoach (*diligencia*). The only visible sign of the modernisation of communications before 1876 was the 5,600 miles of telegraph cable which had been installed.[28]

The railway network represented by far the most significant development in transportation, and it became the most prominent symbol of Porfirian modernisation. Initially it was slow to develop. The first railway concession (for the vital route between Mexico City and the principal Atlantic port, Veracruz) had been granted in 1837, but the line (the Mexican Railway) was not finally completed until 1872. Thereafter, railway construction expanded at a rapid rate. By the time of Díaz's second re-election in 1884, Mexico had 5,731 kilometres of track. This had risen to 12,173 kilometres in 1898, and to 19,280 by 1910, with another 8,000 kilometres of commuter and feeder lines.[29]

The regime's railway policy underwent significant changes during the course of the regime. Initially, the strategy had sought to attract private, initially Mexican, capital as the motor force of railway development. Under the scheme promoted by Vicente Riva Palacio, Minister of Development (1876–80), the initiative was ceded to individual states, with the support of the federal government, to grant concessions for local lines which would ultimately be incorporated into a national network. Over 30 concessions were granted between 1877 and 1880, but construction took place in only eight cases, and even then, no more than a total of 200 kilometres of track was laid.

The absence of domestic capital, the restoration of US–Mexican relations in 1878 and the interest of railway companies in the south of the USA to extend their lines into Mexico prompted a significant shift in policy. In the absence of an alternative source of capital (since debt negotiations with European creditors had not yet been resolved), in 1880 the Díaz government signed contracts with US railway companies for the construction of lines which would link Mexico City with Paso del Norte (now Cuidad Juárez) and with Laredo, Texas. The Mexican Central Railway was completed in 1884, and the Mexican National Railway in 1888, thus heralding the true start of Mexico's railway era and the vital role which foreign (especially US) capital would play.[30]

Foreign investment in railway development has been estimated to represent as much as one-third of total foreign investment in the Díaz era. While most investment (42 per cent) came from US sources, British capital was also prominent (35 per cent). British investors gained a controlling interest in the Mexican Railway in 1881, and had control over the Interoceanic Railway (which linked Veracruz with Mexico City via Jalapa and Puebla) and the Southern Mexican Railway which linked Puebla with Oaxaca after 1892. Mexican capital, however, was by no means invisible during the height of Porfirian railway mania. In the Yucatán, local entrepreneurs built and managed an extensive system of local lines which linked *henequén* plantations with local ports in order to extend the export trade.[31]

If the importance of foreign investment for railway development is uncontested, the benefits which foreign investors received is more controversial. Early analyses concentrated on the transfer of benefits to overseas investors which were judged to have detrimental effects on national development: the fact that railway development relied entirely on imports of locomotives, rails, rolling stock, skilled labour and fuel; the fact that the highest wages within the foreign-owned railway companies went to foreign employees; and, above all, the fact that government subsidies for railway construction were a considerable drain on national resources, consuming a large proportion of government expenditure. It has been estimated, for example, that as much as 50 per cent of the Department of Development's total annual budget between 1880 and 1890, or an average of 16 per cent of total government expenditure, was allocated to railway subsidies. The high level of subsidy necessitated the negotiation of foreign loans and the release of domestic bond issues, which substantially increased the level of public debt and, throughout the 1880s, threatened to bankrupt the government. When interest payments and dividends are taken into account, the transfer of resources abroad has been thought to be substantial.

Nevertheless, the impression that railway construction was of benefit solely or primarily to foreign interests needs some qualification. Alfred Tischendorf's early analysis of the poor level of return for British investors in Mexican railway construction indicated that railway investments did not bring the substantial dividends to foreign investors which has often been supposed.[32] More recent investigations have also indicated that federal subsidies contributed a much lower proportion of the actual costs of construction, implying that foreign railway companies were obliged to make more substantial investments in order to get their railways built. During the final years of the regime, it appears that capital flight represented only a small proportion of total exports, suggesting that the economic benefits which followed from railway development vastly outweighed its cost to the Mexican Treasury.[33]

It is also clear that the Díaz regime became progressively concerned about the potential loss of economic sovereignty which foreign (especially US) control over the railway network represented. As a result, during the final phase of railway development, under the auspices of the newly created *Secretaría de Comunicaciones y Obras*

Públicas (Ministry of Communications and Public Works) created in 1891, there was a new emphasis on increasing state control and regulation of railway development. The new strategy was manifest in Minister of Finance José Yves Limantour's Railway Law of 1899.

The new law sought, first, to integrate the existing network by restricting federal subsidies only to new lines which would link up the disparate parts. Second, the law aimed to reduce the high levels of government subsidy, averaging between 6,000 and 8,000 *pesos* per kilometre. Third, the law aimed gradually to 'mexicanise' the system in order to give the Mexican government the controlling interest in two-thirds of the railway network. By 1907 the government had acquired a majority interest in the Central, National, International and Interoceanic Railways, and created a new company, the National Railways of Mexico.[34]

Limantour explained that the reasons for the shift in policy were rooted in nationalist concerns over the protection of economic sovereignty. In his official report for the Ministry of Finance in 1907, he wrote:

> There is nobody [in Mexico] who thinks that the danger of our main [railway] lines passing into the hands of American lines is illusory. The disastrous consequences for Mexico would be widely felt, both in terms of the exploitation of our railways by foreigners [*extranjeros*], and in terms of the pressure that would be exerted on our most important public enterprises.[35]

The overall impact of the railways on the development of the Mexican economy in the Díaz era is still a subject of contention. All agree that the expansion of the rail network stimulated economic activity, but disagree about what the main benefits were, and for whom. Few would disagree with Enrique Cárdenas, however, that for the Mexican economy, 'the construction of the railroads was the most important event of the last third of the [nineteenth] century'.[36]

Railway expansion certainly stimulated further foreign investment in other sectors of the economy, especially in mining. Some 80 per cent of total US investment in Mexico in the Díaz era (38 per cent of total foreign investment) was concentrated in railways and mining. Improvements in transportation were also directly responsible for the growth of international trade. Mexico experienced positive trade balances every year from 1890 to 1905, with exports exceeding imports by as much as one-third in some years. Freight costs on the railways were reduced by as much as 80 per cent, and freight traffic grew at an average annual rate of 15 per cent between 1873 and 1910.

The expansion of Mexico's export trade was undoubtedly a direct result of railway expansion, but the contribution made by the rapid development of steamship lines in the same period should not be overlooked. Steamships linked Mexican coastal cities to each other and to the global economy. By the end of the 1890s nine steamship lines connected Mexico's gulf ports with the eastern seaboard of the USA and with major European ports (Liverpool, London, Cádiz, Bordeaux, Antwerp and Hamburg), exporting Mexico's tropical exports (dyewoods, coffee, jute and *henequén*), and importing industrial plant and material for railway construction. On the Pacific coast, seven lines connected Mexico to Asia (via San Francisco), and allowed the expansion of silver *peso* exports to the Philippines, China and India, which were central to the revival of Mexico's silver mining industry until Mexico's conversion to the gold standard in 1905.

Until recently, most economic historians have tended to emphasise the negative aspects of railway development. Profit remittances, loan and dividend payments, and high government subsidies, it is argued, drained the domestic economy of resources. It has also been argued that freight and passenger rates remained disproportionately high, thus restricting the movement of goods and labour. The regime's promotion of foreign trade and investment is seen to have distorted domestic development and prevented the growth of national markets, linking Mexico's regional economies more to the global economy than to one another. Above all, it has long been argued that the social dislocations produced by railway development – the encouragement of speculation and acquisition of land, the encroachment on peasant and community smallholdings – prompted rural discontent and rebellion, and thus made a significant contribution to the causes of the Revolution of 1910.[37] It is likely, however, in the light of current trends, that the next generation of economic historians will modify these negative conclusions.

Mining and oil

There is no question that the 'engine of growth' of the Mexican economy during the Díaz era was the export sector. Recent estimates indicate that exports increased at an average rate of 3.9 per cent between 1878 and 1895, and rose to an average annual increase of 6.9 per cent between 1895 and 1910. The most dynamic sector of the export economy was mining, complemented by the development of the oil industry after 1901.

The importance of mining to the Mexican economy pre-dated independence. Mining had been central to the structure of the colonial economy, at the core of a network of agriculture, trade and manufacturing which had expanded rapidly during the late colonial period at the end of the eighteenth century. It would not, perhaps, be an exaggeration to suggest that the economic aspirations of the new Mexican nation in the early nineteenth century had been founded upon the exploitation of Mexico's abundant mineral resources. However, the early and mid-nineteenth-century performance of the mining industry was mostly disappointing, in part because of the loss of capital investment and expertise, and in part because of the loss of regular supplies of mercury (which Spain had previously supplied), which was so crucial to the 'patio' processing of low-grade ores. While foreign – mostly British – capital had been invested, and some modern production techniques, such as steam power, had been introduced, colonial production and labour practices persisted throughout the nineteenth century.[38]

The combination of new technology (with electrification and the development of the cyanide process), railway construction and foreign investment prompted a dramatic revival in the industry during the Díaz era. Foreign investment in mining was greatly stimulated by the legislation passed in the 1880s, which facilitated not only foreign acquisition of mining concessions, but actual ownership of mining properties, hitherto prohibited by Spanish colonial and Mexican law. In 1883, Congress passed a new code which made no reference to the retention of ownership of subsoil deposits by the state. In 1892, a subsequent law removed the requirement that mines had to be worked in order for the concession to be maintained, and eliminated state ownership of the subsoil.

As a consequence of internal reform and external demand, the mining industry experienced a dramatic upturn. This affected not only the traditional mining of gold and silver, but also of hitherto unexploited metals, principally lead, copper and zinc, but also carbon, antimony and mercury. By 1910, production of industrial metals (42 per cent of the total) had surpassed production of silver (39 per cent). New mining centres had developed, particularly in the northern states of Sonora, Chihuahua, Durango and Coahuila, in addition to the traditional centres of Mexican mining production since the colonial period, Zacatecas, Guanajuato and Pachuca.[39]

Mining in Porfirian Mexico was dominated by foreign capital and ownership. The value of US-owned mines in 1911 is estimated as US$223 million, with the British mines valued at US$44 million. By 1909, US companies controlled nearly three-quarters of active mining in Mexico and over 70 per cent of the metallurgical industry. The impact of mining and smelting was particularly strong in the north of Mexico, where large US-owned mining companies, most notably the American Smelting and Refining Company, controlled by the Guggenheim family, predominated. In Chihuahua, a handful of US-mining companies controlled 75 per cent of mining production and over three-quarters of the workforce. Overall, total mineral and metallurgical production increased tenfold during the course of the regime, from a value of 26 million *pesos* in 1877 to 270 million *pesos* in 1910. The most rapid period of growth was the decade after 1900, when mining production doubled.[40]

The period 1900 to 1910 also witnessed a rapid expansion of the oil industry, which was, like the resurgence of mining, viscerally linked to foreign investment and improvements in transportation. The discovery of early deposits at El Ebano, San Luís Potosí in 1904 by Edward Doheny's Huasteca Petroleum Company, for example, was on land which bordered the Mexican Central Railway. The locomotives on Mexico's rapidly expanding network of railways were soon converted to run on Mexican oil, rather than on expensive imported coal, and industrial products from the nascent domestic oil industry (lubricants and fuel oils) were soon supplying the needs of the mining industry.

The domination of US oil companies over the early domestic industry prompted fears that oil exploitation might fall into the monopoly control of US interests. Díaz personally requested that Doheny should not sell his holdings to Standard Oil of California without first giving the opportunity to the Mexican government to buy them. At the same time, the regime granted extensive concessions for oil exploration to British businessman Sir Weetman Pearson, who had no experience of the oil business but who had already proved to be a loyal collaborator with the Díaz government in a number of engineering projects.

Pearson constructed Mexico's first oil refinery at Minatitlán near the terminus of the Tehuantepec National Railway, which his company had reconstructed between 1898 and 1907. The discovery of substantial oil deposits at Dos Bocas in Tuxpan gave Pearson control over Mexico's most productive well. In its nine-year life (1910–19), the well at Potrero del Llano alone produced 104 million barrels of crude. Pearson's *El Aguila* Company eventually controlled half of the foreign investment in Mexican oil, with some 40 per cent controlled by US interests.[41]

In this way, the Díaz government prevented US control over the Mexican oil industry. This was a source of notable resentment in business circles in the USA, and of tension between the US and Mexican governments. US–British rivalry over Mexican oil led, almost inevitably, to an oil price war in Mexico in the years immediately preceding the Revolution. However, the development of Mexico's oil exports, which made Mexico the second largest oil producer after the USA in the decade 1910–20, and which had such a crucial impact on Mexican economic development in the twentieth century, took place only after the demise of the Díaz regime. Given the regime's keen interest in the development of the oil industry, it is not without irony that the day on which the first shipment of Mexican oil for export took place (25 May 1911) was the very day on which Porfirio Díaz sailed into European exile.[42]

Industrialisation and industrial labour

Mining and oil constituted the most important sectors of Mexico's developing industrial base in the Díaz era. Nevertheless, there was also a period of rapid diversification of industrial production after 1890. By 1910, Mexican factories were producing iron and steel, chemicals, soap, glass, cement, textiles, beer, cigarettes, paper, jute and canned goods. By the end of the Díaz regime, manufacturing industry represented 12 per cent of national output and employed 11 per cent of the workforce.

According to Stephen Haber, there were three main features which characterised the nature of Mexican industrialisation in the late Porfiriato.[43] First, the concentration of industrial entrepreneurship among a small group of Mexican financiers (who belonged to the *camarilla* of the *científicos*). This small, close-knit group, led by Finance Minister Limantour, not only had pledged their allegiance to modernity and progress, but also believed that the political stability of the regime was permanent. They became the strongest advocates of the survival of the Díaz regime, since they argued that political stability was the essential ingredient of economic and industrial growth.

Second, Porfirian industrialisation was dependent upon capital-intensive technology and managerial expertise imported from abroad. There was, admittedly, little alternative to dependence upon external sources, given the absence in Mexico of either industrial plant, capital markets or of a trained or skilled workforce. Third, because of the uncompetitive nature of nascent Mexican industry, characterised by low productivity and low returns on investment, Porfirian industrialists sought (and received) from the Díaz regime protection from foreign competition through the imposition of tariffs on foreign imports, and through monopoly control of domestic markets.

Mexican industry in the late Porfiriato was, therefore, inefficient, unprofitable and structurally flawed, sustained primarily by protectionism and monopoly. It was, Haber concludes, an example of 'underdeveloped industrialisation'. Industrial production expanded rapidly in the 1890s, but slumped after 1907, almost as rapidly as it had developed. By 1910, in the context of growing political and economic crisis, what little confidence there had been in the regime's permanence and stability quickly evaporated.

The social and political consequences of industrialisation have received considerable attention but little historiographical consensus. The development of labour organisations representing the growing industrial workforce was certainly an important consequence, but the relationship of organised labour to the regime and, above all, the contribution of organised labour to the political destabilisation of the regime after 1906 has generated controversy.

Before the surge in industrial investment in the 1890s, Mexican labour organisations reflected the pre-industrial, artisan-based, small-scale character of Mexican industry, dominated by a small number of urban sweatshops or factories. The employees in these enterprises, who tended to refer to themselves as *artesanos* (artisans) rather than as *obreros* (workers) were grouped, if they were organised at all, into mutualist, self-help societies which frequently included employers as well as employees. The first indication of the development of a national labour organisation to represent the exclusive interests of industrial workers was the Great Circle of Mexican Workers (*Gran Círculo de Obreros de México*), established in 1872, which by 1876 claimed 28 branches in 12 states and the Federal District (Mexico City).[44]

During the 1890s, there was an increase in the number of industry-specific labour organisations, reflecting the rapid pace of industrialisation. It has been estimated that as much as half of the industrial workforce was unionised by 1905. Particularly active in this period were the Catholic Workers' Circles (*Círculos Obreros Católicos*), which emerged from the Church's broad concern with social Catholicism following the publication of Pope Leo XII's encyclical *Rerum Novarum* in 1891. By 1911, the National Confederation of Catholic Workers' Circles claimed a membership of over 14,000.[45]

Despite the widely-held perception that the Díaz regime was hostile to organised labour, there is evidence of the regime's sponsorship and co-optation of labour organisations, particularly after 1884, and a characteristic preference for negotiation and conciliation in the settlement of labour disputes. In most instances, the regime preferred not to intervene directly, and Díaz encouraged state governors to investigate the causes of local grievances, advocating compromise rather than repression. On some notable occasions (such as the Puebla textile strike in 1884), the regime even intervened in support of the workers' grievances.[46]

The regime's reputation for anti-labour hostility derives primarily from the adoption of authoritarian tactics after 1906 in response to the rapid deterioration of labour relations. Workers' demands became progressively radicalised from primary concerns over wages and working conditions to encompass a range of social and political issues – more equitable distribution of income, and nationalist protests against the foreign domination of industrial enterprises and the iniquity of different wages scales for foreign and Mexican workers. The regime's inept response was to suppress and arrest labour agitators, sometimes with the use of federal troops, and even, in the notorious case of the Cananea Mining strike of 1906, to abuse the sovereignty of the nation by allowing the mine's North American owners to invite a contingent of private US citizens and vigilantes to cross the border from Arizona under the pretext of protecting US lives and property.

Despite the high-profile examples of labour conflicts among mineworkers, railway employees and textile operatives in the 'year of strikes' in 1906, and continuing conflict thereafter, it remains the case that the majority of industrial workers, whether organised into mutualist societies, trade unions or Catholic circles, became actively opposed to the Díaz regime only following the dramatic loss of political authority after 1908. The role played by organised labour in the demise of the regime will be examined more closely in the next chapter. There can be little doubt, however, that the regime's response to growing labour agitation after 1906 exposed its impotence and weakness.

Agriculture and the rural economy

The impact of the economic development under the Díaz regime on Mexico's diverse rural economy has generated an intense and prolonged debate. It is also a topic of intrinsic importance to the understanding of the Díaz era since Mexico in 1910 was still an overwhelmingly rural society, with over 85 per cent of the population living and working in *pueblos* (villages or communities), *haciendas* (large estates), *ranchos* or *rancherías* (smallholdings). Rural development in the Díaz era has received, as a consequence, extensive coverage in the historiography, but it is still, paradoxically, one of the aspects of Porfirian Mexico which is probably least understood.

At the centre of the controversy is the essential character and respective fates of the *hacienda* or large estate and the *pueblo* in the nineteenth century. The image of the *hacienda*, portrayed by late eighteenth-century Enlightenment observers such as Alexander von Humboldt as a feudal institution which exercised a seignorial monopoly over the most productive land, dominion over its estate workers and exploitation of the labour of the impoverished indigenous *campesinos* in the neighbouring *pueblos*, has proved to be remarkably persistent in both the popular and the historiographical imagination. This is all the more remarkable given the existence of a large number of case studies published over recent decades which have successfully proved that the *hacienda* was, since its establishment in the early colonial period, not a 'feudal' institution but one fully responsive to prevailing market conditions and economic circumstances, in symbiotic co-existence (if not always perfect harmony) with its neighbouring *pueblos*.[47]

In addition to the distortions furnished by the traditional image of the *hacienda*, the concentration on the social impact of rural transformation as manifest in the Revolution of 1910 has tended to give a distorted impression of the impact of rural change in the Porfiriato. In other words, because of the rural and agrarian character of Revolutionary mobilisations after 1910, it is assumed that the economic innovations of the Díaz era were universally disruptive and detrimental to Mexico's rural inhabitants. This is not to suggest, of course, that the opposite was the case, that is that the changes were universally beneficial. There were many examples of peasant communities who lost land and resources to property speculators or to acquisitive *hacendados* during the Porfiriato, as the response of the peasant communities in the state of Morelos who joined Emiliano Zapata's agrarian rebellion after 1911 demonstrates. However, the struggle between *hacendado* and *pueblo* in Morelos, significant though it undoubtedly was, did not accurately represent the tremendous diversity of rural structures or rural experiences during the Díaz era. Concentration on *hacendado/pueblo* conflict tends to perpetuate the stereotype of rural Mexico, as criticised in Ramond Buve's recent description, of 'a lunar landscape inhabited by exploiters (the *hacendados*) and their *campesino/*peasant victims'.[48] The starting point, in short, for understanding the transformation of rural Mexico in the Díaz era needs to be the experience of the nineteenth century, not that of the Revolution.

The Díaz regime's vision of agrarian development was fundamentally that of the mid-nineteenth-century liberals of the Reforma. For the majority of liberals, the problems facing rural Mexico were: first, an indolent and ignorant peasantry; second, 'archaic' (i.e. colonial) institutions such as the Church which suppressed individualism and entrepreneurial spirit; and, third, the feudal economic and social relations of production which characterised the 'inefficient' *hacienda*. The solution was to be found in the introduction of agrarian entrepreneurship and capitalist enterprise. This required, as we have seen, the implementation of a series of far-reaching reforms: the privatisation of corporate landholdings, the sale of unexploited public lands (*terrenos baldíos*), the promotion of colonisation schemes, the improvement of inter-regional communication and trade through railway development and tariff reform.

Prior to 1880, successive liberal administrations had made determined efforts to introduce these reforms, but their efforts had been severely constrained by a combination of foreign intervention, domestic political schism and, significantly, waves of rural protest and resistance which began in the late 1840s and recurred in the 1850s, 1860s and again in the 1870s. It was not until the acceleration of economic development and, above all, the consolidation of Díaz's personal authority in the 1880s that agrarian conflict began to decline in intensity.[49]

Díaz's personal approach to agrarian issues has been the subject of much speculation and misinformation. *Anti-porfirista* historiography has, predictably, portrayed him as cynical and ruthless, compliant with the continued rape of the *pueblo* by the rapacious *hacienda*.

'No palliation, no extenuation can be imagined', wrote Eyler Simpson in his 'classic' analysis of the Mexican *ejido*, published in 1937, 'for the cold rape of the *pueblos* and the heartless suppression of the small landowners which Díaz not only countenanced, but openly aided and abetted'.[50]

Díaz's personal correspondence indicates, however, an unequivocal commitment to the liberal goal of rural development. Its implementation, he openly recognised, would require tact, negotiation and compromise. In fact, far from demonstrating cold-hearted aloofness, Díaz showed a good deal of sensitivity to the interests of rural communities over the question of land privatisation. In his correspondence with state governors, Díaz consistently stressed the need for initiatives to respond to local circumstances, and that the benefits of privatisation needed to be explained to rural communities. In July 1890, for example, he explained to the governor of San Luis Potosí, Carlos Díez Gutiérrez, that *pueblos* in his native Oaxaca, which had been notoriously resistant to changes in land tenure, had welcomed the privatisation of municipal lands because it had meant an increase in municipal funds.[51] And he also made it clear that the practice of adjudicating land to those who were not residents of the *pueblos* should be avoided at all costs, and that in all cases 'the rights, and even the whims [*caprichos*] of the municipal authorities should be respected'.[52]

The agrarian grievances of the *municipio* of San Juan Tamazunchale in the Huasteca region of San Luís Potosí make an interesting case study of Porfirian agrarian policy. Violence erupted on a regular basis in Tamazunchale throughout the Díaz era, and although it was clear that Díaz would not tolerate armed rebellion, he personally intervened in an attempt to find a solution which would respect the colonial titles of the villagers in spite of the irregularities in their legal documentation. Equally significant was the fact that, despite his direct intervention in the dispute, Díaz's power to influence local events was limited. It is clear from the experience of the indigenous inhabitants of Tamazunchale that not all of the Porfirian officials entrusted with the implementation of land privatisation shared the President's sensitivity and concern for the welfare of the *pueblos*. Abuse of the process of land privatisation was, therefore, frequent and undeniable.[53]

The most well-known aspect of Porfirian agrarian policy is the policy of selling off unoccupied or vacant lands (*terrenos baldíos*) through private companies which would carry out detailed surveys in return for up to one-third of the land surveyed as compensation. As a result of this process, an estimated 96 million acres of land was privatised during the course of the Porfiriato. It has generally been assumed not only that the process was disruptive and conflictive, but also that the regime actively colluded in unscrupulous practices which allowed speculators to acquire the land of unsuspecting *campesinos*. However, the research carried out by Robert Holden on the activities of the surveying companies suggests a rather different interpretation.[54]

Holden emphasises that the policy was certainly not a free-for-all for speculators or surveying companies, but was strictly regulated by the Ministry of *Fomento*. If surveying companies failed to meet their obligations, the contract was rescinded. As a result, only 40 per cent of surveying companies actually received lands. And, in cases where conflicts with local interests arose, the Porfirian authorities often upheld local protests against the surveying companies. Furthermore, Holden argues that the central purpose of the strategy was not to collude with *hacendados* in the enhancement of their power or wealth, but to raise state revenue in order to finance *Fomento*'s subsidies to railway and public works projects.

Holden agrees with the analysis of Donald Stephens, namely that far from condoning the abusive practices of speculators and surveying companies, the regime embarked upon a significant revision of land policy after 1900. In 1901, amendments to Article 27 of the 1857 Constitution legalised land ownership by Indian villages, while retaining the ban on Church ownership of real estate. In 1902, the process of surveying was brought under stricter central control by requiring the supervision of land surveys by salaried public officials, and forbidding the distribution of land as payment. And a series of decrees in 1909 suspended the granting of new land titles for an indefinite period, in an attempt to temper widespread abuse.[55]

Empirical evidence suggests the need to revise some of the generalisations which have been offered to explain the impact of economic development in rural Mexico under Díaz. Some historians have even been bold enough to propose a positive interpretation of Porfirian agrarian policy. From this revisionist perspective, land privatisation can be seen to have stimulated capital accumulation, the development of infrastructure, the rapid integration of regional and national markets and helped to convert the uncharted northern frontier of Mexican national territory into a dynamic international border.[56] In general terms, agricultural productivity certainly increased

and food supplies generally matched demand. In short, a more positive interpretation of Porfirian rural development would argue that
not just the export sector, but also the domestic market for agricultural products, were the beneficiaries of the overall expansion of
economic activity.[57]

'Revisionist' interpretations of the consequences of rural transformation make the important point that there is still a great deal that
is unknown about the detail of regional agricultural development
during the Díaz era, and that, given the diversity of rural experience,
it is extremely difficult to generalise. It would therefore appear to be
most unwise, and inaccurate, to assume a direct correlation between
land privatisation and agrarian conflict.

Nevertheless, as John Tutino has pointed out, it would be equally
unwise to ignore the fact that Porfirian development brought new
pressures to rural Mexico and new patterns of agrarian conflict and
resistance. For the majority of rural Mexicans, Tutino argues, the
Díaz era brought 'agrarian compression' – in other words, pressures
which arose from a combination of population growth and the simultaneous loss of land and, perhaps most importantly, of security in a
rapidly changing economic environment. Although the regime was
able either to contain or to mediate agrarian grievances throughout
its lifetime, the growing political crisis after 1908, and the rapid collapse of the regime after 1910, unleashed agrarian tensions which
had been growing and, in some cases, festering for some considerable time. Agrarian demands were, therefore, a highly significant
component within the popular insurrection which removed Díaz
from power in 1911.[58]

. . .

NOTES AND REFERENCES

1. P. Díaz, *Informe Que en el Ultimo Dia de su Período Constitucional Da a
   Sus Compatriotas El Presidente de los Estados Unidos Mexicanos Porfirio
   Díaz Acerca de los Actos de su Adminstración*, Mexico City, 1880, p.93.
2. H. Aguilar Camín and L. Meyer, *In the Shadow of the Mexican Revolution:
   Contemporary Mexican History 1910–1989*, Austin, TX, 1993, pp.159–98.
3. J. Coatsworth, 'Obstacles to Economic Growth in Nineteenth-Century
   Mexico', *American Historical Review*, 83, 1978, pp.80–100.
4. R. Randall, *Real de Monte: A British Mining Venture in Mexico*, Austin,
   TX, 1972.

5. V. Bulmer-Thomas, *The Economic History of Latin America since Independence*, Cambridge, 1994, p.46.
6. W. Glade, 'Economy 1870–1914', in L. Bethell (ed.), *Latin America: Economy and Society 1870–1930*, Cambridge, 1989, pp.1–56.
7. J. Bazant, *A Concise History of Mexico*, Oxford, 1977, pp.110–21.
8. F. Madero, *La Sucesión Presidencial de 1910*, Mexico City (reprint, Editorial Epoca), 1988.
9. F. Rosenzweig, 'El desarrollo económico de México de 1877 a 1911', *El Trimestre Económico*, 32, 1965, pp.405–54; J. Hart, *Revolutionary Mexico*, Berkeley, CA, 1987.
10. S. Haber, 'Economic Growth and Latin American Economic Historiography', in S. Haber (ed.), *How Latin America Fell Behind: Essays on the Economic Histories of Brazil and Mexico*, Stanford, CA, 1997, pp.1–33.
11. C. Marichal, 'Obstacles to the Development of Capital Markets in Nineteenth-Century Mexico', in Haber (ed.), *How Latin America Fell Behind*, pp.118–45.
12. P. Garner, 'The Politics of National Development in Late Porfirian Mexico: The Reconstruction of the Tehuantepec Railway 1896–1907', *Bulletin of Latin American Research*, 14(3), 1995, pp.339–56.
13. J. Bazant, *Concise History of Mexico*, p.109.
14. M. Tenorio Trillo, *Mexico at the World's Fairs: Crafting a Modern Nation*, Stanford, CA, 1996.
15. G. Yeager, 'Porfirian Commercial Propaganda: Mexico in the World Industrial Expositions', *The Americas*, 34(2), 1977, pp.230–43.
16. J.Y. Limantour, *Apuntes Sobre Mi Vida Pública (1892–1911)*, Mexico City, 1965, pp.36–40.
17. E. Krauze, *Porfirio Díaz: Místico de la Autoridad*, Mexico City, 1987, p.113.
18. L. Ludlow, 'El Banco Nacional Mexicano y el Banco Mercantil Mexicano: Radiografía Social de sus Primeros Accionistas', *Historia Mexicana*, Vol. XXXIX, 1990, pp.979–1027.
19. Limantour to Matías Romero, quoted in H. Bernstein, *Matías Romero*, Mexico City, 1973, p.327.
20. C. Marichal, 'La deuda externa y las políticas de desarrollo económico durante el Porfiriato: algunos hipótesis de trabajo', in *Pasado y presente de la deuda externa de México*, Mexico City, 1988, pp.85–101.
21. S. Topik, 'La Revolución, el estado, y el desarollo económico de México', *Historia Mexicana*, Vol. XXXIX, 1990, pp.79–145.
22. V. Bulmer-Thomas, *Economic History of Latin America*, pp.114–18; Bazant, *Concise History of Mexico*, p.120.
23. V. Brachet-Márquez, *La Población de los Estados de México en el Siglo XIX*, Mexico City, 1976.
24. R. Holden, *Mexico and the Survey of Public Lands: The Management of Modernization 1876–1911*, DeKalb, IL, 1994.

25. M. González Navarro, *La colonización en México 1877–1910*, Mexico City, 1960, pp.24, 35–6.
26. E. Cortés, 'Mexican Colonies during the Porfiriato', *Aztlán*, 10, 1979, pp.1–14.
27. S. Topik, 'La Revolución', pp.79–145.
28. A. Schmidt, *The Social and Economic Effect of the Railroad in Puebla and Veracruz 1867–1911*, New York, 1987.
29. F. Calderón, 'Los Ferrocarriles', in D. Cosío Villegas (ed.), *Historia Moderna de México* (hereafter *HMM*), 10 vols, Mexico City, 1955–72, Vol. VII, pp.183 634.
30. J. Coatsworth, *Growth against Development: The Economic Impact of Railroads in Porfirian Mexico*, DeKalb, IL, 1981.
31. A. Wells, 'All in the Family: Railroads and Henequén Monoculture in Porfirian Yucatán, *Hispanic American Historical Review*, 72, 1992, pp.159–210.
32. A. Tischendorf, *Great Britain and Mexico in the Era of Porfirio Díaz*, Durham, NC, 1961, p.50.
33. P. Riguzzi, 'Inversión extranjera e interés nacional en los ferrocarriles mexicanos 1880–1914', in C. Marichal (ed.), *Las Inversiones Extranjeras en América Latina 1850–1930*, Mexico City, 1995, pp.159–77.
34. S. Kuntz, *Empresa Extranjera y Mercado Interno: El Ferrocarril Central Mexicano (1880–1907)*, Mexico City, 1995.
35. J. Limantour, 'Política Ferroviaria', in *Memoria de Hacienda y Crédito Público Correspondiente al Año Económico del 1 de julio al 30 de junio de 1907*, Mexico City, 1909, pp.ix–xii.
36. E. Cárdenas, 'A Macroeconomic Interpretation of Nineteenth-century Mexico', in S. Haber (ed.), *How Latin America Fell Behind*, p.77.
37. J. Coatsworth, *Growth against Development*; Bazant, *Concise History of Mexico*, p.113.
38. M. Urrutia and G. Nava Oteo, 'La Minería 1821–1880', in C. Cardoso (ed.), *Mexico en el Siglo XIX (1821–1910)*, Mexico City, 1980, pp.119–43.
39. Coatsworth, 'Obstacles to Economic Growth', p.86.
40. M. Bernstein, *The Mexican Mining Industry 1890–1950*, Albany, NY, 1965.
41. J. Brown, *Oil and Revolution in Mexico*, Berkeley, CA, 1993, pp.7–170.
42. Ibid., p.100.
43. S. Haber, *Industry and Underdevelopment: The Industrialisation of Mexico 1890–1907*, Stanford, CA, 1989.
44. M. Trujillo Bolio, 'Artesanos y trabajadores frente al Estado nacional', in R. Falcón and R. Buve (eds), *Don Porfirio Presidente, Nunca Omnipotente*, Mexico City, 1998, pp.273–95.
45. K. Schmitt, 'The Díaz Conciliation Policy at State and Local Levels', *Hispanic American Historical Review*, 40(4), 1960, pp.513–32.
46. D. Anderson, *Outcasts in Their Own Land: Mexican Industrial Workers 1906–11*, DeKalb, IL, 1976.

47. S. Miller, 'Land and Labour in Mexican Rural Insurrections', *Bulletin of Latin American Research*, 10, 1991, pp.55–79.
48. R. Buve, 'Un paisaje lunar habitado por bribones y sus víctimas: Mirada retrospectiva al debate sobre las haciendas y los pueblos durante el Porfiriato (1876–1911)', in R. Falcón and R. Buve (eds), *Don Porfirio Presidente*, pp.121–51.
49. L. Reina, *Las Rebeliones Campesinas en México 1816–1906*, Mexico City, 1980.
50. E. Simpson, *The Ejido: Mexico's Way Out*, Chapel Hill, NC, 1937, p.29.
51. Díaz to Díaz Gutiérrez, CPD:L66:C8:T18:ff.137–41.
52. Díaz to Chávez, CPD:L41:C8:f.251.
53. D. Stephens, 'Agrarian Policy and Instability in Porfirian Mexico', *The Americas*, 39(2), 1982, pp.153–66.
54. See Holden, *Mexico and the Survey of Public Lands*.
55. Stephens, 'Agrarian Policy', pp.162–3.
56. M. Tinker Salas, *In the Shadow of the Eagles: Sonora and the Transformation of the Border during the Porfiriato*, Berkeley, CA, 1997.
57. S. Miller, *Landlords and Haciendas in Modernising Mexico*, Amsterdam, 1995.
58. J. Tutino, *From Insurrection to Revolution in Mexico: Social Bases of Agrarian Violence 1750–1940*, Princeton, NJ, 1986.

Chapter 8

THE PRICE OF ORDER AND PROGRESS: THE DECLINE AND FALL OF THE DÍAZ REGIME, 1900–11

> Whatever the opinions of my friends and supporters, I shall stand down from power at the end of the current term of office, and I shall not serve again . . . (Porfirio Díaz, Creelman Interview, 1908)

One of the aims of this book has been the attempt to re-evaluate the regime of Porfirio Díaz in the light of new research and of changing historiographical fashion. Above all, it has sought to liberate the interpretation of the Díaz era from the distorting perspective of the subsequent Revolution. The concentration in Revolutionary historiography on the regime's rapidly fading fortunes after 1908 has, inevitably, accentuated its frailties and failures and has distorted the analysis of its achievements.

One of the principal problems in the interpretation of the Díaz era is the fact that too much attention has been paid to the penultimate and final periods of presidential office (1906–10, 1910–11). In these years, the regime struggled to find an adequate response to the political problems caused by permanent re-election, and to the economic and social problems engendered by the rapid transformation of the Mexican economy in the 1880s and 1890s.

As we have seen in the last chapter, during the Díaz regime Mexico had vastly increased the scale of domestic and international trade, had attracted ever-increasing levels of foreign investment, and had embarked upon an ambitious project of railway construction and public works which transformed the economic and social infrastructure of much (but certainly not all) of the country. Not without irony, the years immediately preceding 1910 can be seen, therefore, as a period in which the regime became a victim of its own economic success. The developmentalist economic strategy had

unquestionably made a significant contribution to the consolidation
of the regime but, at the same time, had created a growing number
of problems, related to the uneven distribution of wealth, economic
resources and social benefits, and the failure to broaden the scope of
political participation and democratic legitimacy.

The regime's response to the growing crisis after 1906 was hesitant,
inconsistent, inept and, on certain notorious occasions (such as the
repression of the mining and textile strikes of 1906 and 1907) highly
repressive. The adoption of authoritarian tactics after 1906 was itself
a sign of increasing desperation. Because of the predominance of
heavy-handed tactics adopted by the regime after 1906, there has
been a marked tendency to assume that the repressive character of
the regime during its last years was representative of the regime as a
whole. This analysis, however, provides a distorted picture. Growing
political and economic crisis after 1900 certainly exposed the weaknesses and brittleness of a personalist political system, but it demonstrated above all that the mechanisms and techniques of the type of
patriarchal liberalism which Díaz had skilfully employed since 1884
were no longer appropriate to deal with a changing set of circumstances. In Alan Knight's succinct metaphor, the regime on the eve
of the Revolution resembled a creature that could no longer adapt
to the changed surroundings of its environment: 'like some saurian
monster, the regime lacked a political brain commensurate with its
swollen economic muscle: hence its extinction'.[1]

There is no doubt that after 1906 the regime adopted increasingly repressive tactics in dealing with growing manifestations of
discontent and dissidence. These repressive measures were not only
counterproductive, but also patently unsuccessful in suppressing
political and popular protest which coalesced under the banner of
the Anti-Re-electionist Movement after 1909. What is most striking
is the speed with which the regime collapsed, and it took contemporaries completely by surprise. Only six months after Madero's
call for armed revolution in November 1910, Porfirio Díaz, who
had monopolised political power for more than a generation and had
presided over a regime which had prided itself upon its solidity and
permanence, had resigned and sailed into European exile. The rapid
collapse of the regime created a problem with which historians have
been grappling ever since.

The reasons for the fall of the Díaz regime can be broken down
into two main categories. First, the complex pattern of internal
dislocation and disruption to the structure and fabric of Porfirian

society, both at a national and a regional level, was an important determinant of the popular mobilisation which helped to bring the regime down in 1911. Second, internal schisms progressively undermined the self-confidence of the regime and the fragile equilibrium of elite consensus, which stimulated rivalry, conflict, factionalism and division within the inner circle of the political elite, and between those within the inner circle and those on the margins of Porfirian politics.

Furthermore, no solution had been found to the problem of political succession: a problem which became more pressing as Díaz approached his seventh re-election in 1910. This resulted in an intense power struggle within the inner circle of the regime, and growing opposition to re-electionism from outside the political elite. The problem was made more acute by the deliberate obstacles which had consistently been placed in the way of the development of political institutions or parties, which deprived the regime of an institutional form of succession. As a final consideration, the prodigious energy and the skill and appetite for political manipulation which Díaz had displayed in the maintenance of a highly personalist system had begun to desert him as he approached his eightieth year.

. . .

REVOLUTIONARY HISTORIOGRAPHY AND THE DEMISE OF THE REGIME

Because of the amount of historiographical attention paid to the Revolution of 1910, there is no shortage of explanations for the rapid collapse of the Díaz regime. According to the 'orthodox' or 'popular' interpretation, the key ingredient of the Revolution was its popular origins and base. Peasants, workers and the small but growing urban middle classes mobilised in protest against the unfavourable economic conditions after 1907, which highlighted the monopoly of power and wealth exercised by *hacendados*, factory or mine owners, metropolitan elites and foreigners. For some, the popular revolution was not only agrarian, radical and progressive, but had distinctly nationalist and even xenophobic overtones as a war of liberation from foreign (and especially US) domination imposed by the Díaz regime.[2] For others, the basis of popular mobilisation was broader and more subtle, and responded to the disparity of rural social structures throughout Mexico and of regional experiences during the Porfiriato. Popular mobilisations reflected, in other words, more complex loyalties and identities which were related not exclusively to class, but also to ethnicity, ideology, clientalism and to regional and factional affiliation.

Orthodox interpretations of the Revolution predominated in the post-Revolutionary period and have enjoyed new vigour in the 1980s. They have, however, tended to emphasise the authoritarianism of the Díaz regime in its death throes. Put most crudely, the logic of the orthodox interpretation is that the scale of popular mobilisation and protest after 1910 reflected the degree of dislocation and repression during the Porfiriato. The political excesses of the Díaz regime, especially its repression of agrarian, indigenous or labour protests, and above all its promotion of an economic system which benefited only a small elite and, by implication, caused misery for the mass of the population, explains the extent of popular revolution.

Traditional or orthodox interpretations were increasingly challenged after 1968 by the generation of Mexican and non-Mexican historians who sought to find the roots of their own disillusionment with the betrayal of the ideals of the Revolution in the origins of the Revolution itself. If the post-Revolutionary state, epitomised by the paradox of institutionalised revolution peddled by the ruling Institutional Revolutionary Party, had betrayed the aspirations of *campesinos* and workers, then it was logical to argue that the Revolution itself had perpetrated a similar act of betrayal from its inception. The 'revisionist' approach, which has achieved prominence in recent decades, has, as a result, tended to interpret the power struggles within the Revolution as a reflection of the manipulation and corruption of unscrupulous politicians and *caudillos* who, after 1910, espoused revolutionary rhetoric but mobilised the peasantry and urban workers for their own ends and constructed the post-Revolutionary state to protect their own interests.[3]

While orthodox or revisionist interpretations have dominated the debate, recent contributions to the historiography of the Revolution have shifted attention away from global explanation to focus attention on cultural history, and regional or local history. A growing number of cultural historians, both in Mexico and in the USA, have examined non-institutional manifestations of popular and elite culture – popular religious ritual, fashion, leisure, workplace culture, the construction of historical monuments, public 'discourses' on crime, justice, public morality and public health have been examined in detail. Cultural history has combined here with revisionist analysis in rejecting the traditional periodisation of Porfiriato and Revolution, and their categorisation as separate phenomena. Instead, the tensions and conflicts which characterised late nineteenth- and early twentieth-century Mexico are interpreted as manifestations of a growing cultural clash between a traditional society and the forces of late nineteenth-century 'modernity'.[4]

Regional, 'microhistorical' studies of the Revolution have highlighted very clearly that the Revolution was anything but a homogeneous process. Regional loyalties and, more specifically, loyalties to the village, community or municipality (or the *patria chica*) were often as significant in local, popular mobilisations during the Revolution as conflicts over class, ethnicity or ideology.[5] The proliferation of regional studies of the Revolution has had a marked impact on regional studies of the Porfiriato, since many of those who ploughed the regionalist furrow in the 1980s have realised the importance of understanding the Díaz era in order to understand the Revolution. While regional historiography of the Díaz era is still less prolific than its Revolutionary counterpart, the emerging trend of regional analysis has begun to revise the understanding of the complexity and diversity of Porfirian socio-economic development, and its political implications.[6]

One of the most significant findings of regional research is the fact that the disparity in the pace of regional development appears to have intensified during the Porfiriato. This has significant implications for understanding the fissures and cracks which had appeared within Porfirian society, and why those pressures were acute in some regions and less acute in others. It has also helped to identify the local and regional character of popular mobilisation. There is, therefore, an obvious and important correlation between levels of socio-economic transformation during the course of the Porfiriato and political conflicts in the last years of the regime and during the Revolution. At the risk of over-simplification, it is apparent that it was the north of Mexico, particularly the states which constituted the border between Mexico and the USA, which emerged as the most dynamic of the regions during the Díaz era, as measured in terms of demographic, infrastructural or economic development. It is no coincidence, therefore, that the forces which came to dominate the Revolution during the decade of armed struggle (1910–20) emanated principally (although not exclusively) from the northern states.

By contrast, in the centre and centre/south of the country, which has always been the most densely populated of all the regions of Mexico, the impact of Porfirian modernisation, and especially land privatisation, was varied, but profound. In some cases, the fragile equilibrium of rural social relations was acutely distorted, through progressive encroachment on land and local autonomy. It is this region where the most intense agrarian conflicts of the Revolution occurred, such as the movement led by Emiliano Zapata in Morelos.

By contrast again, the south of Mexico underwent radically different experiences. In some areas, the expansion of commercial agricultural production had a profound impact on economic development and local social relations, most notably in the case of *henequén* in the Yucatán peninsula, or coffee in the Soconusco region of Chiapas. At the other end of the spectrum, other areas of the 'Indian South' experienced limited disruption prior to the Revolution, despite growing evidence of economic and social pressures. In these regions, for the most part, revolutionary activity was a response to the fragmentation of central authority after 1910, and to attempts from the centre and the north to impose unwelcome revolutionary solutions.

It would be most unwise, however, and indeed mistaken, to postulate a deterministic relationship between socio-economic transformation and political conflict, whether during the latter years of the Porfiriato or during the Revolution. There were plenty of areas in the northern, central and southern Mexico where revolutionary activity was muted, both in regions which had, and those which had not, undergone profound transformation. Conversely, pockets of revolutionary activity have been clearly identified in the 'passive' Indian South. As argued in the previous chapter, although changes in land ownership and use, or the impact of 'agrarian compression', certainly had the potential to exacerbate rural grievances, agrarian revolt was far from inevitable.

The panorama is, therefore, immensely varied, and the growing evidence of regional diversity constantly adds new layers to the interpretation of Porfirian modernisation. Perhaps an appropriate way to illustrate the regional disparity in social and economic transformation in Porfirian Mexico, and to indicate the different political responses which it stimulated, is to examine the experiences of two very different regions during the later years of the Díaz era. There is a striking contrast, for example, between the economic and social transformation of the northern Comarca Lagunera region in the 1890s and the much less dramatic experience of the southern state of Oaxaca in the same period. The profound transformations experienced in the Comarca Lagunera and the very much slower and more erratic pace of change in Oaxaca also had important repercussions for local politics, and for revolutionary mobilisation after 1910.

. . .

THE REGIONAL IMPACT OF PORFIRIAN DEVELOPMENT

As William Meyers has shown, the Comarca Lagunera, which encompassed sections of the northern states of Durango and Coahuila, became the showcase of Porfirian modernisation after 1880. The combination of railway construction, foreign investment, internal migration and legislative support for entrepreneurial activity rapidly transformed the region and helped to overcome the obstacles which had plagued the development of the regional economy since independence. At the core of regional development in La Laguna was modern cotton production, but the region also rapidly developed significant textile, cottonseed, *guayule* (rubber), mining and smelting industries, and the towns of Torreón and Gómez Palacio became bustling urban centres. Torreón, for example, increased its population from 3,960 in 1893 to over 40,000 by 1907, transforming a barren and unpopulated plain into a major city in a period of less than 15 years. With a population of 1,500 US citizens, it had become arguably the most North American city in Mexico.[7]

At the same time, the economic transformation of the Comarca Lagunera prompted a series of social and political conflicts in the region, especially after 1900. The cotton planters on the upper, middle and lower sections of the Nazas river, some of whom were old, established families (such as the Maderos), and others were recent immigrants, clashed with each other and with the owners of the Tlahualilo Company (acquired by British and US interests in 1903) in bitter and protracted disputes over access to water rights. With the process of rapid industrialisation and the influx of internal migrants from other parts of Mexico, labour conflicts were frequent, particularly among seasonal workers (*eventuales*) on the cotton estates and in the mines. The economic crisis of 1907 had a particularly profound impact in the Comarca Lagunera. Credit became severely restricted, new businesses closed and unemployment rose. The corresponding intensification of local criticism of government policy, and popular protest at deteriorating economic conditions, gave rise to considerable local political tensions which took on national significance in the context of growing national political insecurity.

Local politics in Coahuila had long demonstrated a tradition of autonomy and resistance to the interference of Mexico City. As a consequence, Díaz had always been cautious of overt intervention.[8] However, local political crisis, especially after 1907, exacerbated long-standing rivalries within the local political elites, especially in Coahuila, between the Garza Galán, Madero and Cárdenas *camarillas* and prompted more direct interference from the centre. Díaz's support for *científico* José María Garza Galán, a protégé of Manuel Romero Rubio, had ensured his election to the governorship of Coahuila between 1884 and 1893 but had alienated rival *camarillas*. The Maderos plotted with Bernardo Reyes, governor of neighbouring Nuevo León and ally of the Cárdenas clan, to oust Garza Galán, which was eventually achieved in 1893. Thereafter, Bernardo Reyes was given a mostly free rein by Díaz to supervise the politics of the state, and his domination of local politics was confirmed by the election of *reyista* Miguel Cárdenas in 1897. Reyes continued to support Cárdenas in the governorship elections of 1905, but his re-election was challenged by both the Madero and Garza Galán factions. It was the elections of 1905 in Coahuila which first raised the anti-re-electionist political consciousness of Francisco Madero.

As indicated in Chapter 5, the more Díaz became fearful of Reyes's ambition and influence, the more he became obsessed with undermining Reyes's influence in both local and national politics. In 1909, Díaz broke with his customary caution and intervened directly in the politics of Coahuila, removing Cárdenas in 1909 and imposing Torreón landowner and businessman Práxedis de la Peña as governor.

Díaz's intervention in local politics in Coahuila in 1909 was a profound mistake, one of many that were made during the last months of the regime and one which provoked the political hostility of important sections of the local political elite. It is, therefore, no coincidence that two of the most prominent national figures of the Revolutionary decade, Francisco Madero (President from 1911 until his assassination in 1913) and Venustiano Carranza (President from 1917 until his assassination in 1920) should have emerged from the provincial political arena of Coahuila after 1905.

By contrast, economic, social and political developments in Díaz's native Oaxaca followed a very different path. In terms of economic development, there was certainly no absence of enthusiasm on the part of national or provincial elites, or from foreign investors in the exploitation of Oaxaca's abundant mineral and agricultural resources during the Díaz era. Oaxaca appeared, in fact, to enjoy distinct advantages over other regions of Mexico, given the active advocacy and promotion by two of her most powerful and influential native sons: the President himself and the indefatigable Matías Romero, Mexican Minister in Washington, who in 1886 had published a detailed analysis of Oaxaca's abundant and untapped resources with the express purpose of attracting overseas, and particularly US, investment.[9]

In other words, the objective conditions for profound transformation of the local economy appeared to be highly favourable. There was substantial foreign investment in mining and commercial agriculture in Oaxaca, to the extent that Oaxaca was accredited with fifth position in the 'league table' of states in receipt of US investment in Mexico in 1902. Between 1902 and 1907, US investment in mining in Oaxaca reached US$10 billion, second only to the state of Guanajuato.[10] In addition to Oaxacan silver, a diversity of cash crops (most notably coffee, tobacco, sugar cane, cotton and *hule* (india rubber)) were produced for the export market. Oaxaca's export development was notably enhanced by the construction of a railway network that, over a very brief period of 16 years between 1892 and 1908, linked Oaxaca City with Puebla and Mexico City (the *Ferrocarril Mexicano del Sur*), the tobacco and coffee plantations of Tuxtepec with Veracruz (the *Ferrocarril Veracruz al Pacífico*), and the gulf and Pacific ports of the Isthmus of Tehuantepec with each other, with Chiapas and with the rest of the country (the *Ferrocarril Nacional de Tehuantepec* and the *Ferrocarril Pan-Americano*).

Matías Romero identified coffee as the new source of regional prosperity, which, he argued, would replicate the success of Oaxaca's late colonial dye trade in the eighteenth century (based upon the export of cochineal or *grana*). He personally invested in a coffee estate (*finca*) on Oaxaca's Pacific coast, in the district of Pochutla. But his expectations, and those of other domestic and foreign investors who invested in commercial agriculture in Oaxaca, proved to have been over-ambitious. Although coffee production in Oaxaca did develop after 1883, it was severely hampered by the successful resistance of indigenous communities to land privatisation, and by severe shortages of labour, capital, transportation and infrastructure. Oaxacan coffee production at the end of the Díaz era still lagged far behind production in the neighbouring states of Chiapas or Veracruz.[11]

The paradox of the Porfiriato in Oaxaca is that despite the best efforts of local elites, with support from central government and the keen personal interest of the President, the returns on the substantial investments made by domestic and foreign entrepreneurs in the exploitation of the state's mineral and agricultural resources were ultimately disappointing. In short, the numerous predictions of a harvest of untold bounty for Oaxaca's mineral and agricultural exports were never fulfilled, and at the end of the Porfiriato both promoters and government continued to write about the potential rather than the proven wealth of the state's resources.

The political implications of this slow and erratic pace of regional development have yet to be fully understood.[12] The available evidence would suggest that the limited socio-economic transformations during the Díaz era were reflected in the reduced levels of political disturbance within Oaxaca during the later years of the regime, in marked contrast to the experience of Coahuila. Internal migration, urbanisation and 'modernisation' had all made their mark in Porfirian Oaxaca, but to a far more limited extent than in Coahuila.

This does not mean that provincial politics in Oaxaca was devoid of conflict, or that Oaxaca was isolated from national political debates during the latter years of the Díaz regime. As one of the states at the forefront of the liberal movement throughout the nineteenth century, this was clearly not the case. Local political disturbances and controversies in Oaxaca in fact reflected national political debates. For example, a serious political conflict developed over the proposed third re-election of Governor Martín González in 1902. González was one of Díaz's oldest and closest military *tuxtepecano compadres*, and the campaign to remove him was orchestrated by young urban middle-class radicals in Oaxaca who supported the candidacy of the President's nephew, Félix Díaz. Despite Don Porfirio's awareness of the corruption and incompetence of his *compadre* González, he was characteristically reluctant to intervene to upset the political status quo, even to support the pretensions of his own nephew. In fact, he was particularly anxious to avoid stimulating criticism of blatant political nepotism. Only when the rival political campaigns of the González and Díaz factions erupted into open hostility and violence in 1902 did Díaz intervene to impose a compromise candidate, the prominent Oaxacan *científico* Emilio Pimentel, whose appointment coincided with the consolidation of *científico* influence at the national level.[13]

Porfirian politics in Oaxaca is therefore notable for the degree of deference which the local political elite continued to show towards

Díaz, even in times of political crisis after 1900. The imposition of Pimentel as governor was accepted with very little protest, in contrast to the hostile reactions of the political elite of Coahuila to the imposition of Miguel Cárdenas in 1905 and Práxedes de la Peña in 1909. The level of deference and support continued until the very end of the Díaz era. The Oaxaca State Congress was, significantly, the only provincial legislature to send a telegram of congratulation and condolence to Díaz as he awaited exile in 1911.[14]

This is not to suggest that there was unanimity within the provincial political elite in Oaxaca prior to the Revolution, or an absence of popular mobilisation after 1910. Popular mobilisation was in fact widespread throughout the state after 1911. Local anti-re-electionist protest, however, certainly by comparison to Coahuila, was muted, and Oaxaca failed to produce revolutionary leaders or revolutionary movements of national prominence after 1911.[15]

To some extent, the muted political response can be explained by the fact that Oaxaca and *oaxaqueños* occupied a unique position within the politics of Porfirian Mexico. Throughout the regime, Díaz maintained close personal relationships with his numerous *compadres* within the state. These close political relationships were consolidated by Díaz's use of fellow Oaxacans within his personal entourage, and in appointments as governors, deputies and senators to other states. Díaz's Oaxacan allies performed the role of Porfirian proconsuls or, as Francisco Bulnes described it with characteristic flourish, the role that Jesuits performed for the Pope, 'charged with the promotion of faith in the Hero of Peace, and the dogma of re-electionism'.[16]

Perhaps the most significant example of the consequences of regional development and the conflicts within local politics is the northern state of Chihuahua. The Chihuahuan revolutionary movement of 1910 and 1911 was a product of mass, popular protest from within a society which had undergone a rapid and profound transition during the Porfiriato. The roots of the movement were to be found, on the one hand, in agrarian discontent, based not simply on land sequestration but on the erosion of the autonomy of Chihuahua's rural communities and former military colonies. On the other hand, the Revolution in Chihuahua reflected the growing protest from broad sections of Chihuahua's urban middle and working classes against the monopoly of political and economic power enjoyed by the Terrazas and Creel clans, the principal representatives of the local *hacendado* oligarchy. In Chihuahua, political opposition was exacerbated, as it was throughout Mexico, by the economic depression of

1907 and a series of financial and political scandals. The combination of political and popular protest, under the leadership of Pascual Orozco and Francisco (Pancho) Villa, meant that Chihuahua became the centre of the most cohesive popular rebellion during the first months of the Revolution. The defeat of federal forces in Chihuahua and the capture of the border town of Cuidad Juárez in May 1911 led directly to Díaz's resignation later the same month.[17]

. . .

NATIONAL POLITICAL CRISIS

Regional disparities in the impact of the economic development during the Díaz era highlight not only the remarkable heterogeneity of Porfirian Mexico, but also the development of regional political tensions which gained momentum after 1900. Throughout Mexico, most notably in Chihuahua and Sonora, but even in loyal Oaxaca, there is ample evidence of the progressive inability of the regime to control or contain political developments in provincial Mexico. This was not only due to the changing dynamic of regional politics, but also symptomatic of a broader political crisis at the heart of the regime.

It is important, however, not to overestimate the extent of the domestic political crisis before 1909. It has often been assumed, particularly by those who have been anxious to uncover the 'precursors' of the Revolutionary movements of 1910 and 1911, that 1900 was the year which marked the beginning of the end of the Díaz era. It is certainly true that 1900 witnessed the emergence of a more coherent opposition movement, with the publication of the radical newspaper *Regeneración*, under the direction of Ricardo and Jesús Flores Magón. The following year saw the establishment of the Liberal Congress by Camilo Arriaga, which met in San Luís Potosí, symbolically on the anniversary of the promulgation of the Constitution of 1857.

However, from the perspective of the Díaz regime in 1900, the dawning of the twentieth century represented, in many respects, the apotheosis of the regime. Railways were under construction in every state in the Republic, foreign investment was pouring into, and exports out of, the country. Public finances were healthy and Díaz had been re-elected for the fifth time without any significant opposition or any major political protest in 1900. The regime was confident enough to allow the publication of 39 editions of *Regeneración* over a period of nine months before there was any sign of official harassment or persecution. Nevertheless, the projection of an image of undisturbed peace, order and stability was, of course, equally misleading. There were important indicators of growing political fissures within the Porfirian political system which would be exacerbated by the economic crisis of 1907.

The roots of the political opposition which would eventually coalesce around the Anti-Re-electionist Movement led by Francisco Madero after 1909 can, in fact, be traced back to 1892. This was a particularly turbulent year for the regime, when the combination of economic recession and widespread regional rebellion threatened to expose the fiction of the *pax porfiriana*. The central political issue was the constitutional amendment of 1890 which had allowed not only successive but permanent re-election of all elected offices within the Republic, including, of course, that of President. As a result, one of the countries which in mid-nineteenth-century Latin America had made conspicuous progress in establishing liberal constitutionalism as the framework and guiding principle of political practice, now proposed to challenge one of liberalism's most sacred principles – that of no re election. The most important consequence was that anti-re-electionism would become the principal focus of opposition to the Díaz system. It was all the more ironic that it was Porfirio Díaz, one of the most prominent *puro* liberals of the Refoma period, who had led two national rebellions against re-election, who should be the perpetrator of the betrayal.

Díaz's justification for recurrent re-election was always based upon his response to the call of public and civic duty. In his reply to those who had endorsed his candidacy in 1892 he replied: 'Some say it is anti-democratic and unconstitutional to seek another re-election, but I cannot refuse a public duty which the majority of my fellow citizens believe I can fulfil.'[18] Permanent re-election remained, nevertheless, deeply offensive to the Mexican liberal tradition, however effective Díaz's political and administrative skills proved to be. It was therefore opposed not only by *puro* liberals, but by prominent members of the political elite who, despite their admiration and support for Díaz, also sought to check executive power.

The vehicle for the challenge to executive power from within the inner circle of the regime was the National Liberal Union, formed in 1892, which developed out of the Central Porfirista Council, formed in the same year to promote the third re-election of Díaz.

As Charles Hale explains, there was no contradiction in supporting the third re-election of Díaz and, at the same time, advocating that re-election should be the exception, not the rule. As Justo Sierra, lawyer, journalist, Mexico's first Minister of Public Instruction after 1905 and one of the leading intellectual figures of the Porfiriato, argued in the manifesto of the Liberal Union: 'If effective peace has been acquired by the strengthening of authority [i.e. in the form of Díaz's re-election], definitive peace will be acquired by its assimilation with liberty.'[19]

Political liberty, Sierra argued, would be strengthened with the reform of the Constitution of 1857, most notably through the creation of the office of Vice-President and the creation of an independent judiciary by making the appointment of judges permanent. The irremovability of judges would replace the practice of the regular election of judges, which meant, in effect, that appointments were made on the basis of political patronage. The ultimate goal of the Liberal Union was to renovate and re-create the Liberal Party as a 'party of government', as a properly constituted national party with a national organisation in which delegates from municipal and states levels would be represented in a National Congress. It was precisely during the polemic over constitutional reform in 1892 and 1893 that the advocates of constitutional reform within the Liberal Union, like Justo Sierra, Limantour, Rosendo Pineda, Joaquín Casasús, Roberto Núñez and Emilio Pimentel, became known by their *puro* opponents within the liberal camp as the *científicos*.[20]

The hopes of the *científicos* of constitutional reform and the restriction of presidential authority under the auspices of the Liberal Union were ultimately thwarted, partly by the opposition of *puro* liberals to amendments to the 1857 Constitution, but also, more importantly, by Díaz's resistance to any encroachment on his absolute personal authority. In characteristic fashion, Díaz made no open public declarations of his opposition, but used his friends in the liberal press, such as Luís Pombo, a lawyer from Oaxaca, and director of *El Siglo XIX*, and his allies and appointees in Congress to block or to eviscerate the legislation. According to Hale, for example, although the revised proposal for the irremovability of judges was passed by Congress in 1893, it was referred by the Senate to committee and was never seen again.[21]

Even though the Liberal Union effectively ceased to be a force in national politics after 1893, its prominent members continued to remind Díaz of the dangers of permanent re-election. In a letter to

Díaz in 1899, Justo Sierra warned that successive re-elections represented the creation of a 'presidency for life, in other words an elective monarchy with a Republican disguise'. Although this might represent stability in the short term, in the longer term it was detrimental to national interests, since the destiny of one man now determined the fate of the nation. 'In my judgement,' he continued, 'statesmen and businessmen in the USA, in England, in Germany, and in France have the abiding impression that in the Republic of Mexico there are no institutions, but one man, on whose life depends peace, productive work, and credit.'[22]

Díaz's reply to Sierra's very real concerns showed a dismissive cynicism, claiming that he was ideologically opposed to re-election, but that circumstances and his sense of duty and responsibility had forced him to continue in office:

> Your views are the same as mine, as I indicated in 1880, when I rejected re-election. . . . If I have subsequently been unable to act according to my political beliefs, it has been for specific reasons in each case. . . . If you were aware of the details, and felt, as I feel, the weight of responsibility for the course of events, it is almost certain that your resolutions in each case would not have differed much from mine.[23]

The failure of the Liberal Union to introduce any restraints on presidential authority would have important repercussions for the ultimate demise of the regime. Díaz's determination to subordinate all institutions to his will, and his ultimate indifference to the implementation of the content, rather than the preservation of the form of liberal constitutionalism, were two of the regime's principal political shortcomings. After 1900 they became increasingly serious obstacles to the functioning of the system. The regime continued to adopt the vocabulary of constitutional liberalism, with constant references to the need to uphold and respect 'the popular will' and 'the sovereignty of the state', but these terms became progressively devoid of meaning. Much more significant as an indication of the true character of the regime was the frequent use of the term 'Supreme Magistrate' (*El Supremo Magistrado*) to describe the President's power. Most significantly of all, while restrictions on the development of political institutions and parties helped to keep opposition under control, they deprived the regime of either an institutional means of succession or a means of channelling the growing demand for wider democratic participation.

When the Liberal Union was revived in 1903, Francisco Bulnes warned the delegates at the Second Congress not only of the dangers of permanent re-election, but also that the mood of the nation had changed:

> After General Díaz, the country does not want men. The country wants political parties, institutions, efficient laws, [and] the free expression of ideas, interests, passions. The country wants the successor of General Díaz to be the law.[24]

The revival of liberal anti-re-electionism and the failure to solve the related question of succession raised the political temperature after the elections of 1900, when Díaz was re-elected for the fifth time on his seventieth birthday. According to Cosío Villegas, Díaz's undeclared intention was to step down from the presidency in 1904, and he therefore attempted to pursue a strategy whereby his trusted but uncharismatic Finance Minister, José Yves Limantour, would become his successor as President, but with the counterbalance of the military influence and popularity of Bernardo Reyes to prevent excessive power becoming concentrated in the hands of the *científicos*. Limantour himself claimed in his memoirs that this had been Díaz's intention even before the elections of 1900. For this reason Reyes was invited to join the cabinet as Minister of War following the election of 1900.

Cosío Villegas states that Díaz's strategy would never have been successful because Limantour was perceived as aloof, aristocratic and unpopular, with no political base outside the narrow elitist *camarilla* of the *científicos*. Limantour himself insisted that he made it consistently clear to the President that he opposed the strategy, on the grounds that he harboured no personal political ambitions, that he lacked the support of the military and that he suffered from persistent ill-health.[25] Most significantly of all, however, it was precisely Díaz's familiar strategy of divide and rule, designed to prevent the emergence of any potential challenge to his personal authority, which undermined the whole enterprise. Díaz certainly did nothing to challenge a press campaign, co-ordinated after 1902 by Reyes's son Rodolfo and financed by the governor of Veracruz, Teodoro Dehesa, and the Minister of Justice, Joaquín Baranda, which argued that Limantour's French parentage – despite the fact that he had been born in Mexico City – made him ineligible to assume the presidency. And Díaz's suspicions of Reyes increased considerably following the successful response to the creation of a civilian volunteer militia (the Second Reserve) which Reyes had introduced as Minister of War in 1900. Díaz could never tolerate a potential political rival, much less one who had command over a civilian volunteer army.

As a result of Díaz's increasing disappointment with Reyes's failure to support his strategy, the Minister of War was obliged to resign from the cabinet in 1902. Ever loyal to Díaz, Reyes obediently returned to the governorship of Nuevo León and the Second Reserve was disbanded. Díaz persisted, however, in his attempt to undermine Reyes's influence and his popularity. The following year, following the death of a number of anti-re-electionist demonstrators in Monterrey, Díaz did nothing to prevent Reyes's appearing before a Congressional tribunal accused of an over-zealous use of force. According to both Cosío Villegas and Bulnes, Díaz allowed Reyes to be prosecuted and thus pilloried, but he did not allow him to be convicted, and thus risk his open enmity. The potential challenge from Reyes would remain one of Díaz's obsessions through the rest of the decade, an obsession which ultimately blinded him to the danger of the challenge posed by Francisco Madero's anti-re-electionist campaign.

In the context of heightened speculation over the succession, and over the careers of Limantour and Reyes, Díaz was prepared to make concessions to his critics. In order to calm political tensions, he first sought a constitutional amendment for a two-year extension to the current term of office, which would now end in 1906 rather than 1904. The subsequent presidential elections would take place, therefore, in 1910. At the same time, Díaz abandoned his previous opposition to the creation of a vice-presidency and appointed *científico* Ramón Corral, the ex-governor of Sonora, now Minister of the Interior (*Gobernación*) to the post for the period 1906–10, in what was, in effect, an additional snub to the anti-*científico* supporters of Reyes. However, according to Limantour, who had closely supported the appointment of a vice-president and the appointment of Corral, Díaz never accepted the need for a vice-president, and proceeded to marginalise Corral from the political decisions and appointments made after 1906, further undermining any attempt at genuine political reform.[26]

The focus of opposition to the regime shifted dramatically in 1906 away from the internal schisms within the political elite towards a series of disputes between workers and their employers, in

a series of well-publicised but badly mis-handled strikes which provided a distinctly negative impression of Porfirian labour relations
and of the social consequences of the export-led economic strategy.
The fact that, in part, the grievances of the workers were aimed at
the advantages enjoyed by foreign employees over their Mexican
counterparts added a nationalist dimension to the disputes at a
period of heightened political sensitivity.

The first flashpoint was the mining town of Cananea in Sonora,
which was, in effect, a US company town belonging to the Cananea
Consolidated Copper Company. A protest over wage differentials
between the 6,000 Mexican employees and their 600 US counterparts led to a riot in which company guards fired on the workforce.
The excessive use of force was compounded by the permission
granted to the company by the governor of Sonora, Rafael Izábal,
to allow 260 Arizona rangers to cross the border to restore order,
in what was widely criticised at the time as an open violation of
Mexican sovereignty.

In the summer of 1906, mechanics on the Mexican Central Railway
shut down the line for over two weeks. Although Díaz refused to
intervene, he advised state governors to investigate workers' grievances and to negotiate with moderate labour leaders. The policy of
conciliation and mediation with labour organisations, however, was
seriously undermined at the end of the 'year of strikes' by the most
violent dispute yet witnessed in Porfirian Mexico. The Great Circle
of Free Workers, which had concentrated its recruitment in the
textile mills of Puebla, Tlaxcala and Veracruz, claiming a membership of over 7,000, called for a series of strikes over pay and conditions which were met by employers' lockouts, even refusing the
workers credit in the company stores (the notorious *tiendas de raya*,
which became a powerful symbol of Porfirian social injustice).

Díaz himself agreed to mediate, and proposed a settlement which
appears to have been accepted, albeit grudgingly, by the majority of
employees. The workers at one of the largest textile mills in the
country, at Rio Blanco in Veracruz, however, refused to return to
work, as a result of which troops and *rurales* were sent to punish the
rebels. The resulting carnage, in January of 1907, left a number of
workers dead and five union leaders executed.[27]

Although the regime attempted to blame the agitation on the
'pernicious' influence of the *Partido Liberal Mexicano* (PLM), the
anarchosyndicalist organisation formed by the Flores Magón brothers
in exile in St Louis, Missouri, in 1905, it was unable to persuade

PORFIRIO DÍAZ

labour organisations, the liberal press, or the regime's political opponents that it was innocent. The simultaneous attempt to persuade the authorities in the USA to be more assiduous in the pursuit and extradition of the regime's opponents in exile was equally unsuccessful. Press criticism mounted, and unfavourable coverage helped to construct an image of a regime which had used the coercive power of the state to massacre Mexican workers on behalf of foreign capitalists.

The interpretation of the broader significance of the labour disputes of 1906 and 1907 for the downfall of the Díaz regime has always been controversial. Those who argue that labour organisations such as the Great Circle of Free Workers, or political organisations such as the Mexican Liberal Party, were significant precursors of the subsequent Revolution have been challenged by those who argue that labour and radical political organisations played only a minor part in the Revolution of 1910, and, indeed, a minimal part in the Revolutionary decade after 1910. Nevertheless, it is clear that the handling of the disputes, and the criticism which ensued, helped to undermine public confidence in the regime's aura of supremacy and its ability to sustain its own promises of stability, order and progress.[28]

. . .

THE CREELMAN INTERVIEW, 1908

In an atmosphere of heightened political tension, the effect of the economic recession of 1907 further undermined public confidence. The fact that the crisis emanated from Wall Street served to emphasise the degree of interrelationship and integration which had developed between the Mexican economy and that of the USA in the Díaz era. The squeeze on capital and credit began to hit Mexico in the summer of 1907. Interest rates rose at the same time as the international price of Mexico's export commodities (sugar, cotton, silver, lead and copper) fell. Factories and mines either scaled down production or were forced to close, and an unexpected drought in northern Mexico not only affected agricultural production but also threatened famine. Sugar production in Morelos, for example, dropped by 10 per cent between 1908 and 1910, and cotton production in the Comarca Lagunera dropped from 300,000 tons to less than 80,000 tons.[29] As a result, with confidence in order already undermined by labour agitation, confidence in progress received a similar blow.

In the midst of growing political and economic pressures on the Díaz regime, US Secretary of State Eliah Root visited Mexico in October 1907. Ostensibly, Root's mission was to continue the dialogue between the Díaz and the Roosevelt administrations over the maintenance of peace in Central America, which, as indicated in Chapter 6, had become an increasingly contentious issue in US–Mexican relations. Given the political difficulties facing the Díaz regime, and the interventionist attitude which the Roosevelt administration had adopted towards the geo-politics of the region, it is entirely likely that, during the course of his visit, Root raised the question of Mexico's political future. It is equally conceivable, therefore, that pressure was placed upon Díaz to clarify his intentions, and even to step down in order to prepare for a peaceful transition of power.

Díaz, for his part, was anxious to retain the support of the Roosevelt administration and to reassure Root that his administration still held a firm grip on Mexican politics. He was also keen to impress upon Washington the need to act over the arrest and extradition of 'seditious elements' within the exiled opposition in the USA (principally members of the PLM). As a result, through the mediation of Enrique Creel, governor of Chihuahua, who had recently been appointed Mexican Ambassador in the USA, Díaz agreed to give an interview to US journalist James Creelman, which was published in March 1908 in *Pearson's Magazine*. Because of the importance of its contents, it was immediately translated and printed in Mexico City newspapers.

There are different views on the importance of the Creelman interview. For some, such as Francisco Bulnes, it was an act of stupidity tantamount to 'political suicide'; others claim that it was an act of cynical manipulation to entice potential rivals out of the woodwork in order to be able to intimidate or suppress them. For Limantour, it was a sincere attempt to gauge the political mood of the nation in order to determine which candidates enjoyed popular support as a basis on which to build a peaceful political transition.[30] Cosío Villegas has suggested that the interview was less significant than has generally been supposed, noting the fact that there was very limited reaction from state governors, who seemed remarkably lacking in curiosity about the implications of Díaz's imminent retirement.[31]

In retrospect, there is little doubt that the impact of the Creelman interview was devastating. While it was meant to reassure the North American government that Díaz was still firmly in control, its reception in Mexico exposed the political contradictions and the fundamental lack of democratic legitimacy of the Díaz regime. As a result, it provided a new stimulus for the revival of anti-re-electionism, which had already gained significant momentum after 1906.

The most sensational revelation in the interview itself was that Díaz declared that he would stand down from office before the next election, thus opening the way for, and even welcoming, the development of democratic institutions, political parties and the free election of his successor. In many ways the interview was remarkably candid. Díaz was quoted as follows:

> It is a mistake to believe that the future of democracy in Mexico has been endangered by the permanence in power of one President over a long period of time. . . . Democracy is the only principle of just and true government, although in practice, it is only possible for nations with a sufficient degree of development. . . . I have waited patiently for the day when the people of the Mexican Republic are ready to choose and to change their government at every election, without the danger of armed revolution and without doing harm to national credit and progress. I believe that this day has now arrived. . . . Whatever the opinions of my friends and supporters, I shall stand down from power at the end of the current term of office, and I shall not serve again. . . . I would welcome a party of opposition in the Mexican Republic . . . and the happy inauguration of a completely democratic government in my country. . . . I do not have the least desire to continue in the presidency; this nation is, at last, ready for a life of liberty.[32]

Although aimed principally at a North American audience, the Creelman interview can be read as an open, even honest, appraisal of the regime's preoccupations and philosophy. Democracy, Díaz declared, was the best political system, indeed the only political system of value, but Mexico had not been ready for it in 1876. Reflecting his own pragmatism and the contemporary creed of positivism, this meant that the regime had had to adopt what Díaz described as a 'patriarchal system' in the exercise of power, to maintain peace and stability as an absolute priority in order for national and material progress to develop unencumbered by the threat of political 'anarchy'.

For those on the margins of the Mexican political elite, whom Díaz himself described in the interview as Mexico's 'new middle classes', the interview was a clear declaration of the democratic deficiency of the regime. Díaz had admitted that permanent re-election ran contrary to the spirit and the letter of liberal democracy and, indeed, contrary to his own principles. Re-election had been necessary, but only because of exceptional circumstances. Now that the country had made adequate material and social progress, Díaz himself recognised that those same liberal principles, and the practice of political democracy, could finally be implemented.

• • • ANTI-RE-ELECTIONISM AND *MADERISMO*

It is richly ironic that the impact of the Creelman interview should have had precisely the effect that Díaz had always striven most to avoid – it disturbed the political peace which the regime had assiduously maintained for nearly three decades, or, in one of Díaz favourite metaphors, it 'frightened the horses' (*alborotó la caballada*). As a consequence, political activity throughout Mexico increased exponentially during 1908, with the publication of a series of books and pamphlets such as Manuel Calero's *Electoral Questions* in 1908, Querido Moheno's *Where Are We Headed?* in 1908 and Francisco Sentíes's *The Political Organisation of Mexico*, also in 1908, which called for the organisation of a Democratic Party. The Party was subsequently established in January 1909 under the leadership of Manuel Calero, Juan Sánchez Ancona and, with significant symbolism, the son of Benito Juárez, Benito Juárez Maza. The Democratic Party launched its manifesto in March 1904 and continued to publish trenchant criticism of the government through its newspaper *El Partido Democrático*, under the guidance of the appropriately-named Diódoro Batalla.[33]

Two of the most significant and influential publications of this period were Andrés Molina Enríquez's *The Great National Problems* (1909) and Francisco Madero's *The Presidential Succession in 1910* (1909). Molina Enríquez argued that the roots of economic backwardness, poverty and political conflict lay in land monopoly and the predominance of the 'feudal' *hacienda*. The influence of Molina's thesis was, arguably, more significant during and after the Revolution than before it, since Molina was himself involved in the drafting of Article 27 of the Constitution of 1917 which firmly established the agrarian question as part of the Revolutionary and post-Revolutionary political agenda. Nevertheless, his analysis constituted a severe critique of the social impact of Porfirian modernisation in rural Mexico.

Madero's book had a more immediate impact on the national political debate. Although he praised the economic and administrative achievements of the Díaz regime, Madero criticised the sacrifice of political liberty for peace and material progress, and urged the implementation of constitutional liberalism in Mexico. As a result of the success of the book, Madero's prestige within the Anti-Re-electionist Movement grew rapidly.[34]

Opposition continued to gather momentum during 1909, reviving a degree of political activity which had not been seen since the elections of 1880. The intensification of political unrest and continuing economic uncertainty eventually persuaded Díaz, in spite of his declarations to Creelman, to accept the nomination made by the National Re-electionist Convention in April 1909 for his seventh re-election. In his official statements, Díaz justified his decision, as he had done since 1892, on the basis that exceptional circumstances required him to assume his patriotic duty to preserve the stability of the nation.

Instead of restoring stability, Díaz's decision unsettled the political situation further. It exposed the extent to which Díaz had increasingly lost his political touch and his ability to assess the national political mood. Suffering increasingly from physical and, according to Francisco Bulnes, mental arteriosclerosis, his age was beginning to take its toll. His gradual physical and mental decline was hidden from public scrutiny but it was certainly apparent to his close associates. Limantour expressed his sadness at the increasingly frequent 'lapses of memory and bouts of nervous tension' which afflicted the President. Sir Weetman Pearson, the British businessman who became a close personal friend of Díaz and his family, commented to his wife after a visit to Mexico in February 1908 that the President was showing distinct signs of old age. 'I am glad to see him working well', wrote Pearson, 'but, of course, each year shows up his age . . . he is alert and attentive, but it is forced now, and not so free and spontaneous as of old.'[35]

While Díaz dedicated his remaining energies to his re-election campaign, opposition activity in 1909 divided into two related, but separate, camps. On the one hand, the moderate or 'loyal' opposition concentrated on the selection of an appropriate vice-presidential running mate for Díaz in the forthcoming elections of 1910, in the belief that the vice-president would be certain to take over as

President. On the other, more radical opposition increasingly advocated the immediate removal of Díaz as President, either through the ballot box or through direct action (as advocated by the PLM).

The two principal factions within the inner circle of the regime – the *científicos*, under the guidance of Limantour, and the *reyistas*, the supporters of Bernardo Reyes – now became locked in an internal power struggle. While continuing to support the re-election of Díaz as President, both *camarillas* attempted to secure their candidate for the vice-presidency and to undermine the chances of their opponents. The nomination of Ramón Corral for the vice-presidency by the National Re-electionist Convention in April 1909 confirmed the influence over Díaz enjoyed by what José López-Portillo later described as the 'bureaucratic brotherhood' (*cofradía burocrática*) of the *científicos*.[36]

The supporters of Bernardo Reyes responded by establishing the Central Reyista Club in June 1909, which proposed Reyes for the vice-presidency. However, the *reyista* challenge to the *científicos* was complicated and weakened by the reluctance of Reyes himself openly to declare his candidacy. In fact, his own public declarations emphasised his loyalty to Díaz and his support for the nomination of Corral as vice-president, in spite of the declarations of his supporters.

Díaz's major fear, as had been the case since 1902, continued to be Reyes's potential challenge to his authority. He therefore adopted his tried and tested method of divide and rule, seeking to undermine Reyes, but also with a view to keeping Limantour's ambitions under close scrutiny. Reyes was criticised for having sponsored press attacks on Limantour and the *científicos*, which served as a double advantage for Díaz in that the reputations of both Reyes and Limantour were simultaneously undermined. In July 1909 Díaz appointed the veteran General Gerónimo Treviño, an old enemy of Reyes, as Commander of the Military Zone which encompassed Reyes's fiefdom in Coahuila, Tamaulipas and Nuevo León. Finally, in November 1909, Díaz executed what he considered his *coup de grace* to the *reyista* campaign. Reyes was despatched on a military mission to Europe, ostensibly to study German military tactics. Reyes, as he had consistently done, meekly obliged and refused to challenge Díaz's authority. He accepted what was effectively a sentence of political exile.

Díaz's obsession with the potential threat represented by Bernardo Reyes was a serious political miscalculation. It not only deprived him of the services of one of his most loyal and effective political allies, but also led him to underestimate the threat posed by the growing Anti-Re-electionist Movement. With the exile of Reyes, many *reyista* supporters now gravitated to the rapidly-growing anti-re-electionist camp.

The Anti-Re-electionist Movement (of which Francisco Madero was initially Vice-President and Emilio Vásquez Gómez President) issued its political manifesto in June 1909. Its slogan '*Sufragio Efectivo y No Re-elección*' (A Real Vote and No Re-election) would become the most significant slogan of the Revolution of 1910. Madero subsequently visited 22 of the 27 states in a highly successful campaign to establish local anti-re-electionist clubs throughout Mexico, which were invited to send delegates to a National Anti-Re-electionist Convention in April 1910. On the eve of the Convention, however, Madero was arrested, thus preventing the Anti-Re-electionist Party from contesting the presidential elections in June.

The arrest of Madero was another of the serious errors committed by the regime during its final months. Although he was released in the early autumn, Madero's opposition to the regime had undergone a significant radicalisation. While the regime indulged in the elaborate celebrations to mark the centenary of independence in September 1910, which culminated in the announcement of the 'electoral victory' of Díaz and Vice-President Corral, Madero proceeded to organise funds for a revolution. In October 1910, Madero launched his revolutionary manifesto, the Plan of San Luis Potosí, which called for an armed uprising against the Díaz regime on 20 November 1910, in what was a classic nineteenth-century *pronunciamiento*, strikingly similar in both structure and content to Porfirio Díaz's own Plan of Tuxtepec of 1876.

The initial response to Madero's call to arms was muted, but the Revolution took root, most notably in Chihuahua, where Pancho Villa made an early and significant contribution, and in Morelos, with the participation of Emiliano Zapata. Díaz's instinct for political survival had clearly not entirely deserted him since he conceded in negotiations with Madero's uncle Ernesto a series of political reforms which would guarantee freedom of suffrage and no re-election and a promise that he would stand down from power once the country had been pacified.[37] But Díaz was also acutely aware of the weaknesses of his position and his growing isolation. Both Reyes and Limantour, formerly two of his strongest allies, were out of the country and unable to advise him, the latter in Paris to negotiate more favourable terms for Mexico's public debt. The Taft administration in the USA, which despite the growing areas of conflict, had always supported the regime, had despatched 20,000 troops to the border, ostensibly to preserve order. Given the highly volatile political context, this was certainly not perceived within Mexico as an indication of support for the regime, but rather as a clear warning to the regime that Washington's support could not be taken for granted. Finally, the weakness, demoralisation and ineffectiveness of the Porfirian army, following years of cutbacks in personnel and its incomplete professionalisation, had been exposed in its failure to contain the early revolutionary uprisings.

Informal and formal negotiations between the government and the *maderista* rebels continued in the early months of 1911 but failed to find a solution to the central *maderista* demand that Díaz's should resign without further delay. The renewal of hostilities, and the surrender of the border town of Cuidad Juárez to the Chihuahuan revolutionaries of Pascual Orozco and Pancho Villa in May 1911, thus represented the final act in the political drama and the coalescence of popular uprising and political failure. Díaz recognised that his position was untenable. On 25 May 1911 he presented a characteristically emotional resignation to Congress:

> The Mexican people, who have so generously showered me with honours, who proclaimed me their *caudillo* during the Wars of Intervention, who supported me in all of my efforts to promote industry and commerce in the Republic, this people, distinguished representatives, has risen up in armed bands, claiming that my presence at the head of the Supreme Executive Power is the cause of their insurrection.
>
> I do not know of anything that I have done which might have caused this social phenomenon: but, recognising and admitting, without agreeing, that I may be unconsciously to blame, that possibility makes me the least appropriate person to analyse and comment on my own culpability.
>
> As a result, respecting, as I have always respected, the will of the people, and in conformity with article 82 of the Federal Constitution, I have come before the Supreme Representation of the Nation to resign unconditionally the appointment as Constitutional President of the Republic, with which the nation has honoured me: and I do so with even more good cause, since to retain it would require the shedding of more Mexican blood, demolishing the credit of the nation, destroying its wealth, shattering its resources, and exposing it to international political conflict.
>
> I hope, gentlemen, that once the passions which accompany every revolution have calmed down, that a more conscientious and accurate

analysis may emerge in the conscience of the nation, a correct evaluation which will allow me to die with the knowledge in the depths of my soul that the respect with which I have throughout my life dedicated, and will always dedicate to my compatriots has found its just correspondence.[38]

At the end of the same month, accompanied by the members of his family and other close associates, Díaz sailed into political exile after nearly 35 years in power. Enigmatic and concise to the last, he is reputed to have made a final comment on the events which had toppled him from power, on the immense difficulties of governing a fragmented nation like Mexico and, finally, on the future of the Mexican Revolution. 'Madero has released a tiger,' he said prophetically. 'Let us see if he can control it.'

· · ·

NOTES AND REFERENCES

1. A. Knight, *The Mexican Revolution*, 2 vols, Cambridge, 1986, Vol. I, p.36.
2. J. Hart, *Revolutionary Mexico: The Coming and Process of the Mexican Revolution*, Stanford, CA, 1989.
3. R. Ruiz, *The Great Rebellion, Mexico 1905–24*, New York, 1980.
4. W. Beezley, *Judas at the Jockey Club, and Other Episodes of Porfirian Mexico*, Lincoln, NB, 1987; W. Beezley, C. Martin and W. French (eds), *Rituals of Rule, Rituals of Resistance: Public Celebrations and Popular Culture in Mexico*, Wilmington, DE, 1994.
5. T. Benjamin and M. Wasserman (eds), *Provinces of the Revolution: Essays on Regional Mexican History 1910–29*, Albuquerque, NM, 1990.
6. T. Benjamin and W. McNellie, *Other Mexicos: Essays on Regional Mexican History 1876–1911*, Albuquerque, NM, 1984.
7. W.K. Meyers, *Forge of Progress, Crucible of Revolt: The Origins of the Mexican Revolution in La Comarca Lagunera 1880–1911*, Albuquerque, NM, 1994.
8. W.S. Langston, 'Coahuila: Centralisation against State Autonomy', in Benjamin and McNellie (eds), *Other Mexicos*, pp.55–76.
9. M. Romero, *El Estado de Oaxaca*, Barcelona, 1886.
10. M. Bernstein, *The Mexican Mining Industry 1890–1950*, Albany, NY, 1965, p.73.
11. D. Spenser, 'Soconusco: The Formation of a Coffee Economy in Chiapas', in Benjamin and McNellie (eds), *Other Mexicos*, pp.123–43; P. Garner, *Regional Development in Oaxaca during the Porfiriato (1876–1911)*, Liverpool, 1995.

12. V.R. Martínez Vásquez (ed.), *La Revolución en Oaxaca 1900–1930*, Oaxaca City, 1985.
13. H. Martínez and F. Chassen, 'Elecciones y Crisis Política en Oaxaca: 1902', *Historia Mexicana*, Vol. XXXVIII, 1989, pp.523–54.
14. J.F. Iturribarría, *Oaxaca en la Historia*, Mexico City, 1955, p.264.
15. P. Garner, *La Revolución en la provincia: Soberanía estatal y caudillismo en las montañas de Oaxaca 1910–20*, Mexico City, 1988.
16. F. Bulnes, *El Verdadero Díaz y la Revolución*, Mexico City, 1921, pp.181–2.
17. F. Katz, *The Life and Times of Pancho Villa*, Stanford, CA, 1998, pp.11–125.
18. D. Cosío Villegas (ed.), *Historia Moderna de México* (hereafter *HMM*), 10 vols, Mexico City, 1955–72, Vol. X, p.600.
19. C. Hale, *The Transformation of Liberalism in Late Nineteenth-Century Mexico*, Princeton, NJ, 1989, pp.103–38.
20. Cosío Villegas, *HMM*, Vol. X, pp.648–58.
21. Hale, *Transformation*, p.121.
22. J. Sierra, *Obras Completas: Epistolario y papeles privados*, Mexico City, 1984, p.96.
23. Cited in E. Krauze *Porfirio Díaz: Místico de la Autoridad*, Mexico City, 1987, p.91.
24. Ibid., p.94.
25. J.Y. Limantour, *Apuntes sobre mi vida pública (1892–1911)*, Mexico City, 1965, pp.106–9.
26. Ibid., p.140.
27. Krauze, *Porfirio Díaz*, pp.97–101.
28. For opposing views, see J. Hart, *Anarchism and the Mexican Working Class*, Austin, TX, 1978, and A. Knight, *Mexican Revolution*, Cambridge, 1986.
29. Meyers, *Forge of Progress*, pp.179–82.
30. Limantour, *Apuntes*, p.145.
31. Cosío Villegas, *HMM*, Vol. X, p.772.
32. Díaz quoted, *inter alia*, in Krauze, *Porfirio Díaz*, pp.129–30.
33. Cosío Villegas, *HMM*, Vol. X, pp.773–85.
34. S. Shadle, *Andrés Molina Enríquez: Mexican Land Reformer of the Revolutionary Era*, Tucson, AZ, 1994; S. Ross, *Francisco I. Madero: Apostle of Mexican Democracy*, New York, 1955.
35. Limantour, *Apuntes*, p.155; Sir Weetman to Lady Pearson, 17 February 1908, Pearson Papers, Science Museum, London, Box A9.
36. J. López-Portillo y Rojas, *Elevación y Caída de Porfirio Díaz*, Mexico City, 1921.
37. Limantour, *Apuntes*, p.151.
38. Krauze, *Porfirio Díaz*, pp.135–7.

. . . . . .
EPILOGUE AND
CONCLUSIONS

The speed with which the Díaz regime collapsed between November 1910 and May 1911 surprised and confounded even the most astute of contemporary political commentators. The regime, which had prided itself on its longevity and had claimed to represent the triumph of political peace and the definitive end of political anarchy in Mexico, had proved to be remarkably fragile and brittle.

Díaz was fully aware that his resignation, which was the principal demand of the Anti-Re-electionist Movement, would mean political exile. Accordingly, he made plans, even before the Ciudad Juárez Treaty had been signed, to make a rapid and unobtrusive (and, in personal terms, highly ignominious) departure from Mexico City. The Díaz family, accompanied by relatives, servants and a military escort, left in the early hours of 26 May 1911 for the port of Veracruz. Díaz spent five days in the residence of British businessman Sir Weetman Pearson (who had recently been elevated to the British House of Lords as Viscount Cowdray), before embarking on the German steamer *Ypiranga*, which arrived at the French port of Le Havre on 20 June 1911 after brief stops at the ports of La Coruña and Plymouth.[1] It is significant, and again not without irony, that his final days in Mexico, and his voyage into exile, should take place under the protection of his European friends and associates, in fear of possible reprisals at the hands of his fellow Mexicans.

Porfirio Díaz would spend the remaining four years of his life in European exile, until his death in Paris on 2 July 1915. He led a far from reclusive life, however, until his health began to fade rapidly in the spring of 1915. Before then, having recovered from the health problems he had suffered during 1911, Díaz lived in comfort, if not splendour, in his Parisian apartment and his summer residences in

Biarritz and St Jean de Luz, surrounded by his immediate family, friends and associates (including fellow exiles José Yves Limantour, Joaquín Casasús and Guillermo de Landa y Escandón). He was courteously treated and lavishly praised by the royal families, aristocracies and governments of Europe, and received a number of military honours and awards. He and his *entourage* travelled to Spain, Germany and Switzerland in 1912, and to Egypt and Italy in 1913. He kept in touch with events in Revolutionary Mexico, waiting for the opportunity to return to his *patria*. But, as the early phases of revolution and counter-revolution in Mexico deteriorated into civil war after 1914, the opportunity failed to materialise.

According to his great-great-grandson, the writer Carlos Tello Díaz, the ex-President was plagued and depressed during his long months of exile by two conflicting sentiments: first, his own culpability for Mexico's rapid return to political instability; and, second, and most of all, his grief and despair at the ingratitude of his fellow Mexicans in failing to recognise the contribution he had made to Mexico's prosperity and progress. As he confessed to the writer Federico Gamboa, who was Mexican Minister to Belgium during Díaz's period of exile: 'I feel wounded. One half of the country rose up in arms to overthrow me, and the other half folded its arms and watched me fall.'[2]

The deliberations of his troubled conscience are an entirely appropriate point of departure from which to assess the legacy of Porfirio Díaz. To what extent can it be said that Díaz was personally responsible for the collapse of the regime? And did he have a right to feel aggrieved at the treatment afforded him by his fellow Mexicans, and their failure to recognise his achievements?

Díaz's personal responsibility for the events which took him into exile was clearly substantial. The analysis provided here has repeatedly stressed the personalist character of the regime, and has focused on the strategies adopted by Díaz and his inner circle in the construction and maintenance of his unassailable authority at the apex of political power. It has also examined the combination of circumstances after 1906, including his own miscalculations, which rendered his personal grip on power increasingly tenuous.

But the analysis of the personal mistakes and the structural factors which exposed the fundamental fragility of the regime in its final months needs to be tempered by an assessment of Díaz's achievement in manipulating the levers of power for over three decades. The central thesis proposed here is that Porfirio Díaz proved to be successful in maintaining a balance between Mexico's dual political cultures of authoritarianism and liberalism. The essential achievement and effectiveness of the Díaz strategy lay in the construction of a *modus vivendi* between the traditions of personal and patriarchal authority represented by *caudillismo*, and the constitutional guarantees and electoral practices advocated by nineteenth-century Mexican liberalism.

Díaz's political career was moulded by the traditions of nineteenth-century *caudillismo*. Throughout his military career, he adapted successfully to the roles of warrior, *patrón*, patriot and, ultimately, republican national hero. Once in office, his accumulation of authority was gradual but, ultimately, unassailable, although never absolute. His power continued to be exercised through a wide network of formal and informal personal relationships, fuelled by patronage and carefully cultivated across a broad social spectrum of Mexican society, and based upon negotiated rather than enforced exchanges of deference and loyalty to the patriarch.

To argue that Díaz possessed the attributes of a *caudillo* and adopted the practices of *caudillismo* does not mean, however, that he should be seen as simply another example in a long line of authoritarian Latin American military leaders who represented the interests of the army in its struggle with civil authority. Indeed, it is possible to argue that the opposite was the case. During his tenure of office, not only did Díaz demonstrate that he was the only nineteenth-century Mexican president who was able to control the military, but he was also most successful in removing the threat of the frequent military interventions in politics which had characterised the post-independence period.

Díaz also must be clearly distinguished from the archetypal *caudillo* in terms of his liberal political convictions. 'Classic' *caudillos* throughout nineteenth-century Latin America were characterised by an absence of personal ideological commitment or, more frequently, were the agents, allies or subordinates of conservative interests determined to preserve the socio-economic or political *status quo*. By contrast, Díaz was, from his early conversion at the age of 18, when he gave up his studies at the seminary to study law at the liberal Institute of Arts and Sciences in his native city of Oaxaca, both a freemason and an ardent supporter of the liberal cause. In fact, when Díaz did eventually take up arms in December 1854, he did so not in pursuit of a professional military career but, significantly, in response to the dictates of his liberal political convictions.

Díaz's commitment to popular and radical liberalism was enhanced by his military experiences as a National Guard commander and federal army officer during the Wars of the Reforma and French Intervention (1858–67). Díaz always demonstrated an awareness of the commitments and sacrifices made by peasant and indigenous communities in south-eastern Mexico (above all in his native Oaxaca) in support of the liberal patriotic cause. Díaz thus became the figurehead of radical 'jacobin' liberalism and, as a result, enjoyed considerable popular support for his political campaigns between 1867 and 1876.[3] Once in office, Díaz's correspondence indicates that he continued to remain sensitive to the demands of rural communities for political, judicial and economic autonomy.

Díaz's personal affiliation to liberalism, including both the radical or conservative versions, was always thoroughly tempered by pragmatism and a good degree of cynicism. It was also clearly subordinate to his relentless quest for political power. Díaz himself openly admitted his scepticism of constitutional or ideological purity. In a telling response to accusations in the press (made in the newspaper *El Partido Liberal*) that the regime had violated the principles of the 1857 Constitution, Díaz chose to draw an analogy with the practice of religion:

> The answer is simple: Catholics violate the 10 Commandments every day, because it is impossible to comply rigorously with every one of them: it is equally impossible for the government to adhere strictly to the letter of the law as laid down in our Constitution.[4]

In spite of the preference for pragmatism, the Díaz regime never abandoned its outward commitment to constitutional liberalism. Its fundamental tenets, enshrined in the Constitution of 1857, were never relinquished – political and religious freedoms, universal (male) suffrage, a secular, representative and federal republic comprising free and sovereign states without corporate structures or privileges. To have done so would have meant a repudiation of the regime's political origins, and the foundation of Díaz's own political career.

Nevertheless, it is also undeniable that, in practice, the regime after 1884 manipulated constitutional and electoral practices, and blocked the creation of institutions (for example, political parties or an independent judiciary) which might have restrained presidential or personal authority. The abandonment of constitutional radicalism must be seen, however, in the context of the transformation of liberalism itself after 1876, when the radical enthusiasms of the 1850s and 1860s were progressively replaced by the elitist doctrine of conservative liberalism, or positivism.[5] The inner circle of the Porfirian elite, led by Finance Minister José Yves Limantour, warmly embraced this fashionable ideology because it provided a doctrine which advocated economic progress and social planning under the control of a technocratic elite, bolstered by an authoritarian government.

There can be no doubt that Díaz fully endorsed the strategy. Long before the end of his presidency, Díaz supported the positivist view that the practice of politics should not concentrate, as liberalism demanded, on the protection of individual freedom, the equality of the individual before the law, or on a guarantee of effective suffrage or democratic representation, but on the protection of social order and the promotion of material (or scientific) progress. As he candidly explained in the Creelman interview in 1908:

> We have preserved the republican and democratic form of government. We have defended the theory and kept it intact. Yet we adopted a patriarchal policy in the actual administration of the nation's affairs, guiding and restraining popular tendencies with full faith that an enforced peace would allow education, industry and commerce to develop elements of stability and unity.

The use here of the pronoun 'we', which Díaz used to trumpet the achievements of his regime, is significant. Although Díaz himself, his contemporary subordinates and *porfirista* historians were more than happy to peddle the notion that he was personally, and even solely, responsible for Mexico's political stability and material progress, it is obvious that the regime benefited from the loyal service of a number of talented and capable individuals from across the spectrum of nineteenth-century Mexican politics. To name only the most prominent: Justo Benítez, Matías Romero, Ignacio Mariscal, Manuel Dublán (all of whom were from Oaxaca), Manuel Romero Rubio, Bernardo Reyes, Justo Sierra and José Yves Limantour all played a significant role in defining the character, and ensuring the survival, of the regime. Three individuals in particular were significant influences during the different phases of Díaz's career: Justo Benítez from the 1850s until Díaz's decision to support Manuel González as his successor in 1880; Manuel Romero Rubio from 1881 until his death in 1895; and José Yves Limantour from his appointment to the Ministry of Finance in 1893 until the Revolution of 1910–11. There is no suggestion here, however, that these individuals played the role of *eminence grise* to the ambitious *caudillo*. Díaz was far too skilful a politician for that. The Díaz regime was, nevertheless, a collective endeavour, and never the work of a single individual. It is also clearly the case that the material progress which Mexico experienced in the Díaz era was not solely attributable to the President's vision, or to the collective efforts of the Porfirian inner circle, but to the character of world trade and finance in the last third of the nineteenth century, and the drive, especially in the USA after 1877, to incorporate Mexico's economic resources and raw materials into the expanding international economy.

The question that needs to be addressed here is whether self-perpetuation in office, and the resumption of an elective dictatorship after 1884, was necessary in order to sustain the pattern of national development which Mexico enjoyed under Díaz, as the regime's apologists have consistently argued. The experience of other Latin American states in this period, which enjoyed similar levels of economic growth without recourse to dictatorship, would suggest that it was not. Ironically, however, not even Díaz himself would have argued that re-election was either necessary or desirable. He consistently argued that he was opposed in principle to re-election, but that his sense of public duty and responsibility had forced him to continue in office. These declarations should obviously not be taken at face value, and should be understood rather as an example of astute, even cynical, manipulation – a means of paying lip service to constitutional principle while abandoning it in practice. Nevertheless, there is very little evidence of a sustained political challenge to the regime before 1908.

Although a number of the individuals in Díaz's inner circle possessed the talent, ability, experience (and ambition) to aspire to presidential office, none of them did so. There was certainly no absence of political conflict or intrigue, and anti-re-electionism remained a core principle of late nineteenth-century Mexican politics. But no individual (other than the maverick intellectual Nicolás Zúñiga y Miranda) was willing to lead an open challenge to Don Porfirio. On the contrary, the leading contenders for the succession after 1892, Reyes and Limantour, consistently refused to endorse a challenge to Díaz's successive re-elections. They not only remained steadfastly loyal to the *caudillo*, but argued that '*el tio*' ('uncle' Díaz, as Limantour affectionately called him) represented the best means of maintaining stability, order and progress.[6] The fact that there was no serious challenge to successive re-election before 1908 cannot, therefore, be attributed solely to Díaz's penchant for manipulation or coercion.

As Díaz himself also admitted in the Creelman interview, the political circumstances of 1908 nevertheless demanded new forms of popular representation and expression – in effect, a change of government. However, the factional divisions within the inner circle of the Porfirian elite made it impossible to reform the system from within, and no alternative strategy was forthcoming. The promises made by Díaz in 1908, including the announcement of his own retirement, aroused enormous expectations and generated intense political activity. But the reforms failed to materialise, and Díaz announced that he would present himself again for his seventh re-election in 1910. It was apparent that no solution had been found to the central and intractable problem of succession. Indeed, it became increasingly obvious that the very nature of Díaz's political authority, and the manner in which that authority had been maintained for so long, prevented a solution from being found. The regime itself therefore constituted the principal obstacle to change.

In short, the open and wilful cynicism shown towards the maintenance of the content as well as the form of liberal constitutional practice, and the failure to solve the problem of succession, became the regime's greatest shortcomings during its final months. While the restrictions on the development of independent political institutions or parties had helped to keep official opposition to a minimum, it had also deprived the regime of an institutional form of succession and of a means of channelling the demand for wider political participation in a society which had undergone a significant transformation by 1910. In addition, the adherence to positivism, by intensifying the ideological and factional divisions within the Porfirian elite, narrowed the ideological base as well as the constituency of support for the regime. It was also obvious to many observers that Díaz, as he approached his eightieth birthday in 1910, no longer possessed the energy or the capacity to sustain the necessary degree of control over a personalist system which had expanded rapidly, but which was now under increasing strain.

From the comfortable but melancholy isolation of his Parisian exile, Díaz thus had good reason to reflect upon his personal culpability in the rapid demise of his regime, and Mexico's return to political anarchy. His regime had emerged from, and still claimed to represent, the traditions of radical, patriotic liberalism. By 1910, as a result of the regime's progressive abandonment of constitutional principle, and its impotence and in-fighting after 1908, it had become widely perceived as incompetent, unconstitutional and inimical to the nation's interests.

Nevertheless, Díaz also had good reason to bemoan the ingratitude and injustice of his fellow Mexicans. By focusing on the multiple shortcomings of the last years of the regime, both contemporary revolutionaries of the decade after 1910 and subsequent *anti-porfirista* historians consistently and deliberately underestimated the achievements of the Díaz regime. For nearly two generations following the death of Porfirio Díaz, the image of his regime which remained in the popular imagination was that associated with the worst excesses of tyranny. Among professional historians, this interpretation has long been superseded. At a popular level, there is plenty of evidence to suggest that official anti-Díaz satanisation is dead or, at least, moribund. It is, therefore, difficult to disagree with the conclusion of historian and polemicist Enrique Krauze, that:

> a more generous interpretation – which has always been absent in Mexico – would concede, without distorting the truth, that Porfirio Díaz made a decisive contribution to the material construction and the national consolidation of his country.[7]

It is only the Mexican government which continues to drag its feet. The final proof of official acceptance, political reconciliation and historical balance will become a reality only when the remains of the old *caudillo* are returned from the Parisian cemetery of Montparnasse to be buried in his beloved Oaxaca.

. . .

NOTES AND REFERENCES

1. C. Tello Díaz, *El Exilio: Un Relato de Familia*, Mexico City, 1993, pp.22–7.
2. Gamboa, cited in Tello Díaz, *El Exilio*, p.30.
3. G.P.C. Thomson, 'Bulwarks of Patriotic Liberalism: The National Guard, Philharmonic Corps, and Patriotic Juntas in Mexico 1847–88', *Journal of Latin American Studies*, 22(1), 1990.

4. J.F. Ituribarría, *Porfirio Díaz ante la Historia*, Mexico City, 1967, p.14.
5. C. Hale, *The Transformation of Liberalism in Late Nineteenth-Century Mexico*, Princeton, NJ, 1989.
6. Limantour to Francisco Mena, 7 May 1900, 2nd series, Roll 1, Archivo José Yves Limantour, Condumex, Mexico City.
7. E. Krauze, *Porfirio Díaz: Místico de la Autoridad*, Mexico City, 1987, p.151.

GLOSSARY

cacique
: The most powerful individual in a region or locality who, through landownership, patronage and, sometimes, political office, dominated local affairs. *Caciques* often acted as intermediaries between local interests and regional or central power. The sphere of influence of the *cacique* was called a *cacicazgo*, and the networks of *cacique* power referred to as *caciquismo*.

camarilla
: A network (often informal) of individuals linked by patronage and loyalty (and often with connections through freemasonry) to further the political ambitions of the group and its leadership.

caudillo
: In Mexico, usually a military figure (such as General Santa Anna) with command over sections of the army, but also at the apex of a broader civilian network of clients and supporters. The *caudillo* used his position to influence and, for much of the nineteenth century, to dominate national politics.

compadre
: Kinship relationship between individuals not related by blood which implies responsibility for members of the *compadre*'s family, and acting as godfather (*padrino*) to the *compadre*'s children. In the broader social context, the institution of *compadrazgo* lies at the heart of clientalistic networks of patronage and loyalty.

hacendado
: Owner of a private rural estate (*hacienda*) which varied enormously in size and range of products

	(principally cereals and livestock). *Haciendas* were both self-sufficient and market-oriented.
juaristas	Supporters of Benito Juárez (used especially after 1867, to distinguish them from their principal rivals in the liberal camp, *lerdistas* or *porfiristas*).
jefe político	Following the 1857 Constitution, the district official (sometimes elected, but usually appointed by the state governor) charged with overseeing municipal affairs (including local elections). Became a byword for corrupt officialdom during the Díaz era.
juchiteco	Native of the Isthmus town of Juchitán in Oaxaca.
lerdistas	Adherents of Sebastián Lerdo de Tejada in his quest for the presidency (1870–71) and during his term of office (1872–76).
mestizo	Product of the racial miscegenation of Indian and Hispanic, but also applied to those members of indigenous communities integrated into Hispanic society (those, for example, who spoke Spanish).
oaxaqueño	Native of the state of Oaxaca in southern Mexico.
porfirista	Supporters of Porfirio Díaz (and opponents of Benito Juárez and Lerdo de Tejada between 1867 and 1876). Used as an adjective to describe the characteristics of the Díaz regime (1876–1911) and, thereafter, is used to describe the apologists of the regime.
pronunciamiento	Military rebellion or *coup d'état*, often led by a military *caudillo*, with the purpose of removing the incumbent president and his administration. The *coup d'état* was launched with a manifesto or *plan*.
pueblo	Usually translated as 'village', but the *pueblo* in nineteenth-century Mexico represented the cornerstone of legal, cultural and economic identity for rural communities. The late nineteenth century was a period of transition and disruption for rural inhabitants as a consequence of the liberal project of land privatisation.
puros	Radical, anticlerical liberals who advocated the implementation of both the spirit and the letter of the Constitution of 1857 and its attack on corporate

	privilege and the Spanish colonial legacy. Also frequently referred to as *jacobinos*.
santanistas	Followers of General Antonio López de Santa Anna (1795–1876).
tehuanos	Native inhabitants of the Isthmus town of Tehuantepec on the Pacific coast of Oaxaca.
tienda de raya	Company store on rural estates or industrial establishments where labourers and workers were obliged to purchase basic goods at company prices. Became a symbol of exploitation and social injustice during the Revolution of 1910–20.
tuxtepecano	Supporters of the Plan of Tuxtepec which brought Díaz to the presidency in 1876. Subsequently, the term referred to those who continued to support the radical liberal agenda in opposition to the regime's gradual abandonment of its radical principles.

BIBLIOGRAPHICAL ESSAY

Given the significance of the Díaz era for the history of modern Mexico, and the recent resurgence of popular interest in Díaz, it is not surprising that bibliographical output on the Díaz era has grown at an exponential rate since 1980. The increase is also a reflection of the professionalisation of historical research in Mexico since the 1970s and the accessibility of new archival sources, most notably the large volume of personal correspondence housed in the Porfirio Díaz Collection at the Iberoamerican University in Mexico City.

The majority of secondary sources on the Díaz era are mostly to be found, predictably, in Spanish. However, sources in English have also increased rapidly, especially as more and more doctoral theses from US universities have been converted into monographs. Biographies of Díaz or of his contemporaries in English are, however, still rare, and there has not been an English-language biography of Díaz published since Carleton Beals's erratic, anecdotal but informative *Porfirio Díaz: Dictator of Mexico* (Philadelphia, Lippincott) in 1932. Because of the preponderance of Spanish-language over English-language sources, this essay will necessarily refer to both, but seeks to highlight, wherever possible, sources published in English.

The broad outlines of the distinct approaches to the portrayal of both Díaz the man and Díaz the regime are discussed in Chapter 1. I have referred to these changes in historiographical fashion as *Porfirismo*, *Anti-Porfirismo* and *Neo-Porfirismo*, each with its respective chronology and interpretative bias. Each has produced its crop of biographies. The most useful of the *porfirista* biographies published before (and during) the Revolution of 1910 are José Godoy's *Porfirio Díaz, President of Mexico: Master Builder of a Great Commonwealth* (New York, G.P. Putnam's Sons, 1910) and James Creelman's

Díaz, Master of Mexico (New York, D. Appleton & Co., 1912). After the Revolution, sympathetic treatments of Díaz and the regime can be found in Francisco Bulnes, *El Verdadero Díaz y la Revolución* (Mexico City, Editora Nacional, 1921), Angel Tarracena, *Porfirio Díaz* (Mexico City, Editorial Jus, 1960), and Jorge Fernando Iturribarría, *Porfirio Díaz ante la Historia* (Mexico City, 1967). A much more critical, generally anti-*porfirista* but informative biography is José López Portillo y Rojas, *Elevación y Caida de Porfirio Díaz* (Mexico City, 1921, reprinted by Editorial Porrúa in 1975). A similarly critical and narrative approach is adopted by Ralph Roeder in his *Hacia el México Moderno: Porfirio Díaz* (2 vols, Mexico City, Fondo de Cultura Económica (hereafter FCE), 1973).

Products of the revived (*neo-porfirista*) interest in Díaz and his regime in the 1980s are Enrique Krauze, *Porfirio Díaz: Místico de la Autoridad* (Mexico City, FCE, 1987), Pedro Pérez Herrero, *Porfirio Díaz* (Madrid, Historia 16, 1987) and Fernando Orozco Linares, *Porfirio Díaz y Su Tiempo* (Mexico City, Panorama Editorial, 1991). Into this same category should be placed Moisés González Navarro's two-volume edition of Díaz's own (distinctly unreliable) account of his life up to 1867 (originally written in 1892 and published for the first time in 1922), *Memorias de Porfirio Díaz* (Mexico City, Conaculta, 1994). The revival of interest in the personal history of Díaz and his family, as manifest in the 1992 TV soap opera (*telenovela*) on the life of Don Porfirio (*El Vuelo del Aguila*), is also reflected in the popularity of the highly readable account of both the early years and the life in exile by Díaz's great-great-grandson, Carlos Tello Díaz, which was reprinted no fewer than eight times in its first year of publication, *El Exilio: Un Relato de Familia* (Mexico City, Cal y Arena, 1993).

Of the more general works which have sought to investigate the regime rather than the man, those written by some of the leading figures of Mexico's post-Revolutionary generation of historians make essential reading. The starting point for a detailed examination of the Díaz era is Daniel Cosío Villegas's ten-volume edited history of the Restored Republic and Porfiriato (1867–1911), published over a 17-year period under the grand and ambitious title of *Historia Moderna de México* (Mexico City, Editorial Hermes, 1955–72). The first three volumes are devoted to the history of the Restored Republic (1867–76), focusing on political, economic and social history, and were published in 1955 and 1956. The remaining seven volumes, each averaging some 1,000 pages, four of which (those dealing with domestic politics and international relations) were written by Cosío Villegas himself, are devoted to the Díaz era (or Porfiriato as he called it) and were published between 1957 and 1972. Equally indispensable is the earlier, but incisive, analysis of the Díaz regime provided by José Valadés in *El Porfirismo: Historia de un Régimen* (3 vols, Mexico City, Porrúa, 1941–48). A very useful general introduction to the character of the Díaz regime is provided by Luís González y González, 'La Dictadura de Díaz', in J. Labastida Martín del Campo (ed.), *Dictaduras y Dictadores* (Mexico City, Siglo XXI, 1986), pp.161–78.

The most useful English sources published in the 1970s are Jan Bazant's chapter on 'The Era of Porfirio Díaz' in his *A Concise History of Mexico: From Hidalgo to Cárdenas 1805–1940* (Cambridge, Cambridge University Press, 1977), and the series published by Northern Illinois University Press on *The Origins of Modern Mexico*, most notably Laurens Ballard Perry's, *Juárez and Díaz: Machine Politics in Mexico* (DeKalb, University of Northern Illinois Press, 1978).

Very significant strides were made during the 1980s in the historiography of the Porfiriato, with path-breaking monographs on key aspects of economic, political, social, regional and cultural history. Many of these monographs were published in English, the vast majority in the USA. A solid and comprehensive general introduction in English to the Restored Republic and the Díaz era is the essay by Friedrich Katz, 'Liberal Republic and Porfiriato 1867–1910', first published in Volume 5 of Leslie Bethell (ed.), *Cambridge History of Latin America* (Cambridge University Press, 1986), and subsequently published in the collection of essays on Mexico taken from the *Cambridge History* and re-published as L. Bethell (ed.), *Mexico since Independence* (Cambridge, 1991, pp.49–125). Katz's principal concern is with political and economic issues, emphasising the importance of land, labour and agrarian conflicts, themes which he had already explored in his *La Servidumbre Agraria en Mexico en la Época Porfiriana* (Mexico City, SepSetentas, 1976). John Coatsworth's *Growth against Development: The Economic Impact of Railroads in Porfirian Mexico* (DeKalb, Northern Illinois University Press, 1981) highlights the centrality of railway development and the economic distortions which it brought in its wake. Stephen Haber's *Industry and Underdevelopment* (Stanford, University of California Press, 1987) provides a thorough analysis of the flawed and 'underdeveloped' character of Porfirian industrialisation.

In the arena of political and intellectual history, Charles Hale's *The Transformation of Liberalism in Late Nineteenth-Century Mexico* (Princeton, NJ, Princeton University Press, 1989) charts the rise of the influence of Comtean positivism on Mexico's political elite and the emergence of the *científicos*, complementing Leopoldo Zea's earlier *El Positivismo en México: Nacimiento, Apogeo y Decadencia* (Mexico City, FCE, 1968). Important aspects of the social history of the period, also published in the 1980s, are John Tutino's analysis of the roots of agrarian unrest, *From Insurrection to Revolution in Mexico: Social Bases of Agrarian Violence* (Princeton, NJ, Princeton University Press, 1986) and Paul Vanderwood's dissection and deflation of the mythological status of the Rural Police Force, *Los Rurales Mexicanos* (Mexico City, FCE, 1981) and his subsequent analysis of rural crime in *Disorder and Progress: Bandits, Police, and Mexican Development* (Lincoln, University of Nebraska Press, 1981). A pioneering and influential analysis of the social and cultural history of the Porfiriato is William Beezley, *Judas at the Jockey Club and Other Episodes of Porfirian Mexico* (Lincoln, University of Nebraska Press, 1986). The social history and political influence of the growing number of Protestant congregations in Porfirian Mexico are analysed in Jean-Pierre Bastian's *Los Disidentes: Sociedades Protestantes y Revolución en Mexico 1872–1911* (Mexico City, FCE, 1989).

One of the major trends in the historiography of the Porfiriato which emerged in the 1980s was the research on regional history, following on from the precedent established by Luís González's hugely influential 'microhistorical' study of his home town of San José de Gracia in Michoacán from the 1860s to the 1960s, *Pueblo en Vilo: Microhistoria de San José de Gracia* (Mexico City, El Colegio de México, 1972), translated into English as *San José de Gracia: Mexican Village in Transition* (Austin, University of Texas Press, 1974). Examples of the new crop of regional studies which began to appear in the 1980s are Mark Wasserman, *Capitalists, Caciques, and Revolution: The Native Elite and Foreign Enterprise in Chihuahua 1854–1911* (Chapel Hill, University of North Carolina Press, 1984) and the volume edited by Thomas Benjamin and William McNellie, *Other Mexicos: Essays on Regional Mexican History* (Albuquerque, University of New Mexico Press, 1984).

Towards the end of the 1980s three very influential studies, all of which sought to explain the crisis and breakdown of the regime and the roots of the subsequent Revolution, were published. As if to illustrate the lack of consensus over the causes and character of the

BIBLIOGRAPHICAL ESSAY

Mexcian Revolution, each came to radically different conclusions. Francois-Xavier Guerra's *Le Mexique, De l'Ancien Régime a la Révolution* (2 vols, Paris, 1985, translated into Spanish, Mexico City, FCE, 1988) stresses divisions within the Porfirian political elite. Alan Knight, *The Mexican Revolution* (2 vols, Cambridge, Cambridge University Press, 1986) focuses on popular discontent with the Porfirian project. John Mason Hart, *Revolutionary Mexico: The Coming and Process of the Mexican Revolution* (Stanford, University of California Press, 1987) concentrates on nationalist reaction to the economic disruptions caused by the rapid influx of foreign capital during the Díaz era.

In the 1990s, studies which fit into the broad categories of regional, cultural and social history of the Porfiriato have predominated. Significant examples of regional history are Mario Cerruti, *Burgesía, Capitales e Industria en el norte de México: Monterrey y su Ambito Regional (1850–1910)* (Nuevo León, Alianza Editorial, 1992); Ricardo Rendón, *El Prosperato: Tlaxcala de 1885 a 1911* (Mexico City, Siglo XXI, 1993); William Meyers, *Forge of Progress, Crucible of Revolt: The Origins of the Mexican Revolution in La Comarca Lagunera 1880–1911* (Albuquerque, University of New Mexico Press, 1994); Gil Joseph and Alan Wells, *Summer of Discontent, Seasons of Upheaval: Elite Politics and Rural Insurgency in Yucatán 1876–1915* (Stanford, University of California Press, 1996); and Miguel Tinker Salas, *In the Shadow of the Eagle: Sonora and the Transformation of the Border during the Porfiriato* (Berkeley, University of California Press, 1997).

In the field of cultural and social history, important new methodologies and fertile areas of research have been opened up in William Beezley, Cheryl Martin and William French (eds), *Rituals of Rule, Rituals of Resistance: Public Celebrations and Popular Culture in Mexico* (Wilmington, DE, Scholarly Resources, 1994); and Mauricio Tenorio-Trillo, *Mexico at the World's Fairs: Crafting a Modern Nation* (Berkeley, University of California Press, 1996). The most significant recent publications on political history have been those studies which have sought to examine the genesis and fate of rural communities and popular or 'grass-roots' movements, and their changing relationship to the emerging central state. Of particular note are Alicia Hernández Chávez, *La tradición republicana del buen gobierno* (Mexico City, FCE, 1993); Florencia Mallon, *Peasant and Nation: The Making of Postcolonial Mexico and Peru* (Berkeley, University of California Press, 1995); and Guy Thomson and David La France, *Patriotism, Politics, and Popular Liberalism in*

Nineteenth-Century Mexico: Juan Francisco Lucas and the Puebla Sierra (Wilmington, DE, Scholarly Resources, 1999). A major contribution to the diplomatic history and international relations of the Díaz regime is Jürgen Buchenau, *In the Shadow of the Giant: The Making of Mexico's Central American Policy 1876–1930* (Tuscaloosa, University of Alabama Press, 1996). A recent volume which highlights the most recent areas of investigation into Porfirian Mexico by historians from Mexico, the USA and Europe is Roman Falcón and Raymond Buve (eds), *Don Porfirio Presidente . . . Nunca Omnipotente: Hallazgos, Reflexiones y Debates (1876–1911)* (Mexico City, Iberoamerican University, 1998).

CHRONOLOGY

1830   Baptism of Porfirio Díaz (15 September) in Oaxaca City, son of José Faustino Díaz and Petrona Mory.

Conservative military rebellion (Anastasio Bustamante, Nicolás Bravo) overthrows President Vicente Guerrero.

1831   Guerrero is executed in Oaxaca.

1833   Birth of his brother Felipe (later Félix), followed by the death of his father.

First Presidency of Antonio López de Santa Anna.

1836   Centralist *Leyes Constitucionales* replace the Federal Republican Constitution of 1824.

Texas declares independence.

1837   Díaz family moves to Casa la Toronja in Oaxaca City.

1838   'Pastry War'. French assault on Veracruz is rebuffed by Santa Anna.

1841   Plan de Tacubaya (Santa Anna) removes Bustamante from the presidency.

1844   Santa Anna is elected President but is replaced by José Joaquín de Herrera.

1845   Annexation of Texas by the USA.

Díaz enters the seminary, under the guidance of his cousin, José Agustín Domínguez (later the Bishop of Oaxaca).

1846   War between Mexico and the USA.

Díaz joins the Trujano Battalion as a volunteer to fight the US invasion.

1847   US troops occupy Mexico City (September).

Caste War erupts in Yucatán.

Benito Juárez becomes Governor of Oaxaca. Separatist rebellion in Tehuantepec.

Díaz 'converts' to liberalism.

1848 Treaty of Guadalupe Hidalgo (US–Mexico) results in the loss of half of Mexican territory.

1849 Díaz enters the liberal Institute of Sciences and Arts, Oaxaca.

1851 Presidency of moderate liberal General Mariano Arista.
Governor Juárez in Oaxaca attempts to suppress the Tehuantepec rebellion by force.

1852 Conservative Plan of Jalisco demands the overthrow of Arista.

1853 Santa Anna returns from exile in Venezuela to assume the presidency.
The USA acquires La Mesilla (Arizona and New Mexico) in the Gadsden Purchase.
Díaz enters the office of Oaxacan liberal lawyer Marcos Pérez.
Santanista Ignacio Martínez Pinillos becomes governor of Oaxaca.

1854 Díaz publicly declares support for the Plan of Ayutla and the rebellion led by Juan Álvarez.

1855 Díaz is nominated to serve as sub-prefect for Ixtlán (August) in the Sierra Norte of Oaxaca by governor Ignacio Martínez under the presidency of Ignacio Comonfort. Promulgation of *Ley Juárez* to abolish clerical immunity.

1856 Díaz is awarded his first military rank as Captain of Infantry in the National Guard by Governor Benito Juárez (December). *Ley Lerdo* forces the sale of clerical and community property.

1857 Promulgation of the Liberal Constitution by President Ignacio Comonfort, Conservative reaction in the Plan of Tacubaya (Félix Zuloaga).
Colonel José María Salado proclaims against the Constitution in Oaxaca, but is defeated by the Oaxaca National Guard under Manuel Velasco at Ixtapa (August).
Díaz is wounded and suffers acute peritonitis.

. . .

WARS OF THE REFORMA, 1858–61

1858 Juárez (President of the Supreme Court) establishes the seat of 'constitutional' government in Guanajuato.
Díaz participates in the siege and capture of the city of Oaxaca, held by Conservative General José María Cobos (January). He is appointed Military Commander and

Governor of the Department of Tehuantepec by Governor José María Díaz Ordaz (April) and is promoted to the rank of Major.

1859 Death of Díaz's mother in Oaxaca. He is promoted to Lieutenant-Colonel.

Conservative forces under José María Cobos occupy Oaxaca. Juárez signs the McLane–OcampoTreaty granting the USA rights of access to inter-oceanic communication across the Isthmus of Tehuantepec. Treaty is rejected by the US Senate.

1860 Díaz suffers his first military defeat at Mitla, Oaxaca (January). Victory at Ixtepeji in the Sierra Norte (May). He is promoted to Colonel. Governor Díaz Ordaz is killed in combat. Interim Governor Marcos Pérez reoccupies Oaxaca (August). Díaz leaves Oaxaca for the first time with the Oaxaca National Guard in campaigns in Central Mexico (Puebla, Hidalgo and Veracruz). The Conservative army is defeated at Calpulapan (December).

1861 Díaz returns to Oaxaca with the Oaxaca National Guard (January). He is elected *diputado* for Ocotlán (Oaxaca) in the National Congress under the restored presidency of Benito Juárez (May). He makes his inaugural (and only) speech to Congress.

Félix Zuloaga claims the presidency and rallies conservative forces (Tomás Mejía, Leandro Márquez). Liberal leader Melchor Ocampo is assassinated.

Juárez government suspends debt payments (July).

Díaz is promoted to Brigadier General, following military action in Jalatlaco (August). Death of his mentor, Marcos Pérez, in Oaxaca (August).

London Tripartite Convention decides on armed intervention, and combined Spanish, French and British forces arrive in Veracruz (December).

. . .

FRENCH INTERVENTION, 1862–67

1862 Spanish and British forces withdraw (April).

Díaz participates in the 'glorious' 5 May, when French troops under Lorencez are defeated by General Ignacio Zaragoza at Puebla. Death of Zaragoza from typhoid.

French reinforcements under General Forey arrive in Veracruz (September).

1863 Puebla is recaptured (May). Díaz is captured but escapes. He declines the post of Secretary of War or Commander-in-Chief of the Army and the governorship of Veracruz. He accepts nomination as Commander of the Army of the Centre (*Ejército del Centro).*

Juárez government takes refuge in San Luís Potosí (June). Díaz is promoted to Divisional General and is entrusted with the formation of the Army of the East (*Ejército de Oriente)* with its base in Oaxaca. Governor of Oaxaca (Ramón Cajiga) clashes with Díaz and resigns. Díaz becomes *de facto* governor and nominates Justo Benítez as Secretary (December).

1864 Archduke Maximilian accepts the Mexican crown and arrives with his wife Carlota in Veracruz (May).

Former *juarista* and *oaxaqueño* Manuel Dublán invites Díaz to join the imperial cause, but he declines.

1865 Díaz (2,800 troops) surrenders Oaxaca to the superior forces of Marshall Bazaine (10,000 troops) and is taken prisoner to Puebla (February). He escapes (September) and engages enemy forces at Tehuitzingo and Piaxtla (Puebla) (September), Tulcingo (October) and Comitlipa (December). He receives support from veteran insurgent Juan Alvarez in Guerrero.

Juárez decrees the extension of his presidential term (December).

1866 Díaz campaigns on the Pacific Coast (*costa chica*) of Oaxaca and Guerrero. Napoleon III withdraws French troops. Empress Carlota leaves Mexico in an attempt to secure funds and support for the imperial cause (July).

Díaz formally declares loyalty to Juárez.

He secures victory at Nochixtlán (September), Miahuatlán and La Carbonera (October), and the recapture of Oaxaca, assisted by his brother Félix and Manuel González (October). He is promoted to the rank of General.

Bazaine offers Díaz the surrender of Mexico City, providing he withdraws support for Juárez, but the offer is declined.

Díaz appoints General Alejandro García as civil and military governor of Oaxaca (December).

He establishes the *Colegio de Niñas de Oaxaca*, the first ever secondary school for girls in Mexico (December).

· · ·

RESTORED REPUBLIC, 1867–76

1867   Díaz orders the execution of the former imperial representative (*prefecto*, *visitador* and *comisario*) of Oaxaca, Juan Pablo
Franco (January).

Díaz nominates Juan María Maldonado as acting civil governor of Oaxaca and his brother Félix as military governor.

Emperor Maximilian offers Díaz, via an intermediary, the
command of the army and his surrender to the liberal cause,
but he declines.

Capture of Puebla (2 April) and the liberation of Mexico
City (20 June).

Final defeat and execution of Maximilian (19 June).
Díaz orders the execution of General Santiago Vidaurri,
Maximilian's Minister of Finance.

He marries his 20-year-old niece Delfina Ortega (April).
Díaz resigns his commission. Juárez issues the *Convocatoria*
which extends the authority of the executive power (including a veto over Congress) and the establishment of a second
chamber (Senate) (August).

Radical liberals denounce the *Convocatoria* as unconstitutional
and promote Díaz's candidacy for the presidency. Juárez is
re-elected.

Brother Félix is elected governor of Oaxaca (November).
State government in Oaxaca awards Díaz status of *benemérito
del estado* and grants him the *hacienda* of La Noria.

1868   Establishment of the first telegraph link between Oaxaca
and Mexico City.

Birth of his first son Porfirio Germán (dies 1870).
Juárez faces regional rebellions (Yucatán, Puebla, Tlaxcala,
Veracruz, Sinaloa, Hidalgo, San Luís Potosí, Michoacán,
Zacatecas and Aguascalientes) and agrarian and peasant rebellions across central and western Mexico, such as those led
by Julio López Chávez (Chalco), Francisco Islas (Hidalgo)
and Miguel Negrete (Tepic).

Juárez persuades Congress to suspend constitutional guarantees for one year.

1869   Plan Político (San Luís Potosí) declares against Juárez.
Inauguration of Puebla–Veracruz Railway (September).
Birth of his second son Camilo (dies 1870).

Governor Félix Díaz in Oaxaca brutally suppresses a local uprising in Juchitán.

1870   Rebellion of General Trinidad de la Cadena in Zacatecas (January).

Díaz stands for President against Juárez and Sebastián Lerdo de Tejada.

. . .

REBELLION OF LA NORIA, 1871–72

1871   Díaz alleges fraud in the July presidential elections, won by Juárez. Confirmation of Juárez as President by the National Congress (October).

Díaz launches Plan of La Noria (8 November) supported by a series of regional rebellions by Generals Treviño (Nuevo León), Trinidad de la Cadena (Zacatecas), Manuel González (Tamaulipas), Luis Mier y Terán (Veracruz), Miguel Negrete (Puebla), and Sonora.

In Oaxaca, Governor Félix Díaz withdraws the state from the Federation and 'reassumes state sovereignty'.

Puebla and Oaxaca are occupied by the Army of the East under General Ignacio Alatorre, who defeats the rebels at San Mateo Xindihui (December).

Miguel Castro is restored to the governorship of Oaxaca and the *Hacienda de La Noria* is ransacked. Díaz brothers are forced to flee Oaxaca. Porfirio seeks refuge in Chihuahua (with Pedro Galván), in San Francisco, California and in Tepic (with Manuel Lozada). Birth of daughter Luz (dies 1872).

1872   Brother Félix is killed in Juchitán, Oaxaca.

Porfirista forces under Gral. Treviño are defeated at the battle of La Bufa (Zacatecas) (March).

Death of Juárez (9 July). Sebastián Lerdo de Tejada assumes the presidency and offers amnesty to rebels (July). Díaz accepts amnesty (October) and 'retires' to the *Hacienda La Candelaria* in Tlacotalpan (Veracruz), the property of Damiano Lara, brother-in-law of his former military companion Juan de la Luz Enríquez, to grow sugar.

1873   Birth of third son Deodato Lucas Porfirio (Porfirito) (October).

Díaz invests in small rural properties in Loma Bonita, San Nicolás and San José Uruapan (Veracruz).

Completion of the Mexico City–Veracruz Railway.

1874 Returns to Congress as *diputado* for Veracruz.

Lerdo's anti-clericalism provokes *cristero* rebellions in the north-west.

Regional revolt by Lozada in Tepic, and the Yaqui rebellion under José María Leyva Cajeme in Sonora.

Lerdo clashes with the *Gran Círculo de Obreros de México* in a series of textile and mining strikes.

In Oaxaca, Lerdo intervenes to remove Miguel Castro and ensure election of *lerdista* José Esperón.

1875 Lerdo offers Díaz the post of Ambassador to Berlin, but he declines.

Birth of second daughter Luz Aurora Victoria (May).

Colonisation Law to encourage immigration.

Political opposition to Lerdo is enhanced by anti-clerical legislation and political centralisation. Lerdo intervenes in Jalisco to depose governor Jesús Camarena.

Díaz leaves Tlacotalpan for New Orleans and Brownsville, Texas, accompanied by Manuel González, to plot rebellion.

.   .   .

REBELLION OF TUXTEPEC, 1876

1876 Plan of Tuxtepec (Oaxaca) is launched in Ojitlán (10 January). Local rebellion from the Sierra Norte in Oaxaca (led by Fidencio Hernández) deposes the *lerdista* governor José Esperón (January) and subsequently endorses the Plan of Tuxtepec.

General Donato Guerra launches a coup against the *lerdista* administration in Jalisco. Insurrections in Puebla and Veracruz (José María Couttolenc and Luis Mier y Terán) (February).

Díaz launches the 'reformed' Plan of Tuxtepec (from Palo Blanco, Tamaulipas) and offers provisional presidency to the President of the Supreme Court, José María Iglesias (March).

Díaz takes the border town of Matamoros (Tamaulipas) on 2 April.

Rebel forces (under General Juan N. Méndez) engage federal troops (under General Alatorre) at the battle of San Juan Epatlán (Puebla) (May). Rebellion spreads to Tlaxcala and Hidalgo (M. Negrete and R. Cravioto).

Military defeat at Icamole (Nuevo León) (May) at the hands of Generals Escobedo and Fuero.

Díaz travels to New York, and during an attempt to return to Mexico in disguise he makes a 'dramatic escape' from capture by jumping ship off Tampico (June).

Lerdo is re-elected President (July), challenged by José María Iglesias, President of the Supreme Court. Iglesias launches his revolt from Salamanca, Guanajuato (October). Battle of Tecoac (Puebla) secures a significant military victory for Díaz (November), following a dramatic and successful rearguard action by Manuel González.

Díaz (through the Convention of Acatlán) offers Iglesias the role of 'provisional revolutionary President', but he declines.

Díaz occupies Mexico City (23 November), assumes executive power by decree (28 November) and nominates General Juan N. Méndez as provisional President.

Lerdo seeks exile in New York, Iglesias in San Francisco.

. . .

THE PORFIRIATO, 1876–1911

I   *The* tuxtepecano *era, 1876–80*

1877   Presidential elections confirm Díaz as constitutional President, with a *tuxtepecano* cabinet: Protasio Tagle, Interior; Justo Benítez, Treasury; Ignacio Ramírez, Justice and Education; Vicente Riva Palacio, Development; General Pedro Ogazón, War; Ignacio Vallarta, Foreign Affairs.

Constitutional amendment preventing successive presidential re-election (May). Senate is reinstated (September). Electoral Reform Law attempts to broaden political participation. Government intervenes in electoral disputes in Puebla, Hidalgo, Michoacán and Chiapas. Elections to Congress secure a majority of *tuxtepecanos* (113), with 35 'independents'.

Mexico makes first payment (US$300,000) to US government in settlement of Mixed Claims Commission.

1878 Manuel González becomes Minister of War (March), and José María Mata Minister of Foreign Affairs.

US government (President Rutherford B. Hayes) recognises Díaz.

Lerdista insurrections in Piedras Negras and Matamoros, barrack revolts in Jalapa and cross-border banditry.

Ex-US President Ulysses S. Grant visits Mexico.

1879 Justo Benítez leaves Mexico for voluntary exile in Europe (January). Series of '*Lerdista*' rebellions in Veracruz results in nine summary executions by Governor Luis Mier y Terán (June).

Carlos Pacheco becomes Minister of War and Ignacio Mariscal Minister of Justice and Education.

Death of Ignacio Ramírez.

Return of Benítez (October) to campaign (*Partido Liberal Constitucionalista*) in forthcoming elections against Manuel González.

Pronunciamientos by Generals Márquez de León (Sonora), Jesús Ramírez (Baja California) and Miguel Negrete (Tepic) are defeated by federal troops under the command of Manuel González (December).

II   *Presidency of Manuel González, 1880–84*

1880 Diplomatic relations with France restored.

Manuel González (11,528 votes) defeats Benítez (1,368 votes) in presidential elections (September). González appoints Ignacio Mariscal (Foreign Affairs), Carlos Diez Gutiérrez (Interior), Ezequiel Montes (Justice), Francisco Landero y Cos (Treasury), General Gerónimo Treviño (War). Díaz becomes Minister of *Fomento* (Development) and elected as President of the Supreme Court.

Death of Díaz's first wife Delfina (April), following the stillbirth of third daughter Victoria Francisca.

1881 Birth of (illegitimate) son Federico.

Death of Gabino Barreda, the 'apostle' of positivism (March).

Díaz resigns from the cabinet (May) and is elected governor of Oaxaca.

Carlos Pacheco becomes Minister of Development.

Díaz marries Carmen Romero Rubio, daughter of prominent *lerdista* Manuel Romero Rubio (November).

New Industries Act attempts to stimulate domestic industry by awarding tax exemptions to local industry.

Political disturbances in Jalisco, Durango and Zacatecas.

General Francisco Naranjo becomes Minister of War.

1882   Díaz is granted permission (*licencia*) to leave governorship of Oaxaca.

Treaty with USA allows reciprocal border crossings.

1883   Díaz is appointed Commissioner General of the Mexican delegation at the New Orleans World Fair. Visits New York, Chicago, St Louis, Washington and Boston.

Article 7 of the Constitution on freedom of the press is amended to allow prosecution of attacks on the government (*delitos de prensa*) in the courts.

Negotiations with Britain over the refinancing of the 'English debt.'

III   *The consolidation of power, 1884–1900*

1884   Mexico restores diplomatic relations with Britain.

New Commercial Code centralises concessions, regulates financial institutions and facilitates foreign investment in mining, railways and colonisation projects.

First railway linking Mexico with the USA is inaugurated.

Díaz is re-elected (unopposed).

Díaz supports María Garza Galán for governorship of Coahuila.

Luis Mier y Terán becomes governor of Oaxaca. New cabinet attempts to reconcile *lerdistas* (Romero Rubio), *juaristas* (Matías Romero, Ignacio Mariscal), *tuxtepecanos* (Carlos Pacheco), positivists (Joaquín Baranda) and conservatives (Manuel Dublán).

1885   Border tensions with Guatemala (President Rufino Barrios). Death of Barrios.

Loan of £10 million secured in London.

Governor Genaro Garza García of Nuevo León is deposed and Bernardo Reyes is installed.

1886   Yaqui rebellion is suppressed. José María Leyva Cajeme is executed (May). Mass deportations of *yaquis* (15,000) to the *henequén* plantations of Yucatán.

Rebellions in Nuevo León, Jalisco, Zacatecas and Sinaloa (Heraclio Bernal and Trinidad García de la Cadena). García de la Cadena is assassinated.

Mexican public debt (the 'English debt') is refinanced. Loan from German banking house of Bleichroeder is secured.

1887 Constitutional amendment allows re-election for one consecutive term. Díaz is re-elected for the second time.

1888 International Boundary Commission, extradition and commercial treaties between Mexico and the USA

Legislation to privatise *terrenos baldíos* (untitled, public land) belonging to municipalities and *pueblos*.

Local uprisings in Sinaloa, Durango and Zacatecas y Nayarit (Heraclio Bernal).

1889 Death of Sebastián Lerdo de Tejada. Buried in Mexico with full military honours. First Pan-American conference in Washington, DC (Matías Romero).

Bid from California for the purchase of Baja (Lower) California is rejected.

Universal Exhibition in Paris.

£2.7 million loan to finance Tehuantepec Railway.

1890 Constitutional amendment removes all restrictions on presidential re-election.

Inauguration of the port works at Tampico.

Final instalment of US debt is repaid. £6 million loan to finance railway subsidies.

1891 McKinley tariff (US) imposes protectionist measures to restrict bilateral trade with Mexico.

Death of Luís Mier y Terán and Minister of Finance (*Hacienda*) Manuel Dublán, and the retirement (and sudden death) of Minister of Development Carlos Pacheco prompts the creation of a Ministry of Public Works and Communications, and a cabinet reshuffle.

Anti-re-electionist disturbances (Coahuila and Guererro) and regional rebellions in Chihuahua (military colonists) and Sonora (*yaquis*) in protest at economic conditions, land privatisation and loss of political sovereignty.

1892 Third re-election. Díaz is now referred to as '*El Necesario*' (The Indispensable). Establishment of the Liberal Union, the future nucleus of the *científicos*.

Anti-re-electionist disturbances in Coahuila. Bernardo Reyes forms the Union and Progress Club.

Popular 'millenarian' rebellion at Tomochic (Chihuahua) led by Cruz Chávez is suppressed with excessive force, resulting in the death of 60 villagers and 500 federal troops.

Mexico is represented at the 1892 celebrations of the 400th anniversary of the 'discovery' of America held in Madrid.

Diplomatic relations with the Chinese Empire.

New Mining code establishes sub-soil deposits are private property.

1893   Economic recession follows the depreciation of silver. José Yves Limantour is appointed Minister of Finance (May).

Inter-state sales tax (*alcabala*) is abolished.

Mexico participates in the Chicago World Fair.

State funeral for General Manuel González.

1894   Rebellion in the state of Guerrero.

Border dispute with Britain over Belize (British Honduras) is settled by treaty. Renewed conflict with Guatemala is peacefully resolved by treaty.

Death of General Juan N. Méndez.

Restrictions on the size of landholdings is removed.

1895   Death of Romero Rubio.

Refurbishment of the Basilica de Guadalupe from public funds.

International Congress of Americanists is held in Mexico City.

First National Census estimates a population of 12.5 million.

1896   Indigenous rebellion in Papantla, Veracruz.

National Porfirian Circle promotes Díaz's fourth re-election. Re-election is challenged by candidacy of Nicolás Zúñiga y Miranda.

Arrival of apostolic delegate Archbishop Nicolás Averardi highlights reconciliation of church and state.

First public enunciation of the 'Díaz Doctrine' of collective responsibility for hemispheric defence of the Americas.

Death of Vicente Riva Palacio.

1897   Death of protesters during governorship elections in Mérida, Yucatán (August). Arnulfo Arroyo attempts to assassinate Díaz during the Independence celebrations in the Alameda Park (September). Arroyo is later 'found dead' in his police cell.

Death of Guillermo Prieto.

1898   USA declares war on Spain over the independence of Cuba. US occupation of Cuba and Puerto Rico.

Death of Matías Romero.

1899   Rank of US and Mexican diplomatic representatives is raised to Ambassador. Mexico participates in the Peace Congress in the Hague alongside the USA, as the only two representatives from the Americas.

Mexico participates in Paris World Fair.

IV   *Apotheosis and nemesis, 1900–10*

1900   Indigenous uprisings in Sonora (Yaqui) and Yucatán (Maya). Governor of Nuevo León, Bernardo Reyes, is appointed Minister of War (January) and Leandro Fernández replaces Manuel Fernández as Minister of Development.

Creation of the volunteer Second Reserve based upon National Guard units by Minister of War Reyes.

Díaz secures fifth re-election.

First edition of opposition paper *Regeneración* in Mexico City, edited by Ricardo Flores Magón.

Construction of port works at Salina Cruz and Coatzcoalcos on the trans-Isthmus railway (S. Pearson and Co.).

1901   First meeting of opposition Liberal Congress in San Luís Potosí (Camilo Arriaga).

Second Pan-American Conference in Mexico City endorses the 'Díaz Doctrine'. Resignation of Minister of Justice Joaquín Baranda, who is replaced by Justino Fernández. Diplomatic relations with Cuba, and the Austro-Hungarian Empire are established.

Mexico participates in the Pan-American Exhibition in Buffalo, USA.

1902   Reyes is forced to resign from the cabinet and is reappointed governor of Nuevo León. Second Reserve is disbanded.

Renewal of *yaqui* rebellion in Sonora.

Disputed governorship elections in Oaxaca (Martín González vs Félix Díaz): Emilio Pimentel is appointed as a compromise candidate.

Iron and steel production begins in Monterrey (*Compañía Fundidora de Hierro y Acero*).

1903   Luis Terrazas becomes governor of Chihuahua and Ramón Corral governor of the Federal District.

Reyes is tried (and acquitted) for excessive use of force in suppressing opposition rally in Monterrey, Nuevo León.

Military campaign against the *yaquis* in Sonora results in mass deportation to Yucatán. Death of Protasio Tagle.

1904 Presidential term is extended for two years.

General González Cosío is appointed Minister of War.

Díaz government recognises the independence of Panama from Colombia.

1905 Mexico converts to the gold standard.

Justo Sierra becomes Minister of Education and Fine Arts.

1906 Sixth re-election. Díaz is supported by the National Porfirian Party (*Partido Nacional Porfirista*) and the Liberal Union Convention.

Office of vice-president is inaugurated (*científico* Ramón Corral).

Strike of workers at the American-owned Cananea silver mines in Sonora is suppressed by state authorities with the help of Arizona Rangers.

Establishment of Mexican Liberal Party in St Louis, Missouri, by the Flores Magón brothers, and the Great Circle of Free Workers, among the textile workers of Mexico City, Puebla, Tlaxcala and Veracruz.

Marblehead Treaty (US–Mexico) secures Mexican co-operation in peacekeeping efforts in Central America in return for greater vigilance of anti-Díaz political activists in the USA.

Death of Ignacio Mejía.

1907 Army is used to suppress a strike of textile workers at Río Blanco, Veracruz, with significant casualties.

Governor of Yucatán Olegario Molina becomes Minister of Development. Inauguration of the trans-Isthmus Tehuantepec Railway (January).

'Mexicanisation' of the railway system and creation of the Mexican National Railways. Economic recession, fall in agricultural production and rise of unemployment. Tensions rise with the Guatemalan government over the assassination of former President Manuel Barrillas in Mexico City (April).

US Secretary of State Eliah Root visits Mexico (October).

Mexico acts as mediator (with US government) in Central American Peace Conference in Washington.

1908 Díaz announces his retirement in 1910 in an interview with US journalist James Creelman and provokes a wave of political activity and debate.

1909 Manuel Calero, Juan Sánchez Ancona and Benito Juárez Maza establish reformist *Partido Démocratico* (January).

Andrés Molina Enríquez publishes *Los Grandes Problemas Nacionales*. Francisco Madero publishes *La Sucesión Presidencial de 1910*.

National Re-electionist Convention in Mexico City launches candidacy of Díaz for President and Ramón Corral for Vice-President (April).

Club Central Reyista 1910 is established to promote the candidature of Bernardo Reyes for Vice-President (June).

Anti-Re-electionist Centre (President: Emilio Vásquez; Vice-President: Francisco Madero) launches political manifesto and the slogan '*Sufragio Efectivo y No Re-elección*' (A Real Vote and No Re-election) (June).

John K. Turner publishes a serialisation of a severe critique of the Díaz regime, later published as 'Barbarous Mexico', in the *American Magazine*.

Reyes is demoted as Commander of the Third Military Zone and is exiled 'on a mission to Europe'.

Re-election of governor Pablo Escandón in Morelos prompts state-wide protest.

Limantour travels to Europe to renegotiate Mexican public debt.

Mexico defies the US by providing asylum for liberal President of Nicaragua, José Santos Zelaya. Meeting between Díaz and US President Howard Taft on the US–Mexican border (October).

V   *Revolution and exile, 1910–15*

1910 Moratorium is declared on the sale of public lands.

Death of Ignacio Mariscal (March).

Madero is arrested on the eve of the National Anti-Re-electionist Convention.

Díaz–Corral are declared the victors in the presidential elections in the National Congress. Lavish public ceremonies mark the centenary of Mexican independence (September). Establishment of the National University (Mexico City).

Madero launches a *pronunciamiento* (Plan de San Luís Potosí) (October) and calls for armed rebellion (20 November). Murder of Aquiles Serdán in Puebla and uprising of Pascual Orozco in Chihuahua.

1911 *Magonista* rebellion in northern Baja California (January). Emiliano Zapata rebels in Ayala (Morelos) (March). 20,000 US troops are despatched to the Mexican border. Fall of Ciudad Juárez (to Pascual Orozco) prompts the resignation of Díaz (25 May). Francisco León de la Barra becomes interim President. Díaz sails to exile in Paris (31 May). Madero is elected President (November). Zapata launches Plan of Ayala against Madero.

1912 Pascual Orozco, Félix Díaz (Porfirio's nephew) and Bernardo Reyes launch separate rebellions against Madero. Díaz travels to Spain, Germany and Switzerland.

1913 Díaz visits Egypt and Italy (January–March). *Decena Trágica* (the Tragic Ten Days) (February) and *coup d'état* led by Victoriano Huerta leads to the murder of Madero and Vice-President Pino Suárez. Rebellions in Coahuila (Venustiano Carranza) and Chihuahua (Pancho Villa). Constitutionalists launch Plan of Guadalupe (November).

1914 US troops occupy Veracruz. Huerta is forced into exile (July). Prussian troops cross into Belgium at the outbreak of the First World War (August). Díaz spends the summer in Biarritz. Civil war follows split in Revolutionary coalition (Carranza and Obregón vs Villa and Zapata). Convention of Aguascalientes (November).

1915 Obregón defeats Villa at Celaya (May). Díaz dies in Paris (2 July).

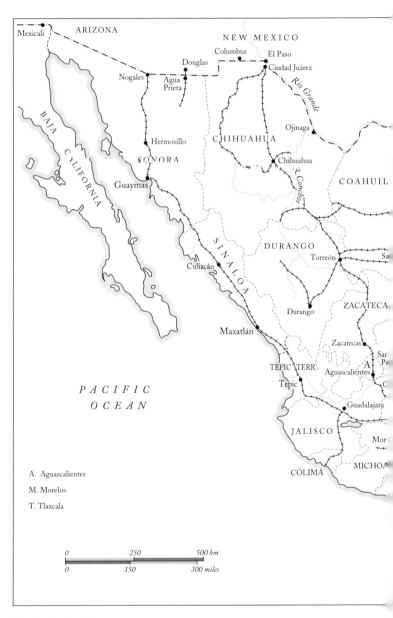

ARIZONA

NEW MEXICO

Mexicali

Columbus

El Paso

Ciudad Juárez

Douglas

Nogales

Agua
Prieta

Río Grande

BAJA
CALIFORNIA

Ojinaga

Hermosillo

CHIHUAHUA

SONORA

Chihuahua

COAHUIL

Guaymas

R. Conchos

SINALOA

DURANGO

Torreón

Sa

Culiacán

ZACATECA

Durango

Mazatlán

Zacatecas

Sar
P.

TEPIC TERR.

A

Aguascalientes

C

PACIFIC
OCEAN

Tepic

Guadalajara

JALISCO

Mor

A. Aguascalientes

COLIMA

MICHOA

M. Morelos

T. Tlaxcala

| 0 | 250 | 500 km |
| 0 | 150 | 300 miles |

Mexico in the Díaz era

INDEX

INDEX